Stories from
the Front Lines

Jane Rumph is a member of the board of directors of Global Harvest Ministries, chronicler of the Spiritual Warfare Network, and an accomplished writer and editor. She and her husband, Dave, live in Pasadena, California.

Stories from the Front Lines

Power Evangelism in Today's World

Jane Rumph

Chosen Books

A Division of Baker Book House Co
Grand Rapids, Michigan 49516

Published by Chosen Books
a division of Baker Book House Company
P.O. Box 6287, Grand Rapids, MI 49516-6287

Printed in the United States of America

Library of Congress Cataloging-in-Publication Data

Rumph, Jane, 1957–
    Stories from the front lines : power evangelism in today's world / Jane Rumph.
        p.   cm.
    Includes index.
    ISBN 0-8007-9238-6 (pbk.)
    1. Evangelistic work. 2. Missions. 3. Miracles. 4. Spiritual healing. 5. Gifts, Spiritual.
    6. Spiritual warfare. I. Title.
    BV3793.R86   1996
    269'.2—dc20   95-42595

Several names cited in this publication have been disguised to protect the individuals involved. All other material facts are true to the best of the author's knowledge.

Contents

116064

Acknowledgments

Sometimes one person's introduction of another can set the course of life down awesome new pathways. In the development and birth of this book, I can trace a direct line of people who connected me graciously to the next person in the chain leading to the volume in your hands. At the end of this chain stands my exceptional editor at Chosen Books, Jane Campbell. Working back along the links, my deepest thanks extend also to Cindy Jacobs, Peter Wagner, Madeline Duncan and Laurel Sherman. Without any one of these, I might never have met the next.

Several people helped midwife this book through their intercession and support, including good friends in the 120 Fellowship class at Lake Avenue Congregational Church and my Monday night kinship group: Diane Fujitani, my prayer partner; Lil Walker, who transcribed interview tapes; Dorothy McCandliss, who brought meals and critiqued part of the manuscript; and numerous others who prayed faithfully and helped carry my other responsibilities during the months of writing.

Thanks also to the women of my monthly writers' critique group: Sheri Bignell, Marty Carmack, Irene Faubion, Kathy Maxwell, Arleta Richardson, Ruth Rodriguez, Pat Verbal and Marilyn Woody.

As a treasury of personal testimonies, this book owes its existence to the dozens of helpful people who shared stories of power evangelism, provided additional story details or gave me referrals to story leads. My profound gratitude to each of them: Fanny Basta, Lok Mani Bhandari, Doug Birch, Edith Breeden, Keith Carey, Len

Cerny, Don Creasman, Stuart Dauermann, David Denunzio, Ranjit DeSilva, Eddie Elliston, Penny Fulton, Bill Gray, Bill Greig, Jr., Keith and Kim Greig, Ted Haggard, Virgo Handojo, Tanto Handoko, David Henry, Kay Hiramine, Cindy Jacobs, Linda Kangrga, Cathy Kiepke, Jack Kilgore, Helen Knight, Michael Koh, Meryl Konrad, Reigh Lang, Aicha Lion, Sharon Manning, Bryan Marleaux, Jack McAlister, Bill McCandliss, Mony Mok, Jim Montgomery, Randy and Edie Nelson, Bob Oehrig, Jim and Ruth Overton, Beverly Pegues, John Robb, Dave Rumph, Bernardo Salcedo, Cathy Schaller, Dan Shaw, Wolfgang Simson, Steve Spaulding, Sophal and Deborah Ung, Jean Vandenbos, Peter Wagner, Laura Williams and Parviz (whose last name is confidential).

Extra special thanks to my family and my husband, Dave, for unconditional love and support, patience and prayers, helpful suggestions and much more. I love you!

Above all, praise and thanksgiving to the Lord Jesus Christ, whose mighty power deserves full credit for each of these stories and for their collection into this book.

Foreword

We live in a remarkable period of the history of the Christian Church. There are no precedents on record for the harvest of souls—the numbers of people coming to Christ and into fellowship with churches—now occurring daily all over the world. We are in the midst of the greatest prayer movement that could ever have been imagined. The center of gravity of world Christianity has now shifted from the Western world to the Third World. The unity of Christians of all stripes has never been greater, at least for 1600 years.

And in the midst of all this, human beings are witnessing the most spectacular outpouring of the power of the Holy Spirit in all of history. Jesus said, "He who believes in Me, the works that I do he will do also; and greater works than these he will do, because I go to My Father" (John 14:12, NKJV). This statement is so remarkable that many of us have had to stretch ourselves considerably in order to take it literally. But in the mid-1990s it is becoming more and more difficult to ignore either Jesus' amazing words or their clear implications for the Church today.

Given the spread of Christianity to virtually every country of the world, and given the huge numbers of followers of Jesus Christ, it can safely be said that although we are deeply impressed with the quantity and quality of the supernatural manifestations we read about in the Gospels and Acts, these were but mere pilot projects in comparison to what the Holy Spirit is doing in our midst today.

My good friend Jane Rumph is one of those who sees this more clearly than most. Over the past years, Jane and her husband, Dave, have shared with my wife, Doris, and me several life-changing paradigm shifts. As Jane describes in detail later, we all started this journey as good, solid, Bible-believing Christians who had hearts bent on pleasing God. We were also observant and inquisitive enough to begin to notice that God was doing some things that seemed to be "coloring outside the lines" of what we had been taught to expect. And we were willing to take risks, not only to observe and appreciate some of these unusual works of God at a distance, but even to move into hands-on participation.

As we did, things began to change radically for us. In our adult Sunday school class, not only were we studying the book of Acts, but we were beginning to see much of the supernatural phenomena recorded there actually happening in our midst. The more we did, the more we believed; and the more we believed, the more we had eyes to see other things which were happening all around us.

Jane Rumph has been participating in a great deal of what God is doing, not only in her own nation, but in many other parts of the world. I am delighted that she has now opened new windows for us to see into the lives and ministries of many of God's dedicated servants who have been moving powerfully, by His grace, in the real world. I know of nothing else like *Stories from the Front Lines* to open your eyes to the wonders of the Holy Spirit in our day and to help you believe that you can participate in these marvels of the Kingdom of God.

As you read, your faith will grow and you will find yourself praising the King of Kings for His mighty works for the salvation of the lost.

C. Peter Wagner
Fuller Theological Seminary
Pasadena, California

1

What in the World Is God Doing?

A week in Argentina turned my life upside-down.

From the first day my husband, Dave, and I arrived in the country—Wednesday, June 13, 1990—I felt as though we had stepped into the pages of a Frank Peretti novel. In the midst of Argentina's ongoing spiritual revival, the invisible realm came alive in almost tangible ways as angels and demons seemed to swirl around us. I could hardly believe everything that was going on, but I could not put the "book" down, soaking up each day's events like a bug-eyed child leafing through pictures of another world.

Dave and I had traveled to South America with Cindy Jacobs, founder of Generals of Intercession, and Doris Wagner, wife of Fuller Seminary church growth professor C. Peter Wagner. Harvest Evangelism, a ministry in the midst of a three-year plan to reach an Argentine city for Christ, had invited Cindy to teach on strategic-level intercession. Dave and I went along with Doris to support and intercede, and I chronicled events on this trip (and two more that year) to write a report afterward.

For the first time I saw an intercessory warfare model in action. Wild? It was like nothing I had ever experienced. As a friend says, I made such a radical paradigm shift that I almost stripped the transmission gears.

My traditional, evangelical background had laid a solid foundation in biblical truth, and I had already begun seeing God's power touch lives through supernatural healing and deliverance. But little prepared me for witnessing firsthand demonstrations of prayer, proclamation and prophetic action intended to help break a demonic stranglehold over a whole city.

Víctor Lorenzo, a Harvest Evangelism staff member, had done research (also called "spiritual mapping") in the city of Resistencia, capital of the northern Argentine province of Chaco. Attempting to get the spiritual lay of the land—studying factors like religion, culture and local history—he had identified what he saw as five evil principalities or "strongholds" pervading the area. One was the cult of San La Muerte, literally "St. Death," a diabolical spirit that adherents believe promises a good death in exchange for allegiance.

Cindy taught extensively during this trip on principles of strategic-level intercession and spiritual warfare. She met with the city's pastors and prepared a team to engage in warfare prayer in Resistencia's central plaza. For someone like me it was a startling, almost unbelievable prayer meeting. All morning the intercessors stood before the Lord or walked to different areas of the open plaza to pray in front of particular statues, artwork or buildings. They sang praises, read Scripture, clapped hands, even pantomimed their prayers and rebuked the demonic strongholds in the name of Jesus Christ. Through worship, individual and corporate repentance and reconciliation, they exercised the authority given believers by the Lord Jesus:

"I have given you authority to trample on snakes and scorpions and to overcome all the power of the enemy; nothing will harm you."
Luke 10:19

After five hours the intercessors experienced a great release of joy that erupted in shouts of victory. The demonic power, they sensed, had been broken.

Six weeks later Edgardo Silvoso, president of Harvest Evangelism, pummeled the kingdom of darkness again when he publicly repudiated and prayed against San La Muerte in a citywide campaign.

Then in October, just before the crusade that climaxed the plan to reach the city, Edgardo got some stunning news.

"You know who died last Saturday?" Víctor, his staff worker, asked him. "Doña Cecilia Medina, caretaker of one of Resistencia's most important temples to San La Muerte."

"She's dead?" Edgardo responded. "What happened?"

"Seems she was smoking in bed and fell asleep—asphyxiated when her bed caught fire. But there's more. A guy from one of the churches was on the emergency team that responded to the fire. Strangest thing, he said. In the whole bedroom, the only things burned were the bed, the woman herself—and her idol statue of San La Muerte."

Edgardo considered this news. They had prayed against the demonic principality itself, not against its followers. Could this development possibly suggest that the powers of darkness were in retreat? Despite all her years of devotion to San La Muerte, Doña Cecilia had suffered a horrible death. Those who prayed to the evil spirit for a good death must have gagged on their *medias lunas* when they read the article in the morning newspaper over breakfast.

The citywide crusade that week drew thousands to hear the good news of Jesus Christ. More than two thousand returned commitment cards. By April 1991, the official end of the three-year plan, Resistencia's church population had doubled—a 102% increase in actual church members. And the plentiful harvest continued. Two years later unofficial figures pegged church growth at 500%, with the total number of congregations jumping from seventy to two hundred.

Did the intercessory warfare against San La Muerte contribute to this amazing change in Resistencia's spiritual climate? Only heaven will tell for sure, but many of those who now trust in Jesus for eternal life would have no doubt.

Power Evangelism

The new Argentine believers came to faith in Christ through a set of circumstances that included *power evangelism*. Pastor John Wimber of the Vineyard Christian Fellowship coined the term, with author Kevin Springer, in their best-selling book of the same name (Harper & Row, 1986). Power evangelism in its widest definition includes any instance in which the demonstrated power of God plays a role in conversion. In a typical power evangelism experience, some kind of supernatural phenomenon breaks through barriers of resistance to the Gospel, empowering the truth about Christ (in whatever way it comes) to penetrate and bring salvation.

Signs and wonders, spiritual warfare, gifts of the Holy Spirit, healing, miracles, dreams, angelic visitations—the Bible speaks of these things, but how often do they happen today? And if they still take place, what is their purpose?

This book showcases the most important purpose served by signs and wonders: bringing people to faith in Jesus Christ. In the following pages, dozens of contemporary stories from all over the world show how God manifests His transcendent power to cut through thickets of spiritual bondage and lead people to the point of conversion.

Power evangelism can take as many forms as the variety of ways God demonstrates His power. Sometimes an unbeliever with a simple headache wants to know Jesus personally after the pain disappears through prayer in Jesus' name. And, on the other end of the scale, incidents of resuscitation from the dead can bring not only individuals but families or even whole villages to faith in Christ.

Make no mistake—signs and wonders cannot save. Only the Holy Spirit bringing conviction of the good news of Jesus Christ— His life, death on the cross and resurrection—can convey God's grace and lead someone into the Kingdom of God. The apostle Paul says in Romans 1:16, "I am not ashamed of the gospel, because it is the power of God for the salvation of everyone who believes. . . ."

Yet the undeniable potency of the Gospel alone can be turbo-charged when it works hand in hand with the power of signs and wonders pointing to Christ. Jesus' own ministry consistently shows effective partnership between the proclamation of the Kingdom and the demonstration of its power: "Jesus went through all the towns and villages, teaching in their synagogues, preaching the good news of the kingdom and healing every disease and sickness" (Matthew 9:35).

Power evangelism hinges on the will of God for a particular time, place and people. Jesus declared while on earth, "I tell you the truth, the Son can do nothing by himself; he can do only what he sees his Father doing, because whatever the Father does the Son also does" (John 5:19). If the Father has no plans to intervene supernaturally, our presumption will not force Him to do so. But perhaps more often, God's sons and daughters miss opportunities to co-labor with Him when we remain oblivious to what He is doing or wants to do. Maximum effectiveness in evangelism comes when those who share the Gospel keep in step with the Holy Spirit and His leading, doing "whatever the Father does," including min-istering in divine power.

In some stories in this book, the Holy Spirit comes in personal, supernatural ways to lead a single individual to salvation. In other stories the demonstrated power of God results in the conversion of people who either witnessed an event or heard firsthand testi-mony. Sometimes the prayers of believers prompt the release of divine power. Other times the Lord seems to act sovereignly. In most of these stories God intervenes for good and blessing, draw-ing people to His love and grace. Occasionally, however, He directs His power against the forces of evil, causing witnesses to revere Him in repentance. In the case of spiritual warfare, as in Resisten-cia, the destruction of demonic strongholds blinding people's minds frees them to respond to the Gospel as never before.

Power evangelism may be new to you. But its potential can rev-olutionize your ministry and mission. At the end of this chapter you will find a list of six ways the implications of the stories in this book can benefit your life and witness.

Read on and take a look at what happened as a result of the simple but courageous obedience of a man stuck with a long airport layover.

Four Hours in an African Airport

On Monday, February 14, 1994, David Henry, an itinerant church-planting coach from Los Angeles, found himself with four hours to kill in Lungi Airport in Freetown, capital of Sierra Leone, West Africa. After finishing seminars on church planting that he had been invited to teach, he had received an unexpected opportunity to minister in The Gambia, about four hundred miles up the coast. David decided to extend his trip, and linked up with four Australians traveling there to assist a mercy ministry with food and medical equipment.

Lungi Airport, not exactly bustling, offered few diversions for the traveler with time on his hands. Sitting with his new friends at a small table, David sipped a cup of coffee heavily spiked with cream and sugar.

Long layovers can be a drag, he thought.

One of the Australians, Ian Farrington, was praying aloud quietly as he left the table and wandered over to a railing overlooking the runway. Before long, this white man who seemed to be muttering to himself attracted the attention of an airport security guard. David noticed the pair talking for a few minutes before they headed over to the table.

"David," said Ian, a new believer of about two years, "this is Moses Konteh. I was over there praying when he came up and asked me what I was doing. I told him I was talking to Jesus, just telling Him how much I love Him. Moses is a Muslim, and the idea of talking to Jesus really seems to astound him. I decided I'd better introduce him to somebody who can tell him about Jesus better than I can."

David set down his coffee cup, but Moses held up a hand. "Wait! Don't say anything yet. I want to get some of my friends."

In moments David and the Australians were surrounded by seven or eight airport employees. David shared a simple message of Jesus' life, death and resurrection.

"Jesus loves Muslims," he concluded, "and He often likes to heal Muslims to show His love. Is anybody here sick or hurting?"

Umar, a baggage-handler, piped up, "I injured my hip and it's in constant pain."

Depending on the Holy Spirit for guidance, David prayed a short prayer for healing in Jesus' name.

Suddenly Umar cried out, "It's gone! My pain is totally gone!" He began to jump and bend while the others gaped at him.

Sensing an anointing from God, David plunged ahead, aware that his methodology would probably mortify traditional Islamic missions strategists. "Would any of you like to receive Jesus as your Savior now?"

Every one of them was ready. They held hands as David led them in a prayer to confess Jesus as Savior. Then he began explaining more of what it means to know the love of God in Christ.

Some of the workers had to return to their duties. But Moses, the security guard who had started all this, hungered for more and went to find his two supervisors. Then they all went to an air-conditioned office.

Both supervisors were already believers, David learned, but they needed healing. One faced possible abdominal surgery. As David prayed for him, his pain and swelling vanished. The other supervisor wanted prayer for chronic pain in his ribs, but David stepped back.

"Moses has just asked Jesus to come into his heart," he told the two men. "Moses, why don't you pray for your boss yourself?"

With a little coaching, Moses laid his hand on his supervisor and told the pain to leave in Jesus' name. It did instantly. A wave of joy spread through the room.

David gave everyone Bibles with study helps as they continued to talk. Then the men returned to their posts.

David was just thinking about a second cup of coffee when Moses telephoned his brother with an urgent request: "Please bring my wife to the airport. There's someone I want her to meet."

The two arrived and David gave another simple account of the Gospel. After Moses told them about the healings, they wanted to receive Jesus, too.

Later Moses asked David when he would be coming back through the airport.

"A week from Wednesday," David answered.

"I'll be looking for you," said Moses, smiling.

So it was that David's next four-hour layover in Lungi Airport promised to be considerably more interesting. You will hear about his ministry in The Gambia in chapter 9. But on his return to Sierra Leone, he taught and ministered to several more people Moses had assembled, giving them Gospel literature and inviting each one to hear an evangelist who would preach in the national stadium the following week.

And David went home praising God for unexpected opportunities. Even an airport layover can be an exciting time of cooperating with "whatever the Father does" and ministering His power to bring souls to Jesus Christ.

Lost in a Sea of Sand

David Henry's story illustrates the interaction between the communication of the Gospel and the demonstration of its power. So does my husband's process of conversion.

For most of his first seventeen years, Dave Rumph clung to atheism and the ideal of self-sufficiency, convinced that scientific rationalism left no room for a Supreme Being who operated outside the confines of time and space. Religion was for mental and emotional weaklings.

But his resolve cracked when he saw friends he respected, strong and intellectual, confess faith in God and His Son, Jesus Christ. He heard them pray and saw answers come. First skeptical, then flabbergasted, he witnessed odd coincidences time and again, too frequent to write off to chance. He began to believe there might be Someone out there bigger than himself.

In the summer of 1975 Dave's Boy Scout troop from suburban Orinda in Northern California spent a week camping at Blue Lake in the Sierra Nevada. One night Dave and other senior patrol leaders put on a skit around the shoreline campfire. He and his fellow actors wore dark glasses, and Dave could see little besides the glow of the fire. But when the skit ended and he took them off, he knew immediately something was wrong. One of his contact lenses had popped out of his eye.

The campfire entertainment continued while Dave felt his guts churn. There was no telling when or where the lens had come out over dozens of square feet of lakeside sand and gravel.

As he turned away in anguish to sit alone under a nearby tree, Dave envisioned boys stepping on the hard plastic lens, cracking it, kicking it deeper into the sand. His math and science training told him that the odds of finding the tiny, clear contact at all (not to mention in good condition) were astronomical.

O God, help! It was a desperate heart cry.

Despite his discouragement, Dave determined to search, even if he had to comb the sand inch by inch, archeologist-style. After the campfire ended, Dave went to his tent, removed the remaining contact lens and dug his thick glasses out of his pack. Returning to the now-deserted campfire ring with a Coleman lantern, he set it down and got on hands and knees. Instantly he caught a glint of something small in the lantern's glow. His lost lens, intact and unscratched, lay in the first place he set his eyes.

Dave sat in silence for a long time before returning to his tent. Waves of relief washed over him while his mind tried to take it in.

This . . . this is a miracle, he had to admit. *This goes way beyond the laws of probability.*

The implications began to hit home. Was this what his friends had been trying to tell him?

God isn't just out there, he realized. *He knows me and my traumas and wants to help. I can turn to Him in situations beyond my control. He's a personal God and worthy of my trust.*

Dave's experience at Blue Lake summer camp proved a turning point in his move toward a relationship with Jesus Christ. All the intellectual arguments and theological apologetics of Christian friends made little impact until he began to see the miraculous power of God at work in ways he could not explain by the laws of nature.

Yet he would not have known who heard and answered his prayer at Blue Lake without his friends' previous testimony. Believers within the Body of Christ had given him the building blocks he needed to lay a foundation of faith grounded not in scientific rationalism but in biblical truth.

Something More?

My own spiritual background could not have been more different. God blessed me with Christian parents. My father, John Novak, came to faith simply by reading and meditating on the Gospel of John. I asked Jesus into my heart at age five when my mother, Zillah Novak, shared the Good News with me.

At the traditional, Bible-believing evangelical church in which I grew up, missions and evangelism received strong emphasis. The youth groups held many outreach events that drew young people to hear contemporary presentations of the Gospel through word, music or drama. People came to Christ. The church grew.

But I learned little until college about the role of the Holy Spirit. And the few stories I heard about remarkable supernatural events always took place long ago or far away.

Change came slowly as I, like Dave, found friends who believed in the immediacy of God's presence in their lives. No flakiness here—these were bright folks who knew the Bible. But they had a personal experience of the Holy Spirit that was new to me. Gingerly I began sampling it.

My approach to evangelism did not change. I still carried a *Four Spiritual Laws* booklet in my purse, took part in the "I Found It!" campaign, invited friends to church and outreach events. But I started discovering a few missing pieces of the puzzle.

In the fall of 1983, two years after we married, Dave and I began hearing about Pastor John Wimber and his Vineyard Christian Fellowship, then meeting in the gymnasium of Canyon High School in Yorba Linda, California. Each service ended with a "ministry time." People shook when prayed for. Others were healed instantly of diseases. Unbelievers were delivered of demons and committed themselves to Christ. The church, mushrooming in size, planned to move to a large leased warehouse in nearby Anaheim.

Within the previous year we had also heard tales of strange goings-on at Fuller Theological Seminary in our hometown of Pasadena. Students packed out a new course called "Signs, Wonders and Church Growth" taught by John Wimber and C. Peter Wagner, professor at Fuller's School of World Mission. And Wagner, we learned, was teaching a class at Lake Avenue Congregational Church called the "120 Fellowship."

From our first visit to 120 Fellowship in January 1984, the new puzzle pieces began coming together. The class took its name from the 120 believers mentioned in Acts 1:15 who joined together in prayer before Pentecost. Dr. Wagner—soon to become "Peter"— showed me how powerful experiences of the Holy Spirit could link with solid evangelical theology in a satisfying, effective partnership. I did not have to stretch the bounds of biblical interpretation to accept signs and wonders as valid for today.

I began reading of other Christian leaders who had come to the same conclusion. Pastors learned from each other, finding common ground. Traditional churches, including the one in which I grew up, added healing services, prayer for the sick and anointing with oil. The new trend, following the Pentecostal movement of the early 1900s and the charismatic renewal beginning mid-century, was dubbed "the third wave of the Holy Spirit."

Staggering Growth

In 1990 the puzzle pieces got rearranged dramatically during my travels to Argentina. For the first time I witnessed a head-on clash of spiritual powers. And when the intercession of the Christians in Resistencia struck a heavy blow against the cult of death strangling their city, I saw how the triumph of God over demonic principalities could help liberate thousands of souls from the kingdom of darkness.

My Argentina adventures opened my eyes to astonishing ways God is exercising divine power all over the world to bring people

to Christ. Frequently in 120 Fellowship we hear news of exciting
global developments. I have been privileged to take part in some
of the Wagners' work as a prayer partner and board member of
Global Harvest Ministries. My horizons expanded further when I
became chronicler of the Spiritual Warfare Network (SWN), part
of the United Prayer Track of the A.D. 2000 & Beyond Movement. The forty United States members of the SWN Founders
Circle represent a wide spectrum of theology and methodology.
(Some of their stories appear in this book.) In October 1993 the
Spiritual Warfare Network held its first international consultation
in Seoul, Korea, with some three hundred representatives from 43
countries and six continents.

The global explosion of spiritual power for evangelism is
unprecedented, as David Shibley notes in his book *A Force in the
Earth* (Creation House, 1989):

> From its humble beginnings at the turn of the century, the move-
> ment of the Holy Spirit has grown to become the most vital force
> in Christianity today. . . . God's Spirit is ever pointing in one direc-
> tion—toward the preeminence of Jesus Christ. And He is ever
> pressing us toward one great goal—the fulfillment of the Great
> Commission. For the first time since the first century, the evange-
> lization of the world is within our grasp. We have been brought to
> the kingdom for such a time as this.
>
> pages 15, 16–17

Dr. Ralph Winter, founder of the U.S. Center for World Mission and president of William Carey International University in
Pasadena, has tracked the phenomenal advance of the Gospel
worldwide and concluded that finishing the task of world evangelization can be accomplished in this generation. Using statistics
from Dr. David Barrett, author of *The World Christian Encyclope-
dia* and head of the Lausanne Statistics Task Force, Winter shows
that "Bible-believing Christians" (in contrast to nominal Christians) are multiplying at a rate more than three times faster than
world population growth.

As recently as 1940, there was one "Bible-believing Christian"
to 32 other people in the world. By 1980 the ratio had improved

to one to sixteen. In 1995 for each believer there were now only eight others (in round figures). This means that close to eleven percent of all people on earth—600 million out of 5.7 billion—confess commitment to Christ (see *Mission Frontiers*, May-June 1995, p. 5).

Patrick Johnstone's handbook *Operation World* (Zondervan, updated 1993) calculates that evangelicals and Pentecostals "are the fastest-growing major religious groupings in the world" (p. 23). Much of their increase comes from conversions, he notes, in contrast to Muslims, whose growth can be traced primarily to high birth rates.

In particular, non-Western harvest fields have yielded a bumper crop in recent years. Johnstone reveals the astonishing facts: "Nearly 70% of the world's Evangelicals now live in the non-Western world and this is likely to rise to 77% by the end of the century" (p. 26).

What about power evangelism? David Barrett hints at the growing acceptance of signs and wonders in evangelism in his article "Global Statistics" in the *Dictionary of Pentecostal and Charismatic Movements* (Zondervan/Regency, 1988). "Massive expansion and growth [of the Pentecostal-charismatic renewal] continue at a current rate of 19 million new members a year or over 54,000 a day," he writes. "One-third of this is purely demographic . . . ; two-thirds are converts and other new members" (p. 811).

In his article "Church Growth" in the same volume, C. Peter Wagner acknowledges that parts of the world are experiencing energetic church growth without accompanying signs and wonders. Conversely, other areas may experience dramatic signs and wonders without, unfortunately, significant church growth. But the sweeping pattern shows a marked correlation between manifestations of supernatural power and bountiful harvests of new believers.

What's in It for You

In this book you will find stories from all over the world illustrating the magnitude and growing significance of power evangelism today. In each chapter I will point out some of the scriptural precedents for particular kinds of power ministry. Even some of the most unusual stories have counterparts in the Bible, particularly the book of Acts.

Many stories raise key issues with wide-ranging implications. Brief observations and interpretations follow to prompt further reflection. I will also note the drawbacks and limitations of power evangelism in various situations.

Why should you read this book? If this book accomplishes all its goals, it will:

- *Expand your vision for the global purposes of God.* God loves all people everywhere and will stop at nothing to make sure that some from even the most obscure and resistant groups will stand before His throne among that great multitude from "every nation, tribe, people and language" (Revelation 7:9).
- *Give you solid reasons to affirm the effectiveness of power ministries in bringing people to Christ in today's world.* Many quarters of the Body of Christ, particularly in the West, have overlooked the potential of signs and wonders for evangelism. But the orientation of some people groups—such as those for whom religion is primarily an issue not of truth but of power—makes them receptive to almost no other kind of evangelism.
- *Encourage you to mediate God's supernatural ministry.* Perhaps that family member who has never responded to your testimony would have a change of heart if he or she experienced the love and power of God through your prayers for healing. The apostle Paul, for one, combined evangelistic methods: "Our gospel came to you not simply with words, but also with power, with the Holy Spirit and with deep conviction" (1 Thessalonians 1:5).
- *Motivate you to intensified prayer for world missions and evangelism.* Does it seem impossible for salvation to come to the Maldivians, one of the least evangelized peoples on earth? Along with interceding for greater openness and receptivity, try praying that God in His power and mercy would work in sovereign, miraculous ways—perhaps through dreams and visions of Jesus Himself proclaiming to them the Good News.

- *Boost your faith in our glorious and almighty God.* Nothing is impossible for the Lord! The Creator of the universe rules and overrules all other powers and principalities.
- *Cause you to join with others in a symphony of praise to God for His glorious acts.* All too often the secular media bombard us with discouraging news. But even the more positive reports from Christian radio, television and magazines cannot keep up with everything the Lord is doing across the globe. Come behind the scenes with me to witness some untold tales of God's grace and power in bringing men and women, boys and girls, into His Kingdom.

In the coming chapters I will reinforce and expand on each of these benefits as we look at the wide potential of power evangelism to accelerate the fulfillment of the Great Commission in our day: Jesus' command to "go and make disciples of all nations . . . " (Matthew 28:19). Already the Spirit of the Lord is sweeping across the world like a prairie wildfire!

More than anything, this book aims to magnify the name of Jesus Christ through testimony to His mighty deeds. The writer of Psalm 96:3 (RSV) might have been giving a mandate for this book:

> Declare his glory among the nations,
>   his marvelous works among all the peoples!

2

"I Am the Lord Who Heals You"

Stories of Divine Healing

The dust swirled in tiny twisters behind Bryan Marleaux's car as he and his wife headed into the hills south of downtown Tijuana, Mexico. The 31-year-old seminarian and itinerant evangelist silently thanked the Lord again for the young woman he had married. Mercedes, an Argentine-American, would minister with him by translating his guest sermon into Spanish as he preached at a local church that Sunday morning in September 1994.

Bryan reflected on the sovereign way God had first linked the two of them to the pastor and congregation at Iglesia Misión Cristiana Plan Libertador.

One day the previous January he had sensed clear direction from the Holy Spirit to take to Mexico some clothing they had received for distribution to the poor. The message was unmistakable: *Today. Go. Mexico.*

Mexico? Brian had asked the Lord in response. *Now?*

But God did not give any more hints. So Bryan and Mercedes had loaded the clothes into their Honda Civic that January day and headed south.

Almost a hundred miles down the coast from their home in Corona Del Mar, California, they crossed the border.

"O.K., Lord, You'll have to guide us from here," Bryan prayed aloud.

The hills just ahead seemed to beckon, and Bryan drove into that area. A turn here and there brought them to a dirt road, which they followed until they came to a little church housed in a converted market with several dozen people clustered outside.

Bryan turned aside to park the car, and he and Mercedes began chatting with the first person they met—the pastor, as it turned out. Their jaws sagged when they learned that the guest speaker that day was a friend of theirs from the United States. How had they managed to show up in this remote neighborhood of Tijuana just in time for their friend's service?

Bryan and Mercedes' friend introduced them to the congregation and invited them to give greetings. They also shared the clothing they had brought.

"Can you come back in a couple of weeks and preach?" the pastor asked the Marleauxes.

In the eight months since then, they had returned several times and forged a warm bond with the pastor and his people. With a partnership established through divine appointment, Bryan and Mercedes had come to expect the unexpected whenever they visited Iglesia Misión Cristiana.

Now, as they reached the church this Sunday morning, September 18, Bryan pulled up to park.

I wonder what God will do today? he mused as he waited a moment for the dust outside to settle.

During the morning service he preached a message on the grace of God, Mercedes at his side, to the congregation of sixty to eighty members. At the end he felt the Lord prompt him with a few words of knowledge about healing needs. Seven or eight people responded and came forward for prayer, lining up shoulder to shoulder in front of the altar.

As he and Mercedes moved to the first person in line on their right, Bryan asked other worshipers to help pray and stand behind anyone who might fall under the power of the Holy Spirit.

A girl about seven years old began shaking as she was prayed for. Then a young man broke out in sobs while the Lord ministered to deep needs.

We need more prayer help! Bryan thought, scanning the congregation.

His eyes lit on Miguel Guerrero, whom just about everyone called Junior. Bryan had met the 28-year-old on previous trips and knew he spoke a little English.

"Junior, why don't you lay your hand on this man," Bryan suggested, "and help us pray for him?"

Clearly the power of God already rested on the young man shaking and weeping in the prayer line. But as Junior extended his hand and placed it on the man's head, Bryan noticed a glazed look come over Junior's saucer-eyed face. Moments later Junior wandered off, waving that same arm like a traffic cop.

Where is he going? Bryan wondered. *We still need his help!*

As he and Mercedes moved down the line praying for others, Bryan spotted Junior sitting in the back of the church with two friends about his age, talking and gesturing with gusto. In a few minutes the trio stood up, and the healing line got longer by two as Junior's friends joined it. Soon Bryan reached the end of the line where Junior stood behind his two friends, one mustached and one clean-shaven, both wearing comfortably worn T-shirts and jeans.

"What would you like prayer for?" Bryan asked them through Mercedes.

The answer took unusually long as Mercedes exchanged words with Junior and his two friends. Finally she turned to Bryan. "His friends say, 'We haven't come for healing. We want to receive the Lord.'"

Bryan's tongue locked in a stammer.

I haven't given an altar call! he marveled. *I didn't even preach an evangelistic message.* He imagined himself joking, "Hey, this isn't how it's supposed to go. You guys sit down and let me give an altar

call. Then you raise your hands and come forward, O.K.? Go back
and let's try this again!"

The Lord, however, had not been caught by surprise. Junior
explained, with Mercedes interpreting, that at the moment he put
his hand on the young man in the healing line, he had felt the
power of God shoot up his arm like a bolt of electricity. He knew
instantly that he had been healed of a long-standing shoulder
injury. With pain-free mobility he had not enjoyed in years, Junior
lost no time explaining to his two friends, Juan Prieto and José
"Che" Rodriguez, what God had done. Although they had never
attended church before, Juan and José recognized God's power and
wanted to give their lives to Him.

"You're sure?" Bryan asked them. "You understand what this
means?"

Indeed, each young man confessed his desire to commit his life
to Christ. Bryan's message about God's grace and the demonstrations of His love in touching and healing others had been enough
for them.

Bryan and Mercedes led Juan and José in the sinner's prayer, asking God for forgiveness and salvation through Christ and pledging their lives to Him. As they finished, the Lord impressed on
Bryan to pray for each to be filled with the Holy Spirit.

Juan's face shone with the peace of the Lord, a heavenly smile
curling up his brown mustache.

José, meanwhile, began to shake. A stream of tears burst forth
and soon his legs gave way. For several minutes he lay on the floor
resting in the Holy Spirit, looking as serene as if soaking in a warm
bath.

Bryan learned later that Juan and José had come out of painful
backgrounds scarred by drug and alcohol abuse. He made sure
Junior and others in the church followed up these new professions
of faith with Bible study and discipleship training.

And Bryan left Tijuana that September day with a fresh sense
of the sovereignty of God in birthing salvation. His theological
training had prepared him for giving orderly expositions of the
Gospel and strategically timed invitations to receive Christ. But
here the Lord had sneaked up on him!

"God doesn't always wait for us to do our little rituals before He acts," he concludes with a smile.

The two new believers in Tijuana, meanwhile, continue to attend church and send strong roots deep into the nourishing soil of the Kingdom of God.

Healing as Love and Power

What moved Juan and José to want to become followers of Christ? That September day at Iglesia Misión Cristiana, they saw something they had never seen with such immediacy: a tangible demonstration of the love, compassion and power of Jesus. The witness proved so strong that a physical healing of their friend Junior—not even their own healing—was sufficient to move them to repentance and conversion.

Healing figured prominently in the earthly ministry of Jesus. Why?

In the first place, the Gospels speak of Jesus' compassion toward the suffering. Mark 1:40–42 chronicles a typical incident from the beginning of His ministry:

> A man with leprosy came to him and begged him on his knees, "If you are willing, you can make me clean."
> Filled with compassion, Jesus reached out his hand and touched the man. "I am willing," he said. "Be clean!" Immediately the leprosy left him and he was cured.

Similarly, near the end of His ministry, Jesus met two blind men sitting by the road outside Jericho. They called to Him, pleading for restoration of their sight. Matthew 20:34 records, "Jesus had compassion on them and touched their eyes. Immediately they received their sight and followed him."

Second, supernatural healing served as a sign of the Kingdom of God, offering powerful validation of Jesus' identity and message. Peter declared in his Pentecost sermon that "Jesus of Nazareth was a man accredited by God to you by miracles, wonders and signs, which God did among you through him, as you yourselves know"

(Acts 2:22). The signs He performed gave evidence of Jesus' divine origin.

Moreover, Jesus Himself pointed to His supernatural deeds as proof of His Messiahship. One day John the Baptist, languishing in prison, sent two messengers to his cousin.

> When the men came to Jesus, they said, "John the Baptist sent us to you to ask, 'Are you the one who was to come, or should we expect someone else?'"
>
> At that very time Jesus cured many who had diseases, sicknesses and evil spirits, and gave sight to many who were blind. So he replied to the messengers, "Go back and report to John what you have seen and heard: The blind receive sight, the lame walk, those who have leprosy are cured, the deaf hear, the dead are raised, and the good news is preached to the poor. Blessed is the man who does not fall away on account of me."
>
> Luke 7:20–23

God still uses supernatural healing today to draw people to Himself through its witness to His love and power. Sometimes (as happened to Junior Guerrero) healing comes as a sovereign, unasked-for act of God, triggering awe in the one healed and others who see and hear of it. At other times God waits for one of His children to ask for healing in a particular situation. When we have courage to approach Him with our requests and not box Him within the boundaries of our expectations or methodologies, the Lord may surprise us.

Prayer for healing, particularly healing of unbelievers, works to greatest effect when intercessors hear God's distinct guidance as to His will and timing. At the beginning of Bryan Marleaux's connection with Iglesia Misión Cristiana, he had sensed the Spirit of the Lord saying to him, *Today. Go. Mexico.*

In the next story, years of sod-busting spiritual warfare helped plow up fallow ground for the Kingdom of God, at which point God arranged an opportunity for healing prayer that sprouted wide consequences.

Hammering Down Walls with Healing Power

Just past midnight an unmarked car cruised quietly through the dark streets of Semarang, Indonesia. Its headlights captured the young women—scores of them—lounging on street corners or in doorways, looking for business. The car slowed but did not stop. No one would have suspected that its occupants were military specialists on an undercover mission.

Pastor Tanto Handoko of Christ the True Shepherd Indonesian Christian Fellowship had begun leading his troops in intercessory "prayer drives" in 1982, when they belonged to the parachurch Sangkakala Mission Fellowship. During the all-night events, thirty or forty intercessors gathered at 9 P.M. and spent three hours in praise and worship preparing for front-line action. At midnight they divided into different vehicles to pray on-site at various targets of need in the city.

Semarang, a metropolis of close to two million on the north coast of central Java, played host to the usual menagerie of urban ills, including a neighborhood notorious as a center of prostitution. The many struggling families who lived in this densely populated area, known as Sri Kuncoro, had steeled themselves to ignore the thriving business carried on by hundreds of their neighbors. But Pastor Tanto and his troops refused to concede this ground to the enemy.

As he drove slowly through Sri Kuncoro, Pastor Tanto and the carful of prayer warriors lifted the residents in prayer to God, murmuring petitions in tongues and in their native Indonesian language. One and then another began to speak out in the authority of Christ: "In the name of Jesus we bind every demonic spirit in this place. We come against a spirit of lust and a spirit of adultery, and command the blinders of darkness to fall from people's eyes. We claim the salvation of these precious souls in Jesus' name. Holy Spirit, we ask You to move in their hearts and bring them to Christ, any way You want to do it."

Month after month, year after year, nocturnal bands of intercessors hammered away at the strongholds of darkness—the persistent presence of practices contrary to God's will. In the visible realm, little seemed to change. But in the spiritual realm, each blow was leaving a hairline crack in a massive brick fortress.

Structurally weakened, the invisible walls of darkness around the prostitution complex finally began to crumble in December 1990 when God performed a dramatic healing.

A Christian businessman in Semarang who owned a shoe manufacturing plant invited Pastor Gaspar Mangke, a colleague of Pastor Tanto, to minister there. One employee approached Pastor Gaspar eagerly.

"Would you be willing to come pray for my father? He's got chronic tuberculosis and has been paralyzed for six years. He needs healing desperately. Will you come?"

When Pastor Gaspar learned that this man's father, Djumadi, lived in the center of the prostitution complex, he knew God was arranging a divine appointment.

Soon afterward, Pastor Gaspar visited the invalid, about 52 years old. Laying hands on Djumadi in the name of Jesus, Pastor Gaspar prayed for complete healing, binding any spirits of infirmity. Immediately Djumadi felt his chest clear and lighten. He began to move his legs. With joy he confessed, "Why, I'm healed!"

Seized by the irresistible love and power of God, Djumadi attended services at Pastor Tanto's church the very next day. In no time the believers there led him to faith and salvation in Jesus Christ. Soon the rest of his family came to the Lord, too.

With this healing God struck a mighty blow for the Kingdom of light. The impact of His spiritual sledgehammer sent cracks spidering in all directions through the walls of darkness surrounding Sri Kuncoro. When Djumadi's flabbergasted neighbors learned what had happened, they too began attending church. Friends told friends, and within a couple of years Pastor Tanto's fellowship had baptized fifty new converts from the prostitution complex, some of them former women of the street. Christ the True Shepherd Christian Fellowship established a medical clinic in the neighborhood that became a preaching point for a satellite congregation.

Now the church offers weekly ministries for all ages: Wednesday evening home fellowships, a Saturday afternoon children's program, a meeting for teenagers each Saturday night and a Sunday morning service.

The church continues to grow and baptize new converts as the Gospel penetrates Sri Kuncoro as never before, transforming lives with the joy and peace of God. Many will never forget the first breakthrough—when the Lord's healing power raised up a sick man.

Healing with Broad Ripple Effects

A single supernatural healing can have broad ripple effects. The book of Acts relates what happened during one of Peter's early preaching trips.

> As Peter traveled about the country, he went to visit the saints in Lydda. There he found a man named Aeneas, a paralytic who had been bedridden for eight years. "Aeneas," Peter said to him, "Jesus Christ heals you. Get up and take care of your mat." Immediately Aeneas got up. All those who lived in Lydda and [the coastal region of] Sharon saw him and turned to the Lord.
>
> Acts 9:32–35

When the witness of one man's healing results in the conversion of an entire city and region, we may wonder if the healing broke through an invisible demonic barrier. 2 Corinthians 4:4 says, "The god of this age has blinded the minds of unbelievers, so that they cannot see the light of the gospel of the glory of Christ, who is the image of God." When the power of God tears off these blinders from unbelievers' minds, they have freedom for the first time to understand and respond to the Gospel of Christ. And when mass conversions take place in an identifiable region, one reason might be gaping new rips in the shroud of darkness over that territory.

Pastor Tanto and his team had targeted the prostitution complex for years of warfare prayer, weakening the evil forces reigning there. Then Djumadi was healed—a healing that may have turned the tide of battle and broken the back of the spirits holding Sri Kuncoro's residents in bondage, allowing people there to see the truth clearly as never before.

Fresh openness to the Gospel means little, however, unless the people of God make the most of the opportunity by sharing the Word of God. Without faithful proclamation of Christ, Djumadi and his neighbors might never have known the Source of the power that healed him. "How can they believe in the one of whom they have not heard? And how can they hear without someone preaching to them?" (Romans 10:14). The new preaching center, coupled with the mercy ministry of the medical clinic, illuminated the message of salvation with the radiance of a floodlight.

Jesus' ministry carefully combined deeds of power with words of power. Matthew 4:23 tells us that "Jesus went throughout Galilee, teaching in their synagogues, preaching the good news of the kingdom, and healing every disease and sickness among the people." The result? "News about him spread. . . . Large crowds . . . followed him" (verses 24–25).

Even those of us not called to large-scale missions or evangelism can boost the effectiveness of our testimony by allowing God to minister His healing power through us.

The young man we will meet next faced years of violent resistance to the Gospel from his parents until God used him to touch each of them with His grace—first in a physical way, then in a spiritual way.

Jesus Christ 2, Buddha 0

One night in April 1982, seventeen-year-old Kay Hiramine gave his life to Christ—a commitment that, just a few hours later, would put him in danger of being murdered by his own father.

The third child of parents who emigrated from Japan in 1956, Kay grew up with his two older sisters in a nominally Buddhist family in Upland, California. Like most first-generation Japanese, his parents maintained a *Butsudan* in their home, a Buddhist altar made of black lacquer and featuring a gold Buddha figure. In front of the altar they placed bowls of rice and other food as offerings to the ancestral spirits. They trained their young children to pray at the Butsudan two or three times a day, although as the years passed the rituals got left behind. Once a year on Memorial Day the family attended temple services together.

Kay knew little about Christianity until he got involved in a Bible study on his high school campus and was befriended by David Emerson, the youth pastor of a local church. Over the weeks, as Kay left for fellowship meetings, he watched his father's mood grow darker.

"I'm warning you, son," he said. "If you become a Christian, the ancestral spirits will come after you. They'll try to kill you."

Kay recognized the reality of these spirits and did not discount the threat. Still, he continued to meet with his new Christian friends. In fact, it was at the Emerson home that April night when Kay spent five hours in tear-filled prayer, confessing his sins and crying out to God for salvation.

At last, with joy and assurance of his newfound faith, Kay returned home at three in the morning. Tiptoeing through the dark house, Kay peeked into his parents' bedroom where his father, Kay Senior, and mother, Hiroko, lay sleeping.

"Lord Jesus," he whispered, "I pray for my mom and dad right now. Please touch their hearts and make them know You as Savior."

Before turning in, Kay also paused in front of the Butsudan. He could almost sense his grandmother's spirit lurking in displeasure nearby.

In a low voice the teenager declared, "In the name of Jesus, if there are any evil spirits here, I say to you that I am a Christian now. I don't want you to have control over my family."

After Kay went to bed, he sensed a dark presence hovering over him intent on his destruction. Evidently something had gotten stirred up. In silent prayer the new believer asked God for protection by the power of the blood of Christ.

Rising unusually early, he came downstairs at 6 A.M. and found his parents already up and sitting at the kitchen table next to the TV room. Before they exchanged a word, Kay Senior turned to his son with a steady gaze.

"You became a Christian last night." It was clearly an accusation. Kay's insides jumped. *How does he know?*

Aloud he answered, "That's right, Dad," and began to explain. But his parents were angry.

They've never been much more than nominal Buddhists, he thought, puzzled. *What's going on here?*

For 45 minutes the confrontation escalated until Kay's father, out of control, sprang from his chair, grabbed a long sushi knife and waved it in front of his son.

"Renounce your faith or die!" he roared.

Terrified, Kay managed to find his voice. "Well, before you kill me, at least let me tell you about Jesus Christ."

The elder Hiramine froze for an instant, as though some unseen force were preventing him from harming his son. Suddenly he threw the knife to the floor. In frustrated rage, he stomped over to the TV area, broke a coffee table with an explosive karate chop and growled, "Leave. You leave this home now."

With trembling hands Kay phoned David Emerson, the youth pastor, asked him to pick him up and feverishly packed three bags of clothes.

Kay stayed with David and his wife, Linda, for about a week. Then Kay's mother cooled down enough to call and allow him to come back and live in a small house at the back of their property. But for many months Kay's father never spoke to him except in occasional curt exchanges.

Kay finished his senior year of high school and in September 1982 moved into a dorm at Occidental College in Los Angeles. Cut off from his family financially, he made his way with the help of grants and loans.

His parents, meanwhile, moved closer to downtown Los Angeles to open a store in Little Tokyo.

One morning early in his sophomore year, his mother phoned. "Kay, your father is dying of cancer."

Touched with new compassion, Kay began reestablishing a relationship with his father, visiting him at home, in the hospital, at his store. His dad started a regimen of chemotherapy for stomach cancer, and Kay sometimes accompanied him on visits to his doctor.

As they left the hospital one day, Kay's father told him, "You know, I'm going to see you graduate."

Don't I wish! Kay thought. Graduation was almost three years away, and the doctors said his dad had just three months to live.

Nevertheless Kay was interceding for his father, even cautiously sharing the Gospel.

Three months came and went. Then one day the elder Hiramine allowed his son to pray for him. After Kay laid hands on his father's head, Kay Senior told him he felt a sensation of warm oil pouring over his head and down his neck onto his shoulders.

"When I pray to Buddha," confessed Kay Senior, "I get no answers. But when you pray to your God, I can tell He's alive."

Months passed. Kay's father fought for survival as his cancer spread. Often when Kay prayed for him, his father experienced the same remarkable manifestation of the presence of God.

During the summer of 1985, between Kay's junior and senior years of college, he joined an outreach program in Japan led by LIFE Ministries. While in Japan he wrote his father a heartfelt letter, asking him to accept Christ as Savior. A few weeks later a response arrived.

"I have come to faith in Jesus," his father wrote.

On Saturday, June 14, 1986, Kay Hiramine, Sr., attended his son's commencement exercises at the Eagle Rock campus of Occidental College. The next Monday he entered the presence of his Lord.

Hiroko Hiramine had witnessed the transformation of her husband. Yet she remained gripped by fear that if she abandoned Buddhism, the ancestral spirits would destroy her. Then in late June 1990 she checked into the hospital, weak and racked with pain. Tests showed leukemia—cancer of the bone marrow.

Kay and Julie, his bride of a year, rounded up a few friends, including Doug Gregg, chaplain of Occidental College, and went out to Northridge Hospital. The cancer had spread so much, especially around the bottom of her rib cage, that Kay's mother could not sit up without excruciating pain.

Kay's friends gathered around the bedside where Hiroko lay back nearly prone.

"You know, Kay," she said to her son, "I remember when you prayed for your dad. He used to get sensations of warm oil on his head and his pain would leave. Can your God do the same thing for me?"

"Of course," Kay replied. "Would you like us to pray for you, Mom?"

She nodded and closed her eyes.

Kay's older sisters, Judy and Anny, staunch Buddhists, stood out in the hall talking with the doctor. The time was right. The team began to pray.

Kay laid a hand on the area above his mother's lower rib cage. In a moment he could feel tremendous heat flowing from his hand into her body. Her eyelids fluttered and she began to glow with perspiration.

As the group finished their prayers, Hiroko Hiramine opened her eyes.

"The pain—the pain is gone," she murmured, her voice filled with wonder.

Then she sat fully upright in her own strength. "Why, the pain is completely gone!" In joyful disbelief she began to laugh and cry at the same time.

Doug Gregg, the chaplain, seized the moment.

"This is the power of God," he explained. "Kay and the rest of us prayed for you in Jesus' name. We don't know what's happened to the cancer, but Jesus has taken away your pain. Would you like to give your life to Him?"

"Yes, I would," she answered. "But—" She hesitated a moment. "I'd like to talk to my daughters first."

Kay called in his sisters from the hallway.

"Judy, Anny," their mother began, "I want you to know I love you very much. I'm going to become a Christian today. Judy, will you take care of the Butsudan?"

The young women were too speechless to argue. Judy, as the oldest child, agreed to inherit the home altar for the ancestral spirits.

Then Hiroko Hiramine was ready for Kay and Doug to lead her in a prayer confessing her sins and asking the Lord Jesus into her heart.

Her doctors had no explanation for the disappearance of Hiroko's pain. A month or two later, after intensive chemotherapy, her cancer went into remission for about a year and a half. Over these months Hiroko learned more about living a life of devotion to Christ. Then in March 1992 she passed from time into eternity.

Although neither of Kay's parents found permanent healing from cancer, their experience of partial remission and a dramatic release from pain convinced them that their son's faith was real and that Jesus is alive.

"Crumbs" of Healing Enough to Satisfy

Divine healing need not be complete or permanent (as the Hiramine family's story illustrates) to touch someone with the transforming love and power of God. The demonstration of God's compassion, especially to someone antagonistic to Him, can prove so overwhelming that humility and acceptance follow as naturally as snowmelt after warm sunshine.

When Jesus declared to the Syrophoenician woman that healing is "the children's bread" (Mark 7:27), she responded that even the "crumbs" of healing for her demonized daughter would satisfy (Mark 7:28). Jesus met the woman's heartfelt desire by pronouncing her daughter well. He seemed to indicate, by identifying healing with such a daily staple of life, that we should not think of healing as an unusual treat, a special-occasion frosted cake that we cannot expect more than once in a great while. The Lord's mercy, more abundant than wheat in a Kansas grain elevator, stands ready to satisfy the hunger of anyone in physical or spiritual need.

God can use even the healing of animals to show how much He loves people. Edgardo Silvoso, the president of Harvest Evangelism whom we met in the last chapter, recounts in his book *That None Should Perish* (Regal, 1994) the story of Señor Alvarez, a grizzled Argentine gaucho who ran a ranch where Ed and his wife Ruth used to go horseback riding.

Although an unbeliever, Mr. Alvarez began attending church sporadically. One Sunday night the preacher expounded on James 5:13–16. Mr. Alvarez heard the part about anointing the sick with oil, the prayer of faith and the Lord's promise to raise him up.

The next morning, by divine coincidence, the rancher woke to find his prize bull dead. As he agonized over the loss, the Word of God sprang to his memory. Mr. Alvarez went to his kitchen, found a can of olive oil, returned outside and poured some on the bull's carcass with a word of prayer. In a moment the animal clambered to its feet, and Mr. Alvarez soon entered the family of believers.

Edgardo Silvoso reflects on this astonishing event:

> Why would God raise a bull from the dead? For the same reason Jesus would do something as unusual as turning water into wine. It was a felt need so real that, once met, it could not fail to open the eyes of the lost to the reality of God's power and love.
>
> page 86

The healing of an animal has a historical precedent in the life of eighteenth-century evangelist John Wesley, founder of Methodism. Traveling on horseback with a companion on a preaching tour, the pair had left the northern English town of Great Smeaton when Wesley's horse went lame. Wesley's journal entry for Monday, March 17, 1746, tells the tale:

> We could not discern what it was that was amiss; and yet he would scarce set his foot to the ground. By riding thus seven miles, I was thoroughly tired, and my head ached more than it had done for some months. (What I here aver is the naked fact; Let every man account for it as he sees good.) I then thought, "Cannot God heal either man or beast, by any means, or without any?" Immediately my weariness and head-ache ceased, and my horse's lameness in the same instant. Nor did he halt any more either that day or the next. A very odd accident this also!

Through the healing of Wesley's mount, the evangelist could continue his travels to the towns and villages where sometimes thousands at a time heard and responded to his preaching.

Healing comes in many forms, and the response of a "pre-Christian" to healing may vary. In the story that follows, a vision and a dream combined with healing—first impermanent, then total—to plant a new believer securely in God's vineyard. But prayer for healing may require persistence.

A Miraculous Meeting with Jesus

Jean and Darell Vandenbos, active laypeople in their sixties, had met Mitra and her husband, Aziz, at their church in Denver in early 1991. The young couple had converted to Christ from Islam separately after leaving their native Iran. As the two couples got acquainted, the Iranians introduced Jean and Darell to family and friends who visited from their home country, as well as Iranian immigrants living in the Denver area.

One of these immigrants was a man we will call Sam, whom Aziz had met in an aviation class. Sam had lived in the States for some fourteen years. But since he had married a Catholic woman, his Shia Muslim parents in Iran had expressed bitter antagonism toward any form of Christianity.

Now in 1993 Sam's parents, Mr. and Mrs. G., had come to the U.S. for several months to visit their son and his family, as well as a daughter also living in Denver. They were interested in American culture but refused to spend any time with Sam's Christian friends, Mitra and Aziz.

Toward the beginning of the summer Sam drove his family to Disneyland in Southern California. Later Jean Vandenbos got an update phone call from Mitra, whose excitement buzzed through the phone lines.

"I don't know what's happened, Jean, but Sam's parents are suddenly open to receiving prayer. They returned from their trip about a week ago and something's changed. Mrs. G. actually gave me a call. She says she's been suffering severe headaches for seventeen years, and now she and her husband are open to prayer. Would you be willing to have them over?"

Jean soon confirmed arrangements to invite the G.'s, along with Mitra and Aziz, for dinner at the Vandenbos home in the foothills west of Denver. Aziz would also bring his mother, in her late fifties, about the same age as Mrs. G.

The guests arrived about three on Sunday afternoon while the summer sun still played high above the Rocky Mountain peaks. Mitra served as English-Farsi language interpreter, introducing Mr. and Mrs. G. to Jean and Darell. Mr. G. wore a long-sleeved shirt

and pants, while his wife clothed herself in a long, dark dress and
stockings, with a dark-brown scarf that covered every bit of her
hair. They received Jean and Darell's hospitality graciously.

The group mingled awhile on the enclosed backyard deck. Then
the two older Iranian women, chatting in Farsi, strolled down to
the stream winding through the Vandenboses' two-acre property,
while Mitra filled Jean in on what she had learned.

"Mrs. G. told me she had an unusual experience when they were
driving back from Disneyland," Mitra began.

Jean listened as Mitra recounted that Mrs. G. had been sitting
next to her eight-year-old granddaughter in the back seat while
Mr. G. had shared the front seat with their son Sam. At one point
Mrs. G. apparently turned to look at the girl and suddenly saw Jesus
where her granddaughter had been, as though covering her. Mrs. G.
recognized Jesus from traditional pictures showing Him with long
hair and a robe. But He frightened her.

"What have you done with my granddaughter?" Mrs. G.
demanded, turning sideways, hands on hips.

Jesus just smiled. When she asked a second time, He disappeared
and the little girl was back.

"Who are you talking to, dear?" Mr. G. inquired from the front
seat.

His shaken wife tried to explain what she had seen. Together
they puzzled over the meaning of the vision, but they were moved
that such an important prophet would appear to them.

"Now Mrs. G. wants prayer for her headaches," Mitra told Jean.
"For seventeen years she's suffered. She says she thinks her sister-
in-law put a curse on her. The pain's gotten so severe she often
can't sleep at night. Sometimes she's even run outside screaming."

When the other guests returned to the deck, Jean had Mitra,
as translator, ask Mrs. G. if she felt ready to receive healing
prayer.

"Jesus is the Healer," Jean explained, "and we're going to pray
in His name, asking and believing that He will heal your
headaches. And if there's any curse—if anyone has wished harm
on you—we're also going to pray for that to be broken in Jesus'
name."

Mrs. G. agreed.

Gently Jean laid a hand on Mrs. G.'s scarfed head and the little group began to pray.

After a while Jean paused. "How do you feel, Mrs. G.? Has the pain left?"

"No, but it's better," she replied through Mitra's translation.

The believers returned to intercession, praying as the Holy Spirit led and asserting authority in the name of Jesus Christ over any demonic forces.

In a few moments Mrs. G. threw up her hands and cried out in Farsi, "It's gone! The pain is gone!"

More hands flew skyward as everyone rejoiced. Jean asked Mrs. G. to be sure to thank Jesus for what He had done.

Then Mitra took the lead in explaining to both Mr. and Mrs. G. the Gospel of Jesus Christ—that through His death and resurrection He reconciles men and women to God.

The G.'s listened carefully as Mitra spoke in their own language. They talked with Mitra, who then turned to Jean. "They say they're ready to ask Jesus into their lives."

"Praise the Lord! You may pray your own prayer," Jean told them through Mitra, "or I can lead you in a prayer of dedication to Christ."

Mr. G. wanted to pray his own prayer. He looked up to heaven from where he sat, and as the words poured forth, the tears flowed with them.

"He said he realized for the first time in his life that he was a sinner," Mitra told Jean later. "The Spirit of God simply convicted him as he opened his heart to Jesus."

Mrs. G. preferred that Jean lead her in prayer. Mitra interpreted. When she opened her eyes afterward, Mrs. G.'s face shone with a light of pure joy. She held out her hands and said, "I feel just like a newborn baby from my mother's womb."

"Why, Mrs. G.," said Jean, "that's a perfect description of what's just happened to you, according to Jesus." And she promised the G.'s that she would find and give them a New Testament in Farsi so they could read Jesus' words in John 3 for themselves.

The group enjoyed dinner and the rest of the evening as new brothers and sisters in Christ. But later that week Mitra phoned Jean again.

"Mrs. G.'s headaches are back," she told her. "The pain is not as severe, but she'd really like some more prayer."

So Jean prayed again, and over the next few weeks phoned a number of times to intercede. She also visited the G.'s where they were staying with their daughter across town. It took Mr. G. just a week to read through the Farsi New Testament that Jean gave them. And during one lunchtime visit, their daughter expressed readiness to receive Christ, too.

But Mrs. G.'s headaches would not stay away more than a few days. Jean asked her pastor for advice, and he fingered spiritual attack as the culprit, speculating that the devil did not want to let go of her.

Jean began praying for God to reveal Himself to Mrs. G. in a powerful way through dreams and visions.

One Friday in late August, Sam took his afflicted mother to the University of Colorado Medical Center for a CAT scan. Doctors discovered several brain tumors. They ordered another scan for Monday morning and recommended surgery as soon as possible.

Mrs. G. returned to her daughter's apartment in tears.

"I don't want surgery!" she cried to Mitra on the phone. But she also told her friend that her daughter had spoken up in newfound faith, which took everyone by surprise: "Mother, God is going to heal you."

Mitra passed the news to Jean, who continued to pray for healing as well as God's supernatural revelation. The torturous pain in Mrs. G.'s head lessened, and she found she could sleep a bit better.

Then that Sunday night Mrs. G. had a dream in which Jesus came to her. He touched her forehead, His face full of love, and said, "I'm healing you."

Mrs. G. stirred from her sleep, and when she opened her eyes in the darkness, she sensed Jesus standing quietly next to her. After a moment He disappeared. Mrs. G. lay back in a sweat, scarcely knowing if she were awake or asleep. Suddenly she realized that the pain in her head had vanished.

In the morning Mrs. G. could hardly wait to tell the story. And after Sam picked up his mother for her appointment at the hospital, the follow-up CAT scan found her brain completely clear of tumors.

Mrs. G. was transformed, physically and spiritually. In the weeks to come she and her husband would endure faith-testing trials, but the touch of God on her body and the memory of the closeness of Jesus provided a well of strength to draw on, especially after they returned to Iran.

Ministering Healing to Internationals

Jean Vandenbos' experience with the G.'s shows the importance of persistence in prayer for healing. God does not always grant remission of illness or disease, but sometimes intended healing gets blocked because of spiritual factors unknown to us. When Jean recognized spiritual warfare as an issue with Mrs. G., she could target her healing prayers more strategically against the barriers to Mrs. G.'s relief.

Jean's story also points out, incidentally, the opportunities of Western Christians to minister to internationals in our midst. In the United States and other countries with freedom of religion, visitors from distant nations may hear the Gospel clearly for the first time. Students, tourists, contract workers, refugees, government employees and many others come for a few days or a few years. Their firsthand impressions, positive or negative, of a so-called Christian nation can mold their receptivity or resistance to the Gospel for the rest of their lives.

Often internationals away from home also suffer feelings of loneliness, isolation or disorientation. When they fall ill, they may have no one to turn to. Believers who offer their time and friendship can have enormous influence on visitors aching for someone to listen and receive them with warmth and acceptance. Jean Vandenbos credits simple friendship and hospitality with helping to soften her Iranian friends' hearts toward God. Many foreigners want to see how Americans live, and when believers open their homes, their guests may begin to let down their defenses against Christianity.

Ministry to internationals can have strategic impact beyond the lives of the visitors themselves. If they come to know Christ while away from home, they will take the Gospel back with them when they return to their countries. In many cases individuals who travel abroad for education, special training or government job assignments are current or future leaders in their homelands, with the potential to affect the lives of many. Especially in nations otherwise hostile to outside religious influence, a new believer returning home will smuggle in the truth about Christ with the explosive power of a bomb.

Giving internationals a copy of Scripture in their native language, as Jean did, can seal a decision for Christ. A Bible or New Testament provides spiritual nourishment for them not only to grow in faith while in their host countries, but to remain strong even after they have gone back to nations where their faith will face the refiner's fire.

When the Syrian army commander Naaman came to Israel seeking healing of his leprosy, the prophet Elisha directed him to wash seven times in the Jordan River (2 Kings 5:1–19). After he finally obeyed this humiliatingly simple instruction, a cleansed Naaman confessed, "Now I know that there is no God in all the world except in Israel" (verse 15).

Naaman's conversion was so unequivocal that he anticipated the conflict he would face back in his home country. He asked Elisha,

"Please let me, your servant, be given as much earth as a pair of mules can carry, for your servant will never again make burnt offerings and sacrifices to any other god but the LORD. But may the LORD forgive your servant for this one thing: When my master enters the temple of Rimmon to bow down and he is leaning on my arm and I bow there also—when I bow down in the temple of Rimmon, may the LORD forgive your servant for this."

"Go in peace," Elisha said.

verses 17–19

Naaman, familiar with only territorial gods, evidently wanted to bring back to Syria some soil from the land of Israel as a token of the Lord God who reigned there. He also knew that unavoidable cultural situations dishonoring to God would crop up, and he begged forgiveness in advance.

May many of today's international visitors to countries where Christ is preached return home with the same kind of commitment! Our prayers of healing for visitors in our midst can make a deep impact, because in every culture, in every corner of the world, human beings grapple with disease, injury and affliction. As a demonstration of God's love and compassion, divine healing touches hearts and lives powerfully in a way that reaches beyond culture.

The Healing of Hogwanobiayo

Hogwanobiayo was sick.

Headaches. Malaise. Achy bones. Hogwanobiayo felt every one of his 45 to 50 years—an old man by the standards of Samo culture. The lowlands Samo people in the Western Province of Papua New Guinea contended with sickness and disease about as regularly as they harvested their staple foods of sago and plantains. Survival was a tough business.

Dan Shaw had been adopted as one of Hogwanobiayo's "little brothers" after he and his wife, Karen, moved to the remote Samo village of Kwobi as missionaries with Wycliffe Bible Translators. Now a professor of anthropology and translation at Fuller Seminary's School of World Mission, Dan learned of his friend's illness during his second term in Papua New Guinea, about 1975. Hogwanobiayo, a good listener, had given Dan stellar help rewording and polishing draft portions of Scripture in the Samo language. Losing him, Dan knew, would be a real blow. But Dan had no personal experience with prayer for healing.

Hogwanobiayo tried to shake his malaise by moving the place where he slept. In traditional Samo culture, the spirit world interacts with the natural world at every point, and it is impossible to take too many precautions.

"If a spirit who knows where I normally lie down sees me in this weakened condition," Hogwanobiayo reasoned, "I could get attacked while I sleep."

But a few nights in a different spot brought no improvement.

Then Hogwanobiayo asked a close relative to lead a *mimi ora* ceremony in an attempt to beat out of him the evil forces (*mimi*) that might be causing his illness. Making a paste with yellow ochre and fashioning a brush from leaves, one of his brothers dipped the leaves in the paste and beat them on Hogwanobiayo's back while chanting spells to evict the evil spirits.

Nothing happened. Hogwanobiayo was still sick.

His family decided to find out what was wrong. They called a spirit medium to conduct an all-night ceremony seeking guidance from the ancestor spirits. While the family sang and chanted to the spirits, the medium in a trancelike state attempted communication with the ancestors to gain information about Hogwanobiayo's illness. Hours passed; no message came.

"The ancestors cannot tell us what's wrong with Hogwanobiayo," the medium concluded. "There seems to be no spiritual influence—he's just sick."

And getting sicker. After several weeks the brothers of his extended village family tried another tack—an all-night party with dancing and drunken revelry. This bash, they hoped, would ward off any evil spirits by mesmerizing them, the way the bird of paradise goes into display to entrance its predators. Enthralled by the riotous scene, the spirits would conclude that everything was fine and leave the revelers and Hogwanobiayo alone.

The hundred or so Kwobi villagers enjoyed a torrid celebration. But Hogwanobiayo only got worse.

In desperation his family moved him to an isolated long house out in the forest, with only his wife and a few attendants. Perhaps removal from any contact with the forces surrounding the village might cut off the disease.

No luck. With resignation Hogwanobiayo moved back to the village. Not a single thing had helped. Even medicine from his "little brother" Dan Shaw had not stopped the course of what by now was pneumonia and probably malaria. Weak with chills and fever, Hogwanobiayo could not face making the two-hour trek through jungle and swamp to the nearest medical facility. He shut himself up in his home, now considered socially dead. People began referring to him in the past tense.

With Hogwanobiayo confined to bed, Dan brought more doses of medicine, along with rough Scripture translations for him to correct.

One afternoon Dan brought a portion that included John 5:1–15, the story of the disabled man at the pool of Bethesda. Dan began to read aloud in the Samo language:

> One who was there had been an invalid for thirty-eight years. When Jesus saw him lying there and learned that he had been in this condition for a long time, he asked him, "Do you want to get well?"
> verses 5–6

As Dan continued reading, Hogwanobiayo became very still. Suddenly he cried out, "That's me! That's me! That's me!"

"What do you mean, that's you?"

"Don't you see? Look at this guy. He's been sick for a long time. He's tried everything. There's nothing more he can do. *I've* been sick for a long time. I've tried everything." His dark eyes fixed on Dan's. "Do you think Jesus can heal me, too?"

"Uh, yeah, Jesus could heal you," Dan replied, knitting his brow. "I don't know how He might do that, but it's possible."

Hogwanobiayo tried to raise his head. "I want *you* to ask Jesus to heal me."

Adrenaline pumped as Dan's theoretical beliefs crashed head-on into the reality of the moment.

Me? he thought in silent desperation. *I'm just a Baptist boy from Tucson. This isn't in my bag of tricks.*

Aloud he asked, "Why me? There are some other believers in the village now."

"You are my little brother," Hogwanobiayo said. "It's the brother's responsibility to be involved in the healing of another brother. I want *you* to ask Jesus to heal me."

With a few gulps and silent pleas for divine help, Dan began to pray aloud. "Dear Lord, here's my brother and he needs Your healing. He says he believes You can heal him, as You healed the man at the pool. We're asking You to do that now for Hogwanobiayo."

After prayer Dan scanned his friend anxiously for any sign of improvement. He saw no change, but Hogwanobiayo thanked him warmly.

Dan went home practically sweating blood. He and his wife prayed together as they had never prayed before: "Lord, You brought us here. These are the moments we read about in mission history. Your name is on the line. *Our* name is on the line. You've got to come through!"

Three or four days passed with little noticeable change. Then one afternoon, when Dan was working in his office, distant shouts reached his ears. Some children from the village ran in crying, "Come and see! Hogwanobiayo is up and around! He's telling everybody that you prayed for him and Jesus healed him!"

Dan followed them and found his friend hobbling around on a cane, skinny and covered with bedsores, but up and out of bed for the first time in a month.

"Look!" he said to Dan. "I've got fresh energy. You prayed and Jesus gave me wonderful new vitality!"

Sincerely happy for his friend, Dan also acknowledged a bit of anthropological skepticism. "You know, Hogwanobiayo, do you think it's possible that all the cultural things you did to try to get well finally accumulated, and now you're getting better?"

Slowly Hogwanobiayo picked up his walking stick and planted it between Dan's ribs. One word at a time, with great deliberation, he croaked, *"Don't—you—believe?"*

Hogwanobiayo's cane seemed to pierce Dan like a hot spear. With tears welling in his eyes, Dan confessed, "Yes, I believe!"

"Before you prayed," Hogwanobiayo went on emphatically, "nothing. After you prayed, I've been getting my strength, and now I'm up and around. Jesus healed me!"

Dan Shaw's eyes were opened to a deeper reality. He found that the healing proved a turning point not only in Hogwanobiayo's conversion, but for the whole village. Hogwanobiayo, like others, had never personalized the message of the Gospel. But now Dan saw a great increase in receptivity among the Samo as a result of the healing—and the witness of a young man named Tiyani, whose story will have to wait until chapter 8.

Stepping Out in the Power of Word and Deed

Hogwanobiayo, elderly as he was, lived for several more years and became a leader in the Samo church. Eventually the people adapted one of their all-night rituals into a Christian ceremony featuring praise to God in song and dance and prayer for the sick.

Dan Shaw's experience illustrates the interaction between the living Word of God and the supernatural power of God. In a situation of desperate need, the Lord quickened Scripture to Hogwanobiayo's heart and faith arose. Then, in the demonstration of God's power to answer prayer (even through a very tentative mediator like Dan), the Samo saw God's supremacy over evil spirits and the true meaning and relevance of the Book the Shaws had come to bring them in their own language.

Dan faced a direct challenge to put his faith into action. We, too, if we want our beliefs to reflect more than abstract theories, need to be willing to step out boldly, however the Spirit leads, to pray for His intervention in the lives of others.

After all, we serve the same God today who declared to the Israelites in Exodus 15:26, "I am the LORD, who heals you." Many in today's world have concluded that a God with both the compassion and the power to heal is a God worthy of unreserved allegiance.

3

"The Secrets of His Heart Will Be Laid Bare"

Stories of Prophetic Messages

Virgo Handojo felt his spirit reenter his body. Coming out of the trance, he collected his amulets and returned them to their secure place in his bedroom. Since his initiation into Kundalini, he had learned how to communicate with the spirit world and use supernatural power for the protection and benefit of himself and others.

In his native Indonesia, nominal Islam and folk Buddhism are woven closely with strong cross-threads of animism. Virgo, although raised in a Buddhist family and baptized into Catholicism, hungered for deeper spiritual power. As a young teenager he became attracted to Kundalini, a form of mysticism rooted in both Hinduism and Javanese traditional beliefs.

During initiation rites his guru introduced him to some of the secrets of the magical arts, as well as the group's strict laws concerning their practice. Virgo knew he risked harm or death should he break Kundalini's mandates, but the superhuman abilities he began to exercise fed his craving like an addictive drug. Over the years he saw fellow Kundalini practitioners levitate, perform supernatural healing, deflect a bullet shot at their bodies and much more. Those who broke the rules died suddenly or were killed in bizarre traffic accidents.

In early 1979 Virgo's friend and neighbor Tiong Gie invited him to a church rally in his hometown of Semarang in central Java. At 22 Virgo had little interest in Christianity. But he went to the rally that Friday, March 2, because a famous Indonesian singer would be performing. His heart was touched but unchanged by the Gospel message.

He returned with Tiong Gie to another church meeting the next day, hoping to make some friends. When someone prayed for him, Virgo felt a kind of electrical energy surge through his body. Still, he went home without making a commitment to Christ.

The following Monday Tiong Gie invited him to a home fellowship meeting and promised him he would meet a lot of good people. Perhaps a hundred people were expected to gather that night at the family house and backyard of Tante Ien and her sister Kiok. Virgo knew Tiong Gie had no idea of his deep involvement in Kundalini, but he saw no conflict and said yes.

Scores of young men and women packed the family room and overflowed into the hall and the outdoor covered veranda. Tante Ien, an older woman with a mother's warmth for her brood, taught briefly. Someone else led in musical worship.

What a strange group! Virgo thought as the evening went on. *I've never experienced anything like this.*

During the prayer and praise Virgo did not understand much. Then he heard Tante Ien speak up in a clear voice.

"I got a vision just now of God telling me there's a young man here who has black magic power," she said.

How interesting, Virgo thought, not suspecting himself. *Kundalini, of course, is good white magic—totally different.*

In a moment two men stood up and moved to his side.

What's happening? Virgo wondered uneasily. *Do they think I'm the one or something?*

They laid their hands gently on his head and began to pray.

Before he could say a word, Virgo felt another current of electricity jolt his body from head to feet. He began shaking. Then he heard the men's prayers take on more authority. One of them commanded, "Devil, come out of him now, in the name of Jesus!"

Collapsing to the floor, Virgo sensed something invisible moving out of his body through his mouth. In that instant he felt as though a black hood had been torn off of his mind. For the first time he realized that Kundalini had deceived him. His supernatural powers had come not from God but from Satan and his dark hordes.

Virgo blinked and sat up, overwhelmed like a newborn emerging into the bright lights of the delivery room. But in a moment another strong power entered his body and he was seized by a spirit of anger and frustration. He cried out, and more people gathered around him to pray and rebuke the demons. No sooner did one evil spirit leave than another took its place. For two hours several members of the group struggled to deliver him.

Finally someone asked Virgo, "Do you own any charms or amulets?"

Virgo nodded weakly. "Yes, they're in my bedroom at home."

Tiong Gie jumped onto his motorbike and sped the mile or two to Virgo's home. Soon, with Virgo's assent, the people who remained at the meeting burned these charms and amulets in the backyard.

Immediately Virgo felt in his body a release from bondage. Worn out but at rest, he listened as Tante Ien and others in the group explained the power of Jesus to save.

Later that night, alone in his room, an exhausted Virgo struggling to fall asleep sensed a dark, accusing presence in his room.

You have broken the law and you are going to die, he heard. *You get up and stand in that corner.*

Confused and afraid, Virgo moved to the spot, feeling helpless to control his response.

Now you have to go here, another voice ordered.

Now go over there.

The tormenting spirits directed him back and forth in his room until something Tante Ien said popped to mind: "If anything happens tonight—if a demon tries to kill you or anything—just pray to Jesus and God will deliver you."

Trembling, Virgo cried out, "God, I don't know what's happening! Please help me."

Instantly the atmosphere in the room changed, and Virgo felt the peace and presence of the Lord.

His mind now clear, Virgo yearned to sleep but continued brooding over everything that had happened in the last several hours. Questions rushed at him like wild animals: *Is Kundalini really from the devil, not from God? Could I have been so deceived? How did I do so much good magic, then?*

Rummaging in his desk, he found a small Bible he had received at school from the Gideons some time before.

God, he prayed, *I don't understand all this. It's hard to believe my guru could be so wrong. Please show me the truth.*

Opening at random, he began to read from Colossians. Several passages burned into him:

> My purpose is that they may . . . know the mystery of God, namely, Christ, in whom are hidden all the treasures of wisdom and knowledge. I tell you this so that no one may deceive you by fine-sounding arguments.
>
> Colossians 2:2–4

> See to it that no one takes you captive through hollow and deceptive philosophy, which depends on human tradition and the basic principles of this world rather than on Christ.
>
> For in Christ all the fullness of the Deity lives in bodily form, and you have been given fullness in Christ, who is the head over every power and authority.
>
> 2:8–10

> Do not let anyone who delights in false humility and the worship of angels disqualify you for the prize.
>
> 2:18

Virgo lay down again, drifting in and out of sleep. Whenever his mind began wrestling with doubts, verses he had just read jumped to his memory and spoke to him, as though God Himself were answering his questions.

In the morning Virgo went to see a friend who understood Kundalini, and told him what had happened.

"The power of this group was amazing!" Virgo exclaimed. "It's as though they could see right into me!"

"How many people were at this meeting?"

"About a hundred."

"A hundred! And you were there all alone? No wonder! Of course your power was defeated—one against so many. If you got more power, or more people, then the Christians would lose."

"Hmm . . . that's—that's right," Virgo pondered, a cloud of confusion beginning once again to descend.

Through the rest of the morning the internal battle raged: *Should I go back to my guru and get more power? But if I do, I've already broken the Kundalini laws—I know I will die. I could go back to this Christian woman, but I don't know if her power is really greater.*

Eventually he contorted himself into a conclusion.

Sooner or later I'm going to die anyway, he reasoned. *If I choose Christianity and it's wrong, maybe I'll be punished less, since a lot more people are following it than Kundalini. Safer to die in ignorance, just following the crowd.*

God can use even twisted logic to lead people to Himself!

Virgo went back to Tante Ien and explained his dilemma, confusion and fear.

Her answer was simple: "Come here every day and we'll read the Bible together."

"That's it? Just read the Bible? Every day?"

That was it.

So every day Virgo drank deeply of the Word of God. Tante Ien and her sister Kiok pointed out its meaning. Soon Virgo committed himself wholeheartedly to Jesus. In fact, before many weeks had passed, he became involved in ministry. He linked with a friend who had also come to Christ out of Kundalini and who served with Sangkakala Mission Fellowship (the parachurch organization we encountered in the last chapter that spawned the church doing intercessory prayer drives in the prostitution district of Semarang, Indonesia).

Virgo grew as a lay leader, helped start many new churches and was ordained as a pastor in the denomination he helped found, Jemaat Kristen Indonesia (JKI). Later Virgo served as chairman of JKI International, a growing movement that now includes about fifty churches ministering to Indonesians in several countries around the world.

Virgo Handojo's life was transformed by the power of the Word of God. First God singled him out with prophetic words of knowledge given to Tante Ien and the young people who came to pray for him. Then the written Word of God, living and active, answered his questions and sealed the truth to his mind and heart. Virgo discovered true spiritual power in a relationship with Christ, satisfying his deepest hunger.

Prophecy and Words of Knowledge

Prophecy, in the biblical use of the term, includes messages for the present as well as the future. The Greek word means not "fore-telling" so much as "forth-telling."

C. Peter Wagner gives this definition in his book *Your Spiritual Gifts Can Help Your Church Grow* (Regal, 1979, 1994):

> The gift of prophecy is the special ability that God gives to certain members of the Body of Christ to receive and communicate an immediate message of God to His people through a divinely anointed utterance.
>
> page 200, fifteenth anniversary edition

The phrase *word of knowledge* is commonly used in much the same way. Paul told the Corinthian church that God can use prophetic messages to convict the hearts of those who do not yet know Him:

> If an unbeliever or someone who does not understand comes in while everybody is prophesying, he will be convinced by all that he is a sinner and will be judged by all, and the secrets of his heart

will be laid bare. So he will fall down and worship God, exclaiming, "God is really among you!"

1 Corinthians 14:24–25

Virgo Handojo did not repent immediately of his involvement in black magic when Tante Ien delivered her prophetic word. But it certainly got his attention. And when God silently identified Virgo to the two young men who came to pray for him, the secrets of his heart soon spilled forth in a dramatic battle for deliverance.

Jesus used a word of knowledge when he met the Samaritan woman at the well in Sychar:

> He told her, "Go, call your husband and come back."
> "I have no husband," she replied.
> Jesus said to her, "You are right when you say you have no husband. The fact is, you have had five husbands, and the man you now have is not your husband. What you have just said is quite true."
> "Sir," the woman said, "I can see that you are a prophet."

John 4:16–19

The woman, apparently flustered when Jesus pointed out part of her private history, tried to change the subject. But His message hit home: "Leaving her water jar, the woman went back to the town and said to the people, 'Come, see a man who told me everything I ever did. Could this be the Christ?'" (verses 28–29). Just hearing her report of Jesus' prophetic words convinced others, too: "Many of the Samaritans from that town believed in him because of the woman's testimony, 'He told me everything I ever did'" (verse 39).

Virgo's story points out the danger of being deceived by supernatural power from demonic sources. It is crucial to wrestle, as he did, with biblical truth to determine the source of the power and therefore how to respond. Those who receive prophetic messages for others should ask the Lord if they have heard correctly (and even then God does not always direct us to speak it forth; more on that later). And those who are given messages from others must seek the Lord for confirmation, aligning the word of knowledge with the written Word of God, not just their own experience.

But a prophetic message from the Holy Spirit, piercing the armor of a heart hardened to Him, can penetrate layers of resistance in one stroke.

Virgo himself, a couple of years later, received a word of knowledge that instantly broke through barriers in a teenage girl's life and led her to Christ.

"Is This a Dagger Which I See . . . ?"

The Bible study seemed to be going very well. Virgo Handojo, leading a group of high school students not many years younger than himself, hoped this fellowship in the town of Ungaran, Indonesia, would form part of the nucleus of a new church in that area of central Java. Each Friday evening throughout 1981 the group had met and grown. And tonight Virgo saw some new faces.

After the meeting, Virgo introduced himself to the visitors. As usual, he inquired about their spiritual backgrounds and whether they knew Jesus personally. His conversation with an ethnic Chinese girl we will call Lanny took an unexpected turn.

"I don't know how much you've thought about eternal things," Virgo ventured, "but we're all going to die someday—no one but God knows when. If you were to die tonight, where do you think you would go?"

In a snap the answer came back. "Hell."

Virgo's mouth dropped open a moment. "Uh, are you sure?"

"Yes, I'm sure."

Virgo studied her face—beautiful, big eyes framed by shining black hair. "Why do you say that? You have so much to live for, and I have good news for you."

"No," came Lanny's blunt and emphatic reply.

Virgo could hardly believe it. *She just doesn't care!*

After a little more discussion, Virgo finally said, "O.K., if you're convinced you're going to hell and have no problem with that, fine. Just let me ask you this: May I pray for you before you go?"

To his surprise, she agreed.

Virgo and two or three other group leaders came alongside Lanny to intercede.

O God, I don't know what's happened to make this girl so hardened, he prayed silently. *Please help me pray according to the truth.*

Aloud he asked Lanny, "May I lay my hand on your head?"

She gave assent.

Almost as soon as his hand touched her hair, Virgo felt a tingling in his palm. From several previous experiences, Virgo knew this probably meant that the person he was praying for had been involved in or influenced by some kind of black magic. Because of his own background, God seemed to have given him a gift of discernment in this area.

Virgo asked God silently for more specific information about Lanny's involvement. Then, as if on the inside lids of his closed eyes, he saw a picture of a Javanese dagger about fifteen inches long, including the handle and wavy curved blade, wrapped in a white cloth sheath tied around the hilt. He knew that Javanese daggers, which could be objects of artistic and cultural interest, were also frequently used in occult and magic rituals.

Virgo questioned Lanny gingerly. "Do you have any kind of experience in witchcraft or something like that?"

"No!"

"How about involvement in magic—with candles, for instance?"

"No," said Lanny, not quite as forcefully.

"Well," Virgo went on, "do you have something in your home, a magic item, like a dagger?"

Lanny's large eyes got rounder.

"Yes," she replied slowly.

"Is it in your room, your bedroom, hanging in a sheath from a nail on the right side of your door frame?"

Eyes snapping wide, Lanny gulped as though she had swallowed a fish whole. "How—how do you know? What—"

Suddenly she stopped and her eyes narrowed back to normal, as if catching herself with her defenses down. "Tell me more. If you know that, tell me where there's another one."

Sending up a quick, silent cry for help, Virgo began to breathe again when God answered with a second picture. "I see another dagger on the top of a closed wooden cupboard, high up on top, above the cupboard doors."

This time the defenses crumbled.

"How do you know?" Lanny cried, her eyes welling up.

"In myself I don't," Virgo said, "but God gave me understanding when I prayed for you."

The dam burst and Lanny began to sob.

"I hate living with my family," she finally gasped out. "I hate it because my father uses that kind of magic with the daggers and all kinds of stuff. I just can't stand it—I feel so oppressed."

Gently Virgo counseled her about the love of God, Christ's sacrifice on the cross for the sins of the world and His supreme authority over all the power of Satan.

"God loves you so much, Lanny," he told her. "He knows all about your situation and wants to deliver you from oppression and give you eternity in heaven, if you'll give your life to Him. Do you want to pray now to ask Jesus to come into your heart?"

Lanny nodded and they prayed together. Afterward Virgo perceived a new softness and radiance shining from her face.

One more issue Virgo had to address. "You know, it seems to me that if God has given this word of knowledge about the daggers and their effect on you in your home, He may also be prompting you to do some spiritual housecleaning."

"But I'm afraid of my father. The daggers belong to him."

"All right, then just tell him what happened tonight. Let him decide. I don't know you and I don't know your father, but when God gives prophetic words like this, it's usually because He wants to give you the freedom and awareness to make the right decision. Maybe when you tell your father your story, God will speak to him about clearing those things out of the house."

Lanny went home and told her father what had happened. A few days later she invited Virgo to come meet with her father. They spent all afternoon in conversation, but Lanny's father resisted suggestions to get rid of the daggers and other occult items.

"Javanese daggers are cultural artifacts," he insisted. "It's impossible to give up everything like that."

"Yes, some daggers are just daggers, but others can be vehicles for demonic power when they are used in magic rituals," Virgo answered. "You've seen the change in Lanny, from how disturbed she was before. Consider the impact on your family. But if you don't want to remove them, that's your decision as head of the house-hold and owner of the items. It's really up to you."

To Virgo's knowledge, the man never got rid of his occult para-phernalia. But Lanny stood her ground in the Lord, growing in freedom and victory as a Christian. She continued attending the fellowship group in Ungaran, which soon became a full-fledged church. Later Lanny married and moved to Jogyakarta, while the Ungaran congregation eventually grew to about two hundred people and planted about fifteen daughter churches. But Virgo never forgot one of its founding members.

Two-Way Communication

Many people who have spiritual gifts in the areas of prophecy, knowledge or discernment learn through years of prayer ministry experience how God typically speaks to them. Over time they iden-tify the idiosyncratic ways they hear God best and the meaning of what they hear.

Two-way communication with God can take place through a diversity of spiritual disciplines, including contemplative prayer, Bible meditation, worship, prayer-filled solitude, fasting and jour-naling. Discovering our own best meeting places with God will help us give priority to those activities in which we hear His voice and guidance most clearly. And the better we know His heart and voice, the more effectively we can pray and intercede.

In specific ministry situations, individuals learn to recognize characteristic signs of the Holy Spirit's special presence with a per-son, including trembling or shaking, fluttering eyelids and a sen-sation of heat. Sometimes the Lord gives an intercessor recurring indications of more specific information. Virgo Handojo knew from past experience, for instance, that a tingling in his palm when he laid hands on someone usually indicated occult influence in that person's life.

In most cases, however, particularly one-on-one ministry, words of knowledge are best shared tentatively, even if the intercessor senses them with great clarity. Asking questions and letting the person being prayed for confirm them (or not) may trigger fewer defense mechanisms than an authoritative *Thus says the Lord*, especially if the prophetic message identifies hidden sins. Recall the oblique way Virgo approached Lanny after the Lord gave him revelation of the Javanese dagger.

Words of knowledge and prophecy, when used with care and sensitivity, can serve as powerful door-openers for the Gospel. Read on for examples from the life of one unusually gifted for this kind of ministry.

Reading Other People's Mail

Cindy Jacobs (whom we met in chapter 1) is president and co-founder, with her husband Michael, of Generals of Intercession, an international prayer network now based in Colorado Springs, Colorado. A petite, high-energy brunette in her early forties, Cindy ministers in personal prophecy and prophetic intercession as a matter of course, the way a postal carrier delivers letters. Her books *Possessing the Gates of the Enemy* (Chosen, 1991) and *The Voice of God* (Regal, 1995) illustrate the importance of intercessors hearing clearly from God for effective ministry.

Several vignettes from her life paint a picture of how God uses divinely anointed prophetic words to convey messages for an immediate time, place and person, changing hearts and lives.

* * * * *

Weatherford, Texas. Thirty miles west and decades distant from downtown Fort Worth, Cindy's former hometown boasts a country-style warmth and charm. About 1983, in the days before God launched Cindy into an international ministry, she spent a Sunday morning across town at the Living Way Church as the guest worship leader.

In the middle of the service, the Lord prompted her with a word of knowledge she could not ignore.

Interrupting herself, she told the congregation of about two hundred, "I sense from the Lord that there's someone here whose heart has been hard toward Him. He's calling you to give your life to Him today.

"It's so urgent," Cindy went on, "that if you don't respond to the Lord's message, you're going to die in a plane crash. In fact, it'll be a mechanical failure—you've got a small plane and you need to check it carefully."

The service continued, and at its conclusion Cindy invited the whole congregation to bow and pray with her as she led a prayer of confession and commitment to God.

Afterward a man of about 46 approached her, his face ashen and intense.

"Cindy, that was me you were talking about," he acknowledged. "I'm a pilot and a Vietnam vet and I've been real hardened against God. I don't even know why I was here today. I'm not a regular churchgoer. But I want you to know I prayed that prayer with you just now and gave my life to Christ. I'm going home where I've got several acres of land outside of town and a grass airstrip, and I'm going to check my plane."

A few days later Cindy got a call from the man's wife. That Sunday afternoon he had found a mechanical problem he would not normally have noticed in the usual pre-flight walkaround inspection. If he had taken his plane up, he would have crashed.

Cindy's word made a big impression on the pilot because he saw the lengths to which God would go to get a message through to him. His life began turning around that day, and although he would struggle through peaks and valleys in his walk with the Lord, he remembered that this demonstration of God's deep love for him had saved his life.

* * * * *

Around the same time, Cindy found herself preaching in the little Texas town of Whitt, 25 miles northwest of Weatherford into cow country. The Lord gave her several prophetic words one after another, almost like a divine roll call, for various people present. Many responded by coming to the altar for prayer.

At one point Cindy turned and waved a hand toward the back of the room, her eye on a tall young man.

"There's a man here, and you think you're a good ol' boy and you can just do what you want during the week, party all night and then show up to church on Sunday. In fact, you have a keg of beer in the back of your truck right now, and you've been out partying last night."

The young man blanched, shot out of his seat and ran to the altar. A lanky dude with cowboy boots and hat, he fell onto his knees and began repenting of his sins. The awe and humility that gripped him were evident; God had read his mail. Cindy prayed with him and he accepted Christ as his Savior.

* * * * *

It was 1982 or 1983. The Jacobs family had just finished vacationing in California. Mike had taken an earlier flight back to Texas to return to work, while Cindy and their two small children stayed an extra couple of days to visit friends.

On their last afternoon Cindy pulled into a gas station near Los Angeles International Airport to fill the tank before returning the rental car. She edged up to the self-service island and got out to pump the gas.

From the nearby sidewalk a young African-American man in his early twenties approached Cindy, bucket and squeegee in hand.

"Can I wash your windows for you?" he asked, apparently hoping to earn a little pocket change.

"Well, no," Cindy answered. "This is a rental car and I'm just on my way back to LAX to catch a plane, so I really don't need the windows washed. But thanks anyway."

Cindy finished pumping and went inside to the cashier. On her way back to the car she noticed the young man again hovering nearby with his bucket. As she looked at him—skinny, forlorn, a bandanna tied around his head—her heart filled with compassion. Simultaneously the Lord anointed her with a prophetic message for him.

She walked over. "You know, even though I don't need the windows washed, there is something I need to tell you."

He looked at her quizzically.

"There's a mighty call of God on your life," Cindy told him. "You've been in a place of imprisonment, and your parents and grandparents are praying for you, and you need to go home. You need to go home to God."

With a clatter the bucket dropped from the young man's hand. His eyes filled with tears.

"That—that's true!" he said, a look of awe on his face. "Everything you said! I just got out of prison, and when I was a little boy I used to kneel at the altar and weep, and my grandfather would pray for me and say, 'One day you're going to preach the Gospel and be a mighty man of God.'"

His eyes brightened. "Lady, I'm going home. I'm going to go call my parents and tell them I'm coming. I'm going home to the Lord and to my parents *today*."

* * * * *

By 1986 Cindy was traveling out of state to preach and teach. Arriving at the Dallas-Fort Worth International Airport one morning, she had just enough time to use the ladies' room before heading to her departure gate. Several travelers crowded the facilities, as well as a cleaning woman pushing a rubbish bin on wheels.

Cindy finished and got halfway down the concourse when the image of the cleaning woman flashed back into her mind like a slide projection—mid-forties, blonde, slightly overweight.

She heard God speaking to her spirit: *Cindy, I want you to go back there and tell that woman I love her, and give her the plan of salvation.*

What, Lord? Cindy protested. *She's going to think I'm crazy. I mean, it was crowded in there, and she could even be gone by now. Besides, I've got a long walk to my gate. I might miss my plane.*

She wrestled a few moments longer, but knew the Lord would not give her peace until she turned back. Returning to the restroom, Cindy was surprised to find it empty of patrons, with the cleaning woman still at work.

"Excuse me, ma'am," she began. "I saw you in here earlier, and God just wants me to let you know that He really loves you."

The woman simply stared at Cindy a moment. Then her face crinkled up and the tears began to flow.

"I just found out that my husband has a brain tumor," she sobbed. "And I have no hope."

For about ten minutes Cindy shared the hope of Christ with her. Briefly she laid a hand on the woman's arm and prayed, then gave her a tract outlining the way of salvation through Jesus.

When Cindy left, the woman's countenance had been transformed from despair to fresh expectancy.

I know I'll see her in heaven! Cindy thought as she hurried to meet her plane.

Then she realized God had protected her conversation with the worker. Not one other woman had entered the ladies' room during the time they had spent talking.

* * * * *

Cindy's international ministry grew quickly. In early May 1991 she made her fourth trip to Argentina to teach at a pastors' seminar in La Plata, the provincial capital forty miles south of Buenos Aires. Before leaving Buenos Aires for La Plata, she accepted an invitation to preach at one of the largest churches in the country.

With Argentina in the midst of revival, church services often featured ministries of supernatural power that strengthened the body of believers and drew countless seekers out of the kingdom of darkness into the kingdom of light.

At this service the Lord impressed Cindy with several words of knowledge for people throughout the audience. One in particular startled everyone.

"There's someone here," she said, speaking through a translator, "and you've decided you're going to go home from this meeting and commit suicide because your life is so incredibly hard. The Lord says to you, 'Don't do it.' Receive His peace and hope tonight."

Cindy went on with the sermon and gave an altar call at the end. But the host pastor wanted to make sure the hurting sheep of his flock got the care they needed.

"Who was that one Cindy spoke about earlier," he asked, "the one who was going to commit suicide? Would you come up if you haven't already done so?"

From far in the back, a small, dark-haired woman in her thirties wearing a white blouse and dark skirt made her way forward. They drew her onto the platform, where she confessed with tears in her eyes, "I have a gun in my purse. I was planning to go home tonight and kill myself and my three children. We're being evicted from our apartment and—oh, I can't tell you the despair I've had," she cried, breaking into huge sobs.

Cindy put an arm around her, stroking her shoulder as the translator gave the interpretation.

"But now I know Jesus cares about me," the woman went on after a moment. "I can see God loves me so much to have brought me this message so dramatically. I want to give my life to Him."

That night she turned her life over to Jesus and her gun over to her pastor.

God's Got Our Number

Without a doubt the Lord can bring unbelievers to faith following a prophetic word simply through the awesome discovery that He knows their names and situations and cares about them personally. What a humbling demonstration of the sovereign Lord's love for an individual! Even when the message may warn of dire repercussions for not heeding, repenting or obeying (as did Cindy's word for the pilot of the small plane), God shows not vindictiveness but compassion in alerting people to natural consequences in time for them to respond.

At the same time, prophetic messages not only evidence the love of the Lord but engender the fear of the Lord. We can hide nothing from Him, and when God substantiates this by giving secret knowledge to one of His servants, the effect can be disorienting. A person graphically confronted with God's omniscience will often be convicted of sins and ready to receive Christ as Savior.

In 2 Timothy 4:2 the apostle Paul advised his young protégé, "Preach the Word; be prepared in season and out of season; correct, rebuke and encourage—with great patience and careful instruction." The more we walk in step with the Spirit, the better prepared we are to share both the written Word and an immediate prophetic word with people who cross our paths. Boldness often pays off. Cindy Jacobs says hardly anyone refuses when she asks, "May I just pray for you a minute?" And anything can happen when we, in our priestly role as intercessors, go to God on behalf of others, seeking His intervention and blessing in their lives.

In addition to giving words of knowledge intended to be shared with others for their response, the Lord may give supernatural revelation meant for the intercessor alone. With this information intercessors can pray and make choices of action they might never have considered. Even though Cindy delivered a simple, generic message of God's love for the cleaning woman in the airport restroom, the fundamental word was the one God gave to Cindy herself—to turn around and minister to this one suffering in silence.

Martin of Tours (c. 335–397), patron saint of France, received a prophetic message through a dream that resulted in the conversion of his mother. According to his biographer, Sulpicius Severus, Martin "was advised in his sleep to go to his native land and in a spirit of religious zeal to visit his parents, who were still pagans." After a difficult, hardship-filled journey to what is now western Hungary, he led his mother to faith in Christ (*Life of St. Martin*, chapters 5 and 6). This was the last time he saw his parents.

From Martin's era to Cindy Jacobs' day, the Lord continues to speak.

Here is another story of a woman to whom God gave inside-track knowledge about someone He wanted to claim for His own.

Squeezing Ripe Fruit

Laura Williams said a warm good-bye to the last guest, then closed her front door slowly in frustration. Another evangelistic Bible study, and no one wanted to make a commitment to Christ.

For several years this 38-year-old mom had been sowing seeds. Along with her husband, Steve, associate pastor at Cornerstone

Community Presbyterian Church in Artesia, California, Laura often talked with unbelievers, inviting them to her home and sharing the Gospel. She enrolled her preschooler, the youngest of her five children, in a parks-and-recreation program, partly to get to know other moms in need of the Lord. She started a women's Bible study for new believers and seekers. People listened pleasantly—but no one ever came to faith in Jesus.

"Lord, I know Your Word is powerful," Laura agonized in prayer one day. "I know Your presence is real. Why do people brush it off like dryer lint? True, You've made me a seed-planter—others will water and someday, I'm sure, a harvest will come. But Lord, could You give me just one piece of fruit? Just let me see someone radically changed as a result of my witness to You, and I'll be content to sow seeds the rest of my life."

About six weeks later, around the first week of May 1990, at 5:30 on a Wednesday afternoon, Laura was preparing a burrito supper in the kitchen of her Bellflower home when the doorbell rang. With Steve not yet home from work and her children playing noisily, Laura did not need another distraction. At that time the Williams household also included the three children of a friend from seminary, Kefa Sempangi of Uganda.

Laura's fifth-grader, Elisabeth, answered the bell. In a moment Laura heard her call out, "Mom, there's someone at the door for you. It's some kind of salesman."

Laura grimaced.

"Oh, Elisabeth, get rid of him," she yelled from the kitchen.

"I can't. You come and do it."

With a sigh Laura put down her knife and washed her hands.

What a rude interruption at dinnertime, she grumbled to herself. *Doesn't he know I'm cooking the evening meal? Doesn't he know I have eight kids in the house?*

She took three steps and heard a voice, clear as a bugle calling reveille: *Don't let him go—he's Mine.*

The voice was not audible, Laura realized, but so distinct she could not mistake it—not her own thoughts, but so familiar it felt a part of her. She knew it was the Holy Spirit.

Her theological background did not allow for receiving contemporary prophetic messages from the Almighty. But the words took hold of Laura from the depths of her being. With excited anticipation, she walked through the family room and turned into the living room toward the front door. *This man is going to become a Christian, I know it! How can I get a hook into this guy?*

Instead of the brusque greeting she would ordinarily have given a door-to-door salesman at that hour, Laura looked carefully into the eyes of the tall, dark-haired young man standing on the front porch hoping to sell books. He returned her gaze, and as he tried to launch into his spiel she began asking him questions: "Hi, where are you from? How'd you get here? Where are you staying?" To her relief, he either had not heard or was not offended by her initial expression of annoyance.

Then Laura stepped outside and invited him to sit with her on the porch, while the burritos took a back seat for the next hour.

His name, Laura learned, was Pat Naughton. He had just arrived from Michigan to take a summer job with a company that gave college students boot-camp training in salesmanship. A 21-year-old student between his junior and senior years at Western Michigan University in Kalamazoo, Pat was staying in temporary quarters with three other budding salesmen.

"You're searching, aren't you?" Laura asked him. "You're out here because you want to find yourself."

Pat stared. "How do you know?"

"It's all over your face. But you're really searching for something bigger than yourself, for truth and meaning in life—isn't that right? You'll find it only if you search in the right place." Laura glanced at his box of book samples. "Do you like to read?"

"I love to read."

"I've got a book for you." Laura went inside and returned with a copy of Kefa Sempangi's *A Distant Grief*. She pointed to the name on the cover. "This man is a friend of ours. It's the story of how he and his wife survived in Uganda in the '70s when many people were being murdered under the dictatorship of Idi Amin. Their three kids are playing in our living room right now. Why don't you read this and then come back and we can talk about it?"

Pat took the volume.

"O.K., thanks," he said.

With a smile and wave he strode off down the street to peddle his books. Laura started praying for him.

Two days later Laura opened the door about 5 P.M. to find her new young acquaintance. As they sat down in the living room, Pat handed back Kefa's book.

"You know," he said, "I'm a philosophy major at Western Michigan, and I have no concept of evil. How can I be educated at a university and never be taught about evil?"

The two talked, and before long Laura's husband arrived home from work.

"Steve, this is that book salesman I told you about, Pat Naughton." Laura put a hand on Pat's arm. "Steve, this was you twenty years ago."

Steve sat down with Pat and, dinner forgotten, presented the Gospel for two hours from Old Testament to New, tailor-made for a searching philosophy student. Pat seemed to soak it up in amazement. But when Steve and Laura asked if he wanted to make a commitment to Jesus Christ, he hesitated.

"No, not yet," he replied.

Eight days passed. Laura's mother-heart yearned to take Pat in and disciple him.

Can we squeeze one more into this house? she wondered. *But I don't know when I'll even see Pat again.*

She knew it was absurd to consider opening her home to a complete stranger, yet this fellow seemed different—honest, deep and truly searching. Laura could even sense somehow the Spirit of God hovering powerfully around him.

Then one day about two in the afternoon, Pat appeared at the door, his face engulfed in misery. Laura sat down with him at the kitchen table where he began to weep.

"I have no peace," he cried. "For over a week I've had no peace. I have to know your God."

He had knocked on countless doors since he had seen her last, he told Laura, and kept discovering Christians who wanted to share the Gospel with him! Now he was more than ready to pray with Laura and ask Jesus into his life.

After prayer Pat looked up. Peace flooded around him and spilled out in a joyful laugh.

"You know, when you answered the door that first day," he reflected, "it seemed like you could see right through me. It was just like a sword piercing my soul, and I felt absolutely naked."

"The Lord had told me about you," Laura answered. "When I looked into your eyes, I could see your search and feel your pain. God loves you so much that He wasn't about to let you go."

Then Laura pushed on. "Pat, why don't you move in with us? This is a crucial time in your life. You need to learn more about what it means to walk with Christ. We can put you in a spare bunk above my son. How about it?"

So for the rest of that summer Pat lived with the Williams family and grew in his faith. He quit selling books; one of Laura's friends found him another job. And he reported that the doubts and worries of his Irish Catholic parents in Michigan regarding his California trip were dispelled quickly by the change in his life.

That fall when Pat returned to college, he recounted to Steve and Laura the comments from curious friends: "What's happened to you? You're totally changed." He joined a Christian fellowship on campus, and after graduation moved back to California, where he stayed with the Williams family again for a year. He met his future bride at a party in their backyard, and now, as a close friend, lives a few miles away in La Mirada. God nailed Pat Naughton the day he rang Laura Williams' doorbell.

God also led Laura and Steve through a series of paradigm shifts about hearing the voice of God. Today Steve, a graduate of conservative Westminster Seminary, is a pastor at the Stadium Vineyard Christian Fellowship in Anaheim, where prophecy and words of knowledge play key roles in the church's ministry.

Laura Williams, seed-planter, finally saw a piece of fruit ripen to harvest.

Asking, Hearing and Obeying

Laura would never have thought twice about the annoying door-to-door book salesman—and Pat might never have found the peace and meaning he was looking for—if Laura had not heard and obeyed God's directive in the word of knowledge He gave her that May afternoon. And perhaps God sent the timely message, and made sure Laura heard it, only in response to her prayer to see fruit from her witnessing. While the Lord cherishes seed-sowing within the cooperative ministry of His Body (see 1 Corinthians 3:6–8), He also understood Laura's frustration and graciously answered. Sometimes, as James 4:2 says, "You do not have, because you do not ask God."

The Holy Spirit brought Pat to salvation primarily through the power of the Gospel that the Williamses and other Christians in their neighborhood shared with the young salesman. But absolute confidence that God had chosen Pat encouraged Laura and Steve to persevere in ministry to him until he surrendered his life to Christ.

When we stay in tune with the Spirit of God, He can point out to us people ripe and ready for conversion. They, in turn, may be deeply touched by our special attention. When Jesus passed through the city of Jericho, a short tax collector named Zacchaeus climbed into a tree to see Him better (see Luke 19:1–10). Although they almost certainly had never met, Jesus stopped and called him by name. "When Jesus reached the spot, he looked up and said to him, 'Zacchaeus, come down immediately. I must stay at your house today'" (verse 5).

A startled Zacchaeus welcomed the Lord into his home, undoubtedly moved that such a prominent leader had singled him out. While they ate dinner, deep conviction of his sins prompted Zacchaeus to announce a complete lifestyle turnaround. And in response "Jesus said to him, 'Today salvation has come to this house . . .'" (verse 9).

A word of knowledge need not pertain to a person in order to result in someone's salvation. Supernaturally derived information about even the natural realm can point people to the true God behind such revelation, as we will see.

Quest for Living Water

Cruising in their four-wheel-drive Toyota Hi-Lux, Keith and Kim Greig and their two Kurdish engineers headed back to their temporary home in Zakho, a city near the Turkish border in the Kurdish Autonomous Region of northern Iraq. For about six weeks the young Australian couple from Brisbane had been working in Iraq under the auspices of the United Nations for an organization called Wells of Life.

Nearly three million people had lost their homes when Iraqi troops destroyed four thousand primarily Kurdish villages. Most water wells were bombed, bulldozed or filled with mines. The Greigs' mission with Wells of Life included finding and installing fresh water supplies for refugees now returning to their village sites. As part of their ministry with Youth With A Mission (YWAM), they also brought with them a Discipleship Training School outreach team of eight other people to help with relief efforts and primary health care in various locations.

On this Thursday, November 5, 1992, the group in the four-wheeler came upon a village fifty or sixty miles out from Zakho in the foothills of the northern mountains. As they drove by, they noticed a small pool, perhaps twenty feet in diameter, thick with mud-gray water.

"Ugh, look at that pond," Kim commented.

As they pulled aside to check it out, a short, slight man of about sixty with fair skin and brown hair approached their vehicle, clearly marked with the recognizable *Wells of Life* logo on the door.

Through Asaad, one of their Kurdish engineers who served as translator, the Greigs learned that this man was chief of the Kurdish village of Brifka, a Sunni Muslim community. The original village, leveled by Iraqi troops and tanks twelve months earlier, had sat about a mile higher up in the mountains. With their wells and water source destroyed, the returning villagers decided to rebuild closer to the main road in hope of connecting with a piped water supply, but their still-remote location dashed this dream.

"I have a thousand people here who began rebuilding three months ago and another thousand waiting in refugee camps to return," the chief explained. "We've spent three thousand U.S. dollars hiring a front-end loader to dig all over our land searching for water, totally in vain. My people are desperate. The children are sick and dying." He looked at them with quiet intensity. "Can you help us at all?"

Keith learned that the muddy pond, almost stagnant, was fed by a tiny spring from the water table below. He also noticed that its location downhill from the village assured that assorted effluent seeped into it. As they talked, women came to wash clothes, shepherds watered their small flocks and children collected drinking water—all from the same polluted pool.

Keith ran a hand through his red hair before answering the chief.

"It's clear you need fresh water," he said as the afternoon sun played off his freckled complexion, "but we're committed to several other well-building projects at the moment. Let me return on Tuesday with another man from our group and we'll survey your situation."

Because of danger from snipers and Communist guerrillas, the team established their base in Zakho, traveling out each day to development sites. That following Tuesday, November 10, Keith and the two Kurdish engineers returned to Brifka with Tim Hermiston, an Australian colleague. At age 27, the dark-haired, six-foot-two mechanic was four years younger and almost a head taller than Keith. His farmer's-style quiet, helpful disposition made Tim a good traveling companion.

When they reached the village, the chief came out and met them. He seemed more discouraged than before. As the men walked and talked, the chief ticked off all the futile efforts and wasted money they had expended.

"We have tried to find water—it's hopeless!" he declared, throwing up his hands. "We have searched everywhere and there is none!"

"We can hire some drilling equipment to explore the area," Keith suggested.

But the haggard chief responded in frustrated despair. "It's no use. You'd be wasting your time."

Not quite sure what to do, the small group walked to a knoll about 330 yards from the village and about ten yards up on higher ground. As Keith and Tim looked out over the area, they began to pray aloud, asking God for direction. Although Asaad did not translate, the chief knew these Wells of Life people prayed to their God, the Jesus of the New Testament.

In the quiet moment after the prayer, Keith spoke up. "Tim, I've got a real strange impression from God, but it's as clear as any-thing—I believe He's telling us we should dig right where we're standing."

"That's just what I was sensing!" Tim exclaimed, turning to stare at Keith. "Weird, isn't it? Who would dig a well for groundwater on the top of a hill? But I heard God just as clearly."

Asaad explained their discussion to the chief. When he heard the translation he again threw up his hands and looked to the sky, shaking his head.

"We have already tried digging only meters from this spot and found nothing! Please," the chief pleaded, his people's suffering etched on his face, "don't waste time or money digging here. It will mean only disappointment."

"I understand your feelings," Keith answered gently. "I know you don't want your hopes dashed one more time. But God has given us an unmistakable message—if we dig right here, we'll find water."

That evening Keith and Tim made arrangements to hire a small front-end loader from Zakho. The next morning, Wednesday, the owner-operator drove the earthmover four hours out to Brifka and began to dig on the knoll. The chief and a handful of village elders squatted nearby, eyeing the operation.

After a couple of hours the heavy equipment had excavated a hole about four feet deep. Suddenly gallons of water—a great, gush-ing stream—came bubbling from the ground. The chief and elders jumped up and began hollering with joyful disbelief.

Keith brought in the rest of his team and got to work building a well, tapping the spring, piping the water down to the village and installing large storage tanks and taps. Every day for about three weeks the new well became Brifka's main social event. Some villagers helped to build while others prepared tea and food for the workers. The polluted pond was filled in and another new well dug nearby—covered, with a hand-operated pump—to provide water for animals and laundry.

The villagers had learned that Keith and his team believed in Jesus Christ, and that they had dug the well in accordance with divine guidance.

As the work went on, Keith approached the chief. "May we have your permission to tell your people about Jesus? Most of them probably don't know anything about Him, but He is the God who provided this water for you."

"By ail means," the chief replied, beaming a smile as wide as his face.

During lunch breaks the believers shared the Gospel with the village elders and others. In addition the YWAM team, with Asaad translating, presented afternoon programs twice a week featuring Bible stories told through puppets and drama, as well as songs and games. The chief cleared out the largest room in his home for the team's programs, and virtually the entire village crammed into the house, at the doors and windows and around the outside, taking in the message of Christ eagerly. The chief was deeply moved by the team's commitment to Brifka and by the miracle of water provided in Jesus' name and through His specific direction.

As Keith, Kim, Tim and the others reflected on this experience, they marveled at the unprecedented receptivity of this village to the Gospel.

"Out of all the villages we've worked in," Keith noted, "Brifka has been by far the most open to the Gospel."

Regrettably, winter came early that year, and by December 10 the team left northern Iraq in the grip of freezing cold and snow. Although the Greigs could not continue contact with the chief and people of Brifka, they knew the water well in its prophetically designated location would remain as a permanent testimony to the love and concern of the Lord Jesus.

With increased conflict in the Kurdish Autonomous Region, many Christian relief workers have since withdrawn from the area. But the Greigs have heard unconfirmed reports of whole villages there converting to Jesus Christ. If Brifka had been one of the first, it would come as no surprise to the Greigs and their team.

Love and Risk

Meeting the needs of people through such avenues as mercy min-istries, relief and development projects often provides instant oppor-tunities for the Kingdom of God to go forth when Christians take leading roles. Jesus commended giving "a cup of cold water to one of these little ones" (Matthew 10:42) at the same time He instructed His disciples on preaching the Gospel. People with vital physical welfare needs who have lost all hope for remedy often express great openness to the Gospel when believers minister to them with the love of God. And when believers are prepared to minister in the supernatural power of God, a great harvest of souls may result.

Jesus, in defining His own mission with a quotation from the Old Testament prophet Isaiah, incorporated the full spectrum of ministry to the poor and oppressed, proclamation of the Gospel and signs and wonders.

> "The Spirit of the Lord is on me,
>   because he has anointed me
>   to preach good news to the poor.
> He has sent me to proclaim freedom for the prisoners
>   and recovery of sight for the blind,
>   to release the oppressed,
>   to proclaim the year of the Lord's favor."
>   Luke 4:18–19

When Keith Greig and Tim Hermiston asked God where to find water for the village of Brifka, they took a risk. Believers who pray for words of knowledge, prophetic messages or divine guidance open themselves to the possibility that God will give specific responses, sometimes unexpected, counterintuitive or costly. Then those receiving the messages must decide whether they will fol-low what they have heard.

The word to dig for water atop a hill in an area already scouted sounded foolish to the village chief. Keith and Tim would have agreed—except they were sure the word came from God. This certainty gave them the courage to obey the message, putting time, money and reputation on the line. Without either the assurance or the obedience, Brifka might never have found its water source, or learned about the Water of Life.

As Jesus said in Luke 11:28, "Blessed . . . are those who hear the word of God and obey it."

4

"Your Young Men Will See Visions"

Stories of Dreams and Visions

Twenty-three-year-old Simba Mohammedovich read the letter from his uncle.

What a great opportunity! he thought.

Already studying economics at a university in his native Turkey, Simba (not his real name) had just learned from his uncle that he could transfer to a school in Russia that trained people primarily of his own ethnic nationality. He had often wondered what life was like for his uncle's family in their ancestral region, a small province of southern Russia in the Caucasus Mountains. Now he could find out.

Simba had grown up in north-central Turkey, on the southern coast of the Black Sea, and practiced the Sunni Muslim faith of his family. But from about age seven, he became aware that he possessed unusual spiritual sensitivity. The figure of a man had appeared to him repeatedly in visions at night, talking with Simba and gaining his confidence. The boy had found that he could tell fortunes to children at school and predict the future with uncanny accuracy. Soon people were coming to Simba asking for spiritual guidance through readings of cards, coffee grounds or their palms.

At night when the spirit figure crept into his room to communicate messages, it had often asked Simba, "Do you love me?"

"Yes, I love you," the boy had responded, "because you help me to help people."

Simba was intoxicated by his ability to understand the supernatural realm and do good for others through the information he received. Now in college, the dark-haired, handsome young man had drifted into practices of "folk" Islam, a popular blend of classical Islam with belief in spirits and supernatural power.

His uncle in southern Russia arranged for a visa, and in the fall of 1991 Simba arrived in the Caucasus city as one of eleven foreign students at the university there. Although his grandfather had been born in this region, Simba spoke only Turkish and spent many months at school in intensive language classes. Nine hours a day he studied—three hours each of Russian, English and the local Caucasian language—and lived with his uncle and family in their second-floor apartment.

Simba also began to make new friends, including Martha, a European Christian working with a Russian Bible mission in the Caucasus region.

One day Simba told her, "You know, I'd like a copy of the New Testament in Turkish."

"I'm so sorry, but I don't have one," Martha apologized, "and it might take me quite a while to get a copy for you. Why don't you come to our Christian meetings on Friday afternoons where we talk about the message of the Bible?"

"I'm not interested in that," replied Simba. "I just want a Turkish New Testament."

Several times more Simba asked Martha for the Scripture in his language. While she worked on it, she again invited him to attend the Messianic Muslim Christian fellowship with people from his ethnic group. Finally he agreed to go.

On a Friday afternoon in late September 1992, Simba walked into the strangest meeting he had ever experienced. As a Muslim he thought he knew all about prayer, a five-times-daily ritual. But normally Simba prayed just for himself, his family or perhaps a close friend. These Christians prayed for anything and everything, even him. It set his mind spinning. Sincere love oozed out like warm honey, and Simba could not help but feel attracted.

On his way home that Friday afternoon, he caught himself singing.

What am I doing? he wondered, almost embarrassed. *Why am I so happy?*

He had no answer, but the next Friday he returned to the fellowship. He listened to the teaching about Jesus Christ and found it different from what he had been taught in Islam. Once again the warmth of the Messianic Muslim believers reached out and wrapped him up. Simba exchanged names and phone numbers with a few new friends.

The meeting ended about 6 P.M., and Simba returned to his uncle's apartment with a light step. Everyone was gone except his uncle, snoring in the bedroom.

A little too much vodka today, I guess, Simba thought with a wry smile.

He fixed himself a bite to eat, then went out on the second-floor balcony to smoke a cigarette and enjoy the fresh air.

What a beautiful day, he mused, gazing over the city as the setting sun glowed warm and yellow.

From inside his soul he felt words stirring—words his mind hardly understood: *O Lord, please show me this way, this faith way. I really need You.*

The next moment a curtain of darkness descended over Simba.

"What's happened to my eyesight?" he mumbled, waving fingers in front of his face.

Wait, Simba, don't panic, he told himself. *Stand up slowly and go inside.*

His left hand groped for the balcony door but he could not get up. All the strength seemed to have drained from his legs.

Suddenly he heard a voice (was it only in his mind?)—a strong, deep voice laughing with icy cruelty.

Ho, ho, ho, ho, it bellowed. *You are mine and you will serve me. Believe me—no one can help you.*

Simba's flesh began to crawl.

"Who—who are you?" he stammered.

From the right side of the darkness in front of him, Simba could make out eyes and the shadow of a face smirking at him. The harsh voice started to laugh again.

"Help! Somebody help me!" Simba cried, scarcely louder than a whisper.

Just then he saw a ball of light rise on his left. Slowly it took shape into a figure so bright that Simba could not keep his eyes on Him, although he longed to. The Man seemed to be dressed in a white robe, and Simba heard a voice like a song, full of mercy, call out, "I'm here."

Then the bright Man turned His attention to the figure in darkness.

"No, he isn't yours!" came the melodic voice, brimming with authority. "He will be Mine. Simba is good and he will serve Me. He's coming to be with Us now."

At this the dark figure on the right writhed and moaned in crazed rage. As Simba watched, he seemed to lunge at his opponent, but the Man in shining brilliance disappeared and everything went black again. Before long the curtain in front of Simba's eyes dissolved.

He stood up, heart pounding, and stumbled inside, where he collapsed into a living room chair.

In a moment he recognized the dark voice hissing again. *See, you're alone. Nobody will help you. Come to me. You'll be mine.*

Something deep in Simba's heart seemed to answer, *No, he won't.*

With a burst of courage he cried out, "No, I won't!"

And the battle was on. Simba's temperature shot up as he felt invisible forces fighting over his very body. Breaking into a sweat, he peeled off some clothes and called feebly, "Help me! Please help me!" But the rumble of snoring from his uncle's room droned on.

Then, like a flare of light, a thought flashed to mind: *Phone that man you met, one of the Messianic Muslim believers.*

Simba felt restrained physically from reaching the telephone, his strength gone.

Please, help! his heart cried out to the bright figure he had seen.

Then he managed to find one of the numbers he had written down at the meeting and pick up the phone.

Now his voice failed him.

"Hello? Hello? Who's there?" said his new friend Mufar on the other end of the line.

After a moment Simba croaked out, "It's Simba. I'm in a very bad way." He gave his address. "Please come."

"What's the problem?" Mufar asked.

Simba could only stammer incomprehensibly.

"O.K., hold on. I'll be there as soon as I can."

Before long Mufar, probably fifteen years older than Simba, arrived. The door was open, and he found Simba sprawled out, breathing hard.

"What's wrong, Simba?"

The young man began to cry uncontrollably.

"I don't know, it's just so bad—so bad," he gasped. "I can't even describe it, it's just so bad."

Mufar knitted his eyebrows and started to pray. After a while he paused. "I feel a dark, evil force in this room. It would really be better if more than one person prayed for you. Do you think you can come to another believer's home where we can get two or three intercessors together?"

Simba nodded weakly, but the evil voice kept tormenting him as they made their way across town.

Nobody can help you, the dark voice growled. *I'm stronger than Jesus. You're alone. Believe me!*

Every time Simba's spirit answered, *No, I won't!* he felt physical pain, as though the demon were beating, stabbing, shaking him.

Mufar and a weeping, nauseated Simba reached the apartment of a younger believer, who soon left to fetch the pastor of their group. While he was gone, Simba suffered another demonic attack that left his limbs stiff.

In a panic he implored Mufar, "Call an ambulance!"

Mufar dialed anxiously but did not know the building number. So he helped Simba downstairs, where they waited on the street to flag down the emergency vehicle.

Simba did not dare tell the medic about the voice, but the man seemed to discern the truth. After checking Simba's blood pressure and finding it normal, the medic ventured, "You know, I think this is not a medical problem but a spiritual problem."

Simba agreed.

Just after the ambulance left and the pair returned to the apartment, the host arrived with their pastor, whom Simba had met at the Christian fellowship. For some time the three believers prayed for him, stopping often to explain truth from the Word of God. The more they talked and prayed, the more Simba began to relax and feel at peace.

"Don't be afraid," the pastor told him. "Jesus will help you, and He's stronger than anything the devil might try to do to you."

Eventually conviction of this truth rose in Simba's heart. When he was ready, he prayed to repent of his sins and confess his new-found faith in Jesus as deliverer and Lord. Then he saw another vision, this time of white doves fluttering from the sky and into his heart. His body felt warm again, but now the heat brought a feeling of joy, almost exhilaration.

Close to two in the morning, Simba, Mufar and the pastor headed for home.

"If the devil tries to harass you again," the pastor advised Simba, "rebuke him in the name of Jesus."

Just after going to bed, Simba heard the dark voice whisper a few parting shots.

"No, I'm *not* alone," Simba called out quietly but firmly. "Be gone, in the name of Jesus."

He heard a sound like a door slamming shut, and then felt the room fill with peace and joy.

Simba, a new believer in Jesus Christ, slept well that night.

God Speaks through Dreams and Visions

Until recently Simba's ethnic grouping had no native Christian testimony and was considered an unreached people group. Now an indigenous church movement has begun, partly through the effects of power evangelism, as the Lord forges ahead with His purpose of saving some from every tribe, tongue and nation on earth.

Does God—who incarnated His revelation of Himself through His Son, Jesus Christ—still speak through dreams and visions? The apostle Peter's address on the Day of Pentecost following Jesus' ascension, when the New Testament Church was born, suggested that He would not only continue but expand this kind of communication.

Peter explained the unusual goings-on that morning by proclaiming the fulfillment of Old Testament prophecy:

"These men are not drunk, as you suppose. It's only nine in the morning! No, this is what was spoken by the prophet Joel:

"'In the last days, God says,
    I will pour out my Spirit on all people.
Your sons and daughters will prophesy,
    your young men will see visions,
    your old men will dream dreams.
Even on my servants, both men and women,
    I will pour out my Spirit in those days,
    and they will prophesy.'"

Acts 2:15–18

In the Old Testament, dreams and visions remained primarily the province of prophets, priests and kings. Prophets were called "seers" because they frequently received their divine messages through dreams or visions. But as early as Job's day, people recognized that God sometimes used night visions to speak to ordinary people, even unbelievers, warning them out of paths of destruction:

For God does speak—now one way, now another—
    though man may not perceive it.

In a dream, in a vision of the night,
    when deep sleep falls on men
    as they slumber in their beds,
he may speak in their ears
    and terrify them with warnings,
to turn man from wrongdoing
    and keep him from pride,
to preserve his soul from the pit,
    his life from perishing by the sword.

Job 33:14–18

A dream or vision that results in the salvation of the one who receives it may hold quite idiosyncratic content. The vision can come as a word of warning, as encouragement or comfort, as direction or guidance, as an answer to prayer, revelation of spiritual reality or any number of other forms. Dreamers and visionaries may see demons or angels (a specific subcategory we will look at in chapter 5), heaven or hell, often Jesus Himself.

One of the most dramatic conversions in the Bible centers around the appearance of Jesus in a vision—Saul's encounter on the road to Damascus. As a zealous persecutor of the early Church, Saul traveled to Damascus seeking the imprisonment and eventual execution of the Lord's disciples. The book of Acts tells the story:

> As he neared Damascus on his journey, suddenly a light from heaven flashed around him. He fell to the ground and heard a voice say to him, "Saul, Saul, why do you persecute me?"
>
> "Who are you, Lord?" Saul asked.
>
> "I am Jesus, whom you are persecuting," he replied. "Now get up and go into the city, and you will be told what you must do."
>
> The men traveling with Saul stood there speechless; they heard the sound but did not see anyone. Saul got up from the ground, but when he opened his eyes he could see nothing. So they led him by the hand into Damascus. For three days he was blind, and did not eat or drink anything.

Acts 9:3–9

God got Saul's attention. Yet it took the ministry of a believer to "complete" Saul's conversion through baptizing and incorporating him into the Church. Ananias of Damascus received a vision directing him to the exact street and house where Saul was staying, so he could pray for Saul to be healed of his blindness and filled with the Holy Spirit (verses 10–19). Simultaneously God gave Saul another vision that a man named Ananias would come to him (verse 12).

Through the divine intervention of three separate visions, Saul's life took a 180-degree about-face, and the firebrand Saul became the apostle Paul.

"Jews Want a Sign from Heaven"

"Lord God, please tell me the truth about Your Son. I won't hear it from anyone else, but I want to hear it from You. Please give me a sign."

Meryl Konrad prayed her usual prayer for the umpteenth time. Ever since she had begun attending Ahavat Zion Messianic Synagogue in Beverly Hills, California, she had asked God to reveal the truth. No one else—not her husband, not her rabbi, not a person or a book—could persuade her that Jesus was the Messiah. She would accept it only directly from God.

Ahavat Zion served as a compromise congregation for Meryl and her husband, since neither was a Messianic Jew. Bill came from a Lutheran family and Meryl was Jewish, raised as a Reform Jew in Skokie, Illinois. They met while attending the University of Illinois at Champaign/Urbana and married right after graduation in June 1977—Meryl at age 21 with an undergraduate degree, and Bill, three and a half years older, with a degree from law school.

Neither of their families felt completely delighted about the marriage, but each set of parents soon came to accept their new daughter- or son-in-law. For several years Bill and Meryl avoided all religious services. It seemed easier to do nothing. Gradually, however, they both began to sense a need for spirituality in their lives.

About two years after moving to California in 1979, they discovered Ahavat Zion, where they started attending Shabbat (Sabbath) services. Each got something out of the experience. Bill liked the sermons centered on Yeshua Hamashiach (Jesus the Messiah) and Meryl enjoyed the traditional Jewish worship. They also found it amusing that many people assumed Bill was the Jewish partner in their mixed marriage, with his darker complexion, dark hair and beard.

Change came on the heels of the most frightful crisis of their lives. Their first child, Allison, born May 28, 1986, became dangerously ill just after her parents brought her home to El Segundo. Bill and Meryl rushed Allison, only twelve days old, to the neonatal intensive care unit at Torrance Memorial Hospital, where doctors gave them the grim diagnosis: spinal meningitis.

As the doctors ran tests and gave Allison various medications, the Konrads' friends and their families in Illinois drew a circle of care around the anxious couple. Meryl's family offered love and moral support, and her father traveled out to be with them—a great blessing. Bill's family and the congregation at Ahavat Zion offered something extra—prayer for healing in Jesus' name.

Meryl was moved by the intercession of the Messianic Jews and Christians. Although she had no relationship with Yeshua, she, too, lifted her daughter to God in prayer.

During three and a half weeks in intensive care, Allison recovered progressively. The doctors pinpointed her condition, gave the right treatments and adjusted her medications expertly. The Konrads' tiny daughter got better and stronger, passed all the tests—and finally came through with absolutely no side effects.

"Blessed are You, O Lord God, King of the universe!" Meryl and Bill rejoiced with their families and congregation over the Lord's intervention. Bill was growing firmer in his faith, and Meryl had seen the power of prayer in action for the first time.

During the following months, Meryl kept going to God with her petition: "Please show me the truth about Your Son. If Yeshua really is Messiah—I will accept this only from You, Lord."

In April 1987, with Allison about six weeks shy of her first birthday, Meryl found herself watching an Easter movie on television and began reflecting on the life of Jesus, the stories of His death and resurrection.

One night that week, in the dark and quiet of the wee morning, Meryl lay sleeping when her mind filled with a heavenly vision. In her dream she saw Yeshua standing before her dressed in dazzling white garments. He shone with a light so brilliant she could not make out the features of His face. Because of her angle of view, looking up at Him, Meryl realized later she must have been kneeling at His feet.

The vision, brief but crystal-clear, hit her consciousness with the impact of a tidal wave and jolted her awake. Meryl recognized this not as a dream she had concocted but a message from God Himself. Immediately she woke her husband.

"Bill, I believe in Yeshua!" she exclaimed. "I just saw Him in my dream!"

When she described her vision, her husband murmured sleepily, "Praise the Lord! I've been praying for this."

In the morning the indelible image remained seared on her brain. She had no doubt her dream had come from God.

Lord, You've answered my prayer of all these years, Meryl acknowledged in awe. *You heard my cry and knew what I needed in order to believe. Thank You, Lord! Thank You, Yeshua!*

She told Bill's family eagerly and the friends from Ahavat Zion who, she learned, had been praying for her.

"I've become a believer in Yeshua Hamashiach!" she testified.

Later, after much prayer and pondering, she told her own family.

As Meryl began studying the Bible, certain passages blazed with meaning, especially part of the first chapter of 1 Corinthians:

I know very well how foolish it sounds to those who are lost, when they hear that Jesus died to save them. But we who are saved recognize this message as the very power of God. For God says, "I will destroy all human plans of salvation no matter how wise they seem to be, and ignore the best ideas of men, even the most brilliant of them."

So what about these wise men, these scholars, these brilliant debaters of this world's great affairs? God has made them all look foolish, and shown their wisdom to be useless nonsense. For God in his wisdom saw to it that the world would never find God through human brilliance, and then he stepped in and saved all those who believed his message, which the world calls foolish and silly. It seems foolish to the Jews because they want a sign from heaven as proof that what is preached is true; and it is foolish to the Gentiles because they believe only what agrees with their philosophy and seems wise to them. So when we preach about [Messiah] dying to save them, the Jews are offended and the Gentiles say it's all nonsense. But God has opened the eyes of those called to salvation, both Jews and Gentiles, to see that [Messiah] is the mighty power of God to save them; [Messiah] himself is the center of God's wise plan for their salvation. . . .

For it is from God alone that you have your life through [Messiah] Jesus. He showed us God's plan of salvation; he was the one who made us acceptable to God; he made us pure and holy and gave himself to purchase our salvation. As it says in the Scriptures, "If anyone is going to boast, let him boast only of what the Lord has done."

verses 18–24, 30–31, TLB

God answered Meryl's sincere prayer for divine validation of the truth about Messiah by sending her a dream. By meeting her graciously at her point of confusion and need, God ensured that Meryl was born one of His chosen people—again.

Dream, Vision or Reality: Is There a Difference?

What is the difference between dreams and visions, trances and visitations? In modern Western thought we try to make neat categories for each of these terms. We may suggest, for example, that a dream occurs while we are asleep and a vision while we are awake, or that a trance is a private encounter, while a visitation is seen by more than one person simultaneously. But in both Old and New Testaments, this sort of language often appears interchangeably to describe like kinds of experiences.

In Hebrew thought, the terms *dream* and *vision* frequently identified different sides of the same perception, *vision* referring to the content of the message and *dream* referring to the usual vehicle through which the vision came. In several places the Bible refers to a dream experience as a "vision of the night" or otherwise seems to equate the two (see Job 20:8, 33:15; Isaiah 29:7; Daniel 2:19, 28, 4:5, 7:1–2; Zechariah 1:8; Acts 16:9, 18:9).

Regarding divinely sent perceptions that occur during waking moments, a Westerner might also be tempted to ask, "Was it a vision or was it real?" Such an inquirer wants to know whether Jesus or the angel (or whatever figure was seen) actually stood in the room, or whether everything took place in the mind. This question may have scientific validity, but the person with the experience would not likely make this distinction. Most of the world, in fact, does not confine the term *reality* to physical or sensory perceptions. Nonphysical reality, such as the content of a dream or vision, can be just as objective to the inner eye as physical reality is to the outer eye.

People who receive dreams or visions they perceive to have supernatural origin or meaning often experience deep emotional responses. In terms of the Gospel of Christ, a person can move from resistance to receptivity literally overnight. The early theologian Origen (c. 185–c. 254) wrote, "Many have come to Christianity as it were in spite of themselves, some spirit having turned their mind suddenly from hating the gospel to dying for it by means of a vision by day or by night. We have known many instances like this" (*Contra Celsum*, 1:46).

Even if such instances were rare, imagine the exciting possibilities—especially for countries currently closed to missionary endeavors! Intercessors who believe God can still work this way today will include prayer for divine dreams and visions among their arsenal of intercessory strategies for the lost.

Read on for a story from another woman who attends Ahavat Zion Messianic Synagogue, one with a background very different from that of Meryl Konrad.

An Ex-Buddhist Arab Among Jews

Chanting over and over, Aicha Lion repeated her Buddhist prayers. She believed that humankind, through daily chanting and meditating on God, could attain world peace and unity. Aicha also found that as a Buddhist she could chant for particular things she needed, like money or a job, and they would come to her.

But the more answers to prayer she received, the more Aicha's pre-Buddhist analytical mind kicked in. Each day after she finished chanting, Aicha added a final prayer: "God, who is behind this? Why am I getting what I ask for? Who's giving this to me?"

Buddhism represented a new discipline for Aicha Lion. Born in France of Algerian Arab parents, she had grown up in a family headed by a Muslim mother and an atheist father. The short, slight, olive-skinned young woman spoke French and Arabic fluently. With a goal of pursuing success in acting, she immigrated to Los Angeles in 1984 at age 25 to study and improve her English language skills.

Around September 1985 she met her future husband, Jim Lion, a tall, blue-eyed blond one year older, a new convert to Buddhism. Aicha became involved immediately in his group, Nichiren Shoshu of America, now known as Soka Gakkai. She spent many hours chanting in their apartment in West Hollywood.

Yet God had not left Himself without witness. Aicha's next-door neighbors were believers in Jesus Christ. When Aicha chatted with Cara and Dan, she told them about her practices.

"The Buddhist philosophy is very good," she said. "Every day I chant for world peace. In fact, I've chanted a lot for financial needs, too, and when I do, it always seems like money arrives from unexpected sources."

Her neighbors listened with interest.

"Who do you suppose is answering those prayers?" Cara asked her.

Aicha shifted uncomfortably.

"Well, that *is* the biggest question I have," she admitted.

"You need to be careful," Cara said, "because there are evil spirits as well as good spirits. The only Person you want to pray to is Jesus."

Cara and Dan encouraged Aicha to try worshiping at a Christian church. They themselves attended The Church On The Way, north across the Santa Monica Mountains in the San Fernando Valley. But they recommended a good congregation just down the road, First Presbyterian Church of Hollywood.

"You should try it," Cara urged her. "You'd really like Pastor Lloyd Ogilvie."

Aicha declined their suggestion but reluctantly accepted a Bible they gave her.

By the time Aicha and Jim married in June 1987 at a Buddhist temple, Aicha's perplexity over the source of power behind her prayers made her increasingly uncomfortable with Buddhism. When she finished chanting she continued to pray, "God, am I doing the right thing? Please show me who's giving me these answers when I chant. Because if it's the wrong thing, if it's not from You, I don't want it."

Not long after their honeymoon, Aicha's anxiety escalated. She quit chanting and no longer visited the temple. But instead of relief, she found her spiritual discomfort heating from a simmer to a full, rolling boil. Once in the middle of the night she sensed evil spirits in the bedroom urging her to kill her husband. An unfamiliar fear haunted the apartment.

Aicha knew that two or three times a year, including during the month of August, the Buddhists held campaigns in which the faithful came to the temple and prayed fervently for all former Buddhists to return to the fold. She sensed that many of her troubles stemmed from a spiritual battle for her soul. Overwhelmed, Aicha began to chant her Buddhist prayers again.

About mid-September Aicha lay sleeping when a voice spoke to her in a dream. She saw no one but heard a voice clearly: *Aicha, you have to come back. You need to come home to Me. I am answering your prayer.*

When she woke up, fear gripped her.

Who's talking to me? she wondered with alarm.

"I don't know," she said later to Jim and her Buddhist acquaintances, "but I think maybe God spoke to me in a dream."

They dismissed the idea as crazy.

Two or three weeks later Aicha was resting on the couch early one afternoon when the Lord spoke again. This time she saw a vision with her eyes open in a glassy gaze as if she were in a trance. As she stared toward the ceiling, a picture emerged of a bright white figure standing as though in a doorway. She could not discern the face, but the figure held open the door and told her, "Come in."

Too scared to respond, Aicha only looked blankly at Him.

He repeated the invitation: "Come in the door, Aicha."

This time she saw herself step forward and go through the doorway from dark to light.

Now Aicha knew God was giving her a message. When Jim came home from work and heard her description of the vision, he seemed impressed.

"It sounds like you went to a high level of enlightenment," he commented.

"Oh, but Jimmy, this is God speaking to me," Aicha replied. "He asked me twice to get in the door, and the first time I didn't move. I think that represents the voice I heard a couple of weeks ago that I thought was Him but didn't respond to. Now He gave me another chance. Now I have to obey. He showed me that I wasn't chanting for Him, that it wasn't right.

"I'm quitting Buddhism, Jimmy," she added. "This time I'm not going back."

Jim grumbled over Aicha's decision but did not argue with her.

Although Aicha had never read the Bible, the next morning she picked up the copy her neighbors had given her.

God, if You're really true, she prayed, help me to understand the Bible.

She opened at random and, to her astonishment, found the Lord speaking to her through the passage she read.

Every morning for the next several weeks, as soon as Aicha woke up, God seemed to show her what to read, and the passage always had direct application to the issues she faced that day.

Aicha told Cara and Dan what was happening, and took them up on their recommendation of Hollywood Presbyterian Church. One Sunday in October 1987 she met with a woman counseling after the service and prayed to give her life to Jesus Christ. She began to attend a Sunday class as well as the worship service, and returned Sunday nights for Bible teaching. Shortly afterward she was baptized and became a member of the church.

Every day Aicha prayed for her family as well as for Jim, who continued his Buddhist chanting. Their home became a spiritual battleground. But as demonic presences attacked Aicha with fear and illness, she turned to the church for peace and strength. She enjoyed the fellowship in her Bible classes, although she felt a little lost in the crowd at the large worship services.

One night in late 1990, Aicha dreamed the Lord spoke to her again.

I want you to worship with the Jewish people on Saturdays, He said. *What!* Aicha protested. *Lord, I can't! I'm an Arab! They're never going to accept me.*

Yet she sensed God persisting gently: *Just go and I will open the door for you.*

Aicha pondered and prayed over this message for two or three weeks. Throughout her life she had known and shared friendship with many Jews, in Paris as well as in Los Angeles, but she could not imagine finding a synagogue where she would fit in, much less one that worshiped Jesus.

Then one day Aicha mentioned this unusual behest to a friend who had phoned. Marcie Glickman's husband was Jewish and had recently come to acknowledge Jesus as his Messiah.

"Aicha, I know just the place for you," said Marcie eagerly. "It's right nearby you, too."

Marcie herself lived many miles away and had only visited, but told Aicha about Ahavat Zion Messianic Synagogue in Beverly Hills. A few weeks later Aicha dropped by and—again, to her surprise—found a warm welcome.

For about a year she wavered between the Saturday synagogue services and the Sunday services at Hollywood Presbyterian, but the Lord prodded her again one Saturday: *Aicha, you belong here. This is your place where I want you to pray and worship Me.*

Aicha devoted herself to the synagogue and felt the Lord's blessing. In October 1993 she also began ministering in the role of a chaplain at Hollywood Presbyterian Medical Center, visiting and praying with patients. Many people received a touch of God's grace, including at times divine healing, as she encouraged them to trust the Lord.

Jim did not know what to make of Aicha's involvement at the synagogue, but he agreed to attend with her once, partly just to see the strange sight of Jews worshiping Jesus. He discovered he enjoyed the singing and returned a number of times, even as he continued his Buddhist chanting at home.

One Saturday the rabbi, Stuart Dauermann, challenged him, "Why don't you ask the Lord to show you if He's really real?"

Jim began to pray for the Lord to come and manifest Himself. Two nights later he had a dream of a huge, bright light that filled the apartment. He woke up trembling, seized with awe, and immediately roused Aicha to tell her what he had seen. From then on he never went back to Buddhism.

Given their religious pedigrees, Aicha and Jim struggled through spiritual pits and pinnacles in their ongoing journeys with Christ. Evil spirits—tempting, accusing, deceiving—tried to pull them away from their walks with the Lord. Nevertheless, they grew. Aicha in particular learned better how to discern the voice of God and minister in the power of the Holy Spirit. God led this ex-Buddhist Arab, through three heaven-sent dreams, from a Muslim/atheist family to a family of Jews worshiping Jesus as Messiah.

Dreams, Dangers and Discernment

From Bible times through today, God has on occasion used dreams and visions to turn people from the kingdom of darkness to the Kingdom of light. Morton T. Kelsey gives a historical example in his book *Dreams: The Dark Speech of the Spirit, A Christian Interpretation* (Doubleday, 1968):

> All through the Middle Ages the delightful story of Theophilus of Adana and the salvation he received in a dream was kept alive. This saint had been tempted and had promised his soul in writing to the devil. But he repented, and when the Virgin appeared to him in a vision, he saw that he wanted no part of the deal. His prayers were answered that night; he received back his bond in a dream, and awoke to find the paper lying on his breast. This story circulated in one Latin translation after another until it was set down in final form by the Bollandist fathers in the Acta Sanctorum.
>
> page 172

For Aicha Lion, dreams not only pointed her to salvation but gave her guidance and direction in following God's will.

Why should God speak through dreams? For many people, the soul, or seat of the emotional life, is least shackled and most open to unexpected ideas when the analytical mind lies dormant. The Gospel of Jesus Christ is by no means anti-intellectual, but rational thought does not constitute the only means of knowing. The Lord might choose at times to reveal Himself in dreams when no other kind of communication can get through.

An unconscious dream state in which the sleeper may be receptive to spiritual messages can, on the other hand, open an individual to the danger of visions implanted by demonic influence. Believers seeking guidance through dreams should make a point of praying for the Holy Spirit's protection over their minds and souls before going to bed. In addition, intercessors who pray for Christ to reveal Himself to nonbelievers in dreams would do well to ask the Lord to bind the enemy from bringing confusion or deception.

The apostle Paul mentions "all kinds of counterfeit miracles, signs and wonders" (2 Thessalonians 2:9) that will accompany the diabolical work of the Antichrist at the end of the age. Satan wields authentic supernatural power, and although it pales in comparison to the power of almighty God, the devil can deceive and enslave people with impressive demonstrations of transcendental capability. Only the Holy Spirit can reveal the truth, and the people of God need to pray earnestly for the gift of discernment of spirits—for themselves as well as for others God wants to bring into His family.

The next story illustrates clearly the capacity of dreams and visions to communicate other-worldly messages from both demonic and divine sources.

The Diviner's Dream

Nangodia stirred and woke. As he lay still on the camel hide covering the sandy floor of his hut, his quickened spirit alerted him to the significance of the dream he had just had. All in all, another night's work for a man who made his living practicing divination.

The Turkana people of remote northwest Kenya—dark-skinned, tall, slender—depended on diviners for guidance on all kinds of questions pertaining to daily life. In their belief, humankind long ago offended the Creator God, Akuj, and now shouldered the Sisyphean obligation of trying to placate Him through repeated animal sacrifices. If they earned His favor, so they thought, He would share essential knowledge and bring life-giving rain.

Although some settled Turkana lived in very small towns, many of them fishing for a living, the nomadic Turkana in particular depended on seasonal rains to sustain their herds. Wherever and whenever the rains came, the nomadic clans picked up and headed out looking for pastureland. Because of Nangodia's occupation, however, he almost always remained at his homestead where people needing his services could find him.

In a little space of desert called Lorengalup, 22 barren miles from the nearest town of Lodwar, Nangodia and his extended family of about forty people had pitched their loosely woven palm-leaf huts, shaped like squat beehives. About eight feet high and twenty feet in diameter, Nangodia's hut was flanked a few steps on each side by huts for each of his two wives and their children. A little farther away lived his widowed mother, unmarried sisters and other relatives.

As a son of the most powerful diviner in the district, Nangodia had inherited at his father's death a portion of his mystical ability, shared with ten brothers scattered up to fifty miles away in different homesteads throughout the area. Not yet thirty years old, Nangodia already wielded strong influence among the nomadic Turkana in his region and had grown wealthy as clients brought goats and other animals as fees for his services. In addition to dreaming, Nangodia sometimes read animal intestines or threw sandals to receive messages from the spirits of dead relatives.

Tonight's dream, however, seemed different. On this night in late 1976, Nangodia sensed an unusual presence. In the morning he talked about it with one of his wives, Amanakwar.

"I've never had a dream like this before," he told her. "I dreamed a foreigner will come to visit with an important message from God that must be accepted and obeyed. What could it mean?"

They could only guess, since non-Turkana people almost never came out to the villages, and since the Turkana held deep suspicions of outsiders. Word of the new dream buzzed through the family over the next few days.

Not long afterward, Amanakwar needed to journey to Lodwar to buy a supply of cornmeal. Occasional treks to town furnished almost the only setting for the Turkana to mix with people from other tribes, using a few words of Swahili as a trade language. Amanakwar took her new baby with her, and in the crowded marketplace caught the attention of a lighter-skinned, stocky Kikuyu man.

"Beautiful baby you have," he complimented her.

They exchanged a few words in Swahili. Then the man's interpreter companion began to translate into Amanakwar's Turkana tongue.

"I am a college student doing a senior research project," said the man we will call Kamau. "I'm here to learn more about the Turkana culture. Do you know any Turkana diviners I could interview?"

Nangodia's wife eyed him warily. "You want to talk to a diviner?"

"Yes," Kamau replied. "It's an important project, and I'd like to talk directly with a diviner if I could."

Amanakwar looked at the Kikuyu in silence as she remembered Nangodia's dream.

Certainly he's a foreigner, she thought. *Could he be the one bringing the message from God?*

After a moment she ventured, "My husband is a diviner. If you come to our home, you may talk with him."

They left Lodwar in Kamau's vehicle and made their way across the desert to the little settlement of Lorengalup.

Once home, Amanakwar told Nangodia of the market encounter. His eyes grew large as he looked from his wife to the stranger and his interpreter. Then Kamau offered Nangodia food gifts such as tea, sugar and cornmeal, and the diviner welcomed the men into his hut.

For three weeks Kamau, who was studying at Daystar University, a Christian school in Nairobi, stayed as Nangodia's guest. Many conversations took place, with Nangodia's extended family present to hear all of them. Kamau learned about Turkana culture, and in turn shared the Gospel through his interpreter.

"When God sent His Son, Jesus," Kamau explained, "He gave us the highest kind of friendship gift, just as you Turkana do when you give a camel or other gift as a sign of your commitment to your friend. God gave us His most precious Son, who died and rose again as a perfect sacrifice to take away our sins, and all we need to do to be His friends is accept His gift of Jesus."

Nangodia recognized Kamau and his message as the fulfillment of his dream, and told Kamau about it.

"Except for that dream," Nangodia said, "I would probably never have been willing to talk with you. But I'm convinced you came here sent by God. The dream also insisted that your message be accepted and obeyed. I want to be a friend of God—I'm ready to receive His Son, Jesus."

And Kamau prayed with Nangodia as he turned his life over to Christ.

When Kamau's three-week visit came to an end, Nangodia presented him with a camel—an expression of the most important kind of friendship. Over the coming months Kamau returned to Lorengalup for a few more stays before his graduation from Daystar. By that time fourteen members of Nangodia's immediate family had become Christians.

"Please send others to come and teach us more about the Gospel," Nangodia urged Kamau. "I would like my whole tribe to hear this message about Jesus."

A year or two after finishing his degree at Daystar, Kamau came to the United States and enrolled at Biola University in La Mirada, California. The amazing openness he had found among Nangodia's family continued to excite him. He also saw several other cultural factors that pointed to growing receptivity to the Gospel among the nomadic Turkana. With everything coming together, the time for mission outreach seemed right. The Holy Spirit was blasting a hole through the walls of spiritual opposition to the Gospel surrounding this people group. Now, with Nangodia's invitation, someone needed to seize the opportunity to charge through the breach with the Kingdom of God.

In early fall 1979, Kamau was introduced to a young American couple at a get-together for dessert one evening at Biola. Friends invited Randy and Edie Nelson, newlyweds already interested in missions to the Turkana, to meet Kamau and hear his perspective on evangelistic opportunities among this people group—including the story of the diviner's conversion.

"Because of Nangodia's dream," Kamau told Randy and Edie, "he was wide open to the Gospel when I shared with him. He's such an influential man in his area that I'm sure many more would come to Christ if someone went in with the Word of God to disciple him and his family. Why don't you go and finish the job?"

Randy and Edie prayed about this opportunity. Besides their own Christian Missionary Fellowship, they knew that other mission agencies were already working with some of the fishing and settled Turkana. But most of the nomadic peoples had never heard of Jesus. Even when they came into the towns briefly to trade, most of their contact with Christians or churches was negligible.

In October 1979 the Nelsons traveled to Kenya to participate in survey trips to Turkana lands. The next month a Kenyan Christian bush pilot took them on an aerial survey over the desert in a small plane. They landed on an airstrip near Nangodia's home, where the former diviner welcomed them warmly.

In December the Nelsons and a handful of other believers from Kenya rejoiced to witness fourteen baptisms of Nangodia and his immediate family members in the crocodile-infested waters of Lake Turkana, several miles east near Kerio town. That night the new believers made a bonfire and burned their fetishes and amulets as a sign of their commitment.

By January the Nelsons moved to Turkana and established their base in a small town on a truck route where they could catch occasional transportation in and out.

During their first term Randy and Edie took regular camping trips to Lorengalup, often with a missionary doctor colleague, to teach and train the new believers there. Nangodia grew in his faith, and his testimony touched many others powerfully. By 1983, some six years after his conversion, Nangodia and Randy baptized 79 more Turkana people.

When Randy and Edie returned after furlough for their second term in July 1984, now with infant and toddler sons, they built a wooden prefab house at Lorengalup. There they lived for the next six years as guests on Nangodia's land. As more of the nomadic Turkana became believers through contact with Nangodia, the Nelsons taught them from the Bible, using Scripture recordings on hand-cranked tape-players to train church leaders. By early 1986 seven churches had been established and 245 nomadic Turkana baptized in the region between Lorengalup, Kerio and Kangatosa.

Today there are well over a thousand believers in that area of Turkana. Edie estimates that Nangodia has been a key influence in several hundred of these conversions. The story of his dream and the witness of his changed life continue to open Turkana hearts to the good news about Jesus.

But Nangodia's dream was by no means the only supernatural event to bring salvation to members of his tribe. Other people came to Christ after something strange happened one day to the Nelsons' windmill—a story that will be told in chapter 7.

Fulfilling God's Destiny

In most cases, when the Lord gives a dream to someone who is not yet a believer, it takes gifts of wisdom and discernment from one of God's people to interpret the night vision in order for its message to result in conversion.

The Lord gave to Daniel not only the interpretation of King Nebuchadnezzar's dream but the revelation of the dream itself, which the king had apparently forgotten after waking. When Nebuchadnezzar heard Daniel's explanation, he gave honor to the one true God: "The king said to Daniel, 'Surely your God is the God of gods and the Lord of kings and a revealer of mysteries, for you were able to reveal this mystery'" (Daniel 2:47).

In the case of Nangodia, one of God's people needed to come not simply to interpret his dream but to fulfill it. Kamau, unaware of the diviner's night vision, set out faithfully to complete the research work God had set before him. Only later did he discover how God had prepared the way for a spiritual breakthrough among the Turkana, and that his arrival represented in itself the sign Nangodia was looking for.

The Lord also gives dreams and visions to His own children to guide them in ministering most effectively to the lost. Shortly after the apostle Paul's conversion, he had a vision or trance in which God revealed both Paul's target mission field and the field he should avoid at that time. Paul recounted the story for the crowd in Acts 22:

> "When I returned to Jerusalem and was praying at the temple, I fell into a trance and saw the Lord speaking. 'Quick!' he said to me. 'Leave Jerusalem immediately, because they will not accept your testimony about me.' . . .
> "Then the Lord said to me, 'Go; I will send you far away to the Gentiles.'"
>
> verses 17–18, 21

Years after this vision, on his second missionary trip, Paul received additional detailed guidance. As he and his companions traveled through central Asia Minor, they felt specifically prevented by the Holy Spirit from preaching in the province of Asia and in Bithynia (see Acts 16:6–8). Reaching the western seacoast, they learned what God had in mind instead:

> During the night Paul had a vision of a man of Macedonia standing and begging him, "Come over to Macedonia and help us." After Paul had seen the vision, we got ready at once to leave for Macedonia, concluding that God had called us to preach the gospel to them.
>
> verses 9–10

Still later on the same trip, God used a vision to encourage Paul that despite abusive opposition in Corinth, a harvest of souls awaited him there:

> One night the Lord spoke to Paul in a vision: "Do not be afraid; keep on speaking, do not be silent. For I am with you, and no one is going to attack and harm you, because I have many people in this city." So Paul stayed for a year and a half, teaching them the word of God.
>
> Acts 18:9–11

Dreams and visions remain a possible avenue for divine revelation even today. God's children who desire to bring the good news of Christ to the nations would do well not to discount every unusual dream as the aftereffect of last night's pizza. If we are listening, God can speak precisely about when, where and how we are to labor in His vineyard to yield much fruit.

Reports from around the world in recent years suggest that God has been giving dreams and visions with increased frequency to people not yet believers, particularly Muslims. The story in chapter 2 of Jean Vandenbos' Iranian friend Mrs. G. included, in addition to healing, a waking vision and a dream that played a role in Mrs. G.'s conversion. (Chapter 9 includes more such stories.)

At the same time, Christians should not look to these kinds of supernatural revelations as quick and easy substitutes for the painstaking work of cross-cultural missions. The 1995 booklet "30 Days Muslim Prayer Focus," published by the organization of the same name, notes on Day 27,

> Throughout history there are countless testimonies of Muslims receiving dreams and visions of Jesus. Often these visions are the result of years of prayer and labor by God's people, including martyrdom.

Even when God apparently intervenes sovereignly in an unbeliever's life, it is almost certain that someone, somewhere, at some time, "prayed the price" at some level. From the intercession of a grandma in her prayer closet in London or Chicago, to the Bible translation or church-planting work of pioneer missionaries in Africa or Asia, to the martyrdom of faithful witnesses in Ecuador or Iran, God's praying people have paved the way for supernatural breakthroughs of the Gospel, sometimes many years later.

If we want the Lord to continue speaking in dreams and visions that result in the salvation of the lost, we will persevere in devoting not only our intercession but our very lives to the spread of the Good News in every form God may choose to convey it.

5

"An Angel of the Lord Appeared"

Stories of Angelic Visitations

The nineteen-year-old gangster had just pulled off his boots to get ready for bed on a Wednesday night when he remembered the dinner invitation. He groaned at the thought. It was past 9:30 P.M., he had already eaten dinner and another downpour threatened his notoriously rainy home city of Pokhara, Nepal. Lok Mani Bhandari might have chucked his date with destiny then and there. But he knew that Markku Vortilainen and his family would still be waiting for him.

In the fall of 1983 Lok served as president of one of the 4-H Clubs Markku had founded all over Nepal, offering agricultural training and support. Markku, a Finnish missionary with the United Mission to Nepal, worked under government edicts permitting Western missionaries to enter the country for educational, medical or development purposes only.

Lok, from a high-class Hindu Brahmin family, his father a well-known political figure in West Nepal, enjoyed many privileges and dreamed of someday leading his country. But during his teenage years the role of a gangster, street-fighter and guerrilla militarist had seduced him with the lure of power. At age 18 muscular Lok had become national champion ("Mr. Nepal") in the martial art of *tae kwon do* and was hired by anti-government political leaders as a bodyguard. Lok's lifestyle was marked by leather jackets, motorcycles and crime.

Yet something would not let Lok brush off this dinner commitment. Much as he yearned to pull the bedcovers over his head, an inner voice badgered him, *You must go! They're waiting for you! Go! Go!*

He yanked on his boots and went out to get his motorcycle, but the heavens had opened again with cold rain and wind. Leaving the bike, Lok walked out to the highway and flagged down a taxi.

As they headed for downtown Pokhara, Lok saw that large sections of the city had lost electricity in the storm. About six miles later the taxi braked to a halt where several inches of water flooded the streets.

"Looks like this is as far as I go," said the cabby.

Lok did not press him. As a gangster he needed to keep on good terms with the taxi drivers, who often helped him make quick getaways. He got out and watched the cab turn back, its taillights disappearing into the darkness. Then Lok slogged on, turning north toward the mountains through the flood and driving rain.

Drenched like a street cat, he shivered miserably and began to rag on himself. *This is crazy! What am I doing out in this weather? Markku must have finished dinner long ago. I'm not sure I can even find the place. Why don't I just turn back?*

In the year or two he had known Markku, Lok had attended many 4-H training sessions at a school near the missionary's home. Through his motorcycle escapades he was well familiar with the neighborhood. But he had never been to Markku's house.

Lok traversed out of the flooded area and came to a crossroads, with the Vortilainen home still more than a mile to the north. Then out of the darkness, from a road to the right, strode an unusually tall figure in a coat with a big, black umbrella—the first person the teenager had seen on this stormy night since leaving the taxi.

"Say, where are you going?" the man asked.

Lok looked him up and down. "Well, I was going to this missionary's house for dinner, but it's pretty late now."

"Oh, which one?"

Several foreigners lived in the neighborhood, Lok knew. "Markku, a Finnish missionary."

"I know that man's house," the umbrella-holder replied. "I can take you there if you want."

"Well," said Lok, glancing at the umbrella, "I wouldn't mind."

The man clapped an arm around Lok's shoulder and they headed north together.

Any self-respecting teenage gangster would have felt a little humiliated by this intimacy, but Lok stuffed his pride and took advantage of the bit of shelter from the downpour.

It was nearly 11 P.M. when the tall stranger guided Lok to a house with a tiny porch, close to the street, and windows that revealed the faint glow of candles flickering inside.

The electricity must be out here, too, he thought.

Lok's companion stood behind, still holding the umbrella over both of them, while Lok stepped onto the porch, tried the dead electric doorbell, then knocked.

In a moment his friend Markku opened the front door and looked out through the screen. "Lok Mani! Lok, please come in! We were hoping you would make it."

"Thank you," Lok answered as Markku held open the screen door. "Just a minute. I'd like you to meet—"

Lok's words stuck in his throat as he turned around to stare at the blank space behind him.

Well, where did he go? The street looked deserted. Suddenly he realized he was getting even more soaked.

"Is something wrong?" Markku asked.

"Uh, no," said Lok. He stepped quickly inside, hoping he did not look as strange as he felt.

The fair-skinned, blond missionary in his early thirties asked his wife to find Lok a complete change of clothes. Then Lok met another couple the Vortilainens had invited, Satoshi Mori and his wife from Japan. They, too, worked with United Mission to Nepal.

The group was enjoying a late dessert with coffee. Lok joined them since he had already eaten dinner. Then Markku raised a question: "Lok, do you know that one day everyone will be held accountable for their lives?" And the missionary read to him from Matthew 25:14–30, the parable of the talents.

Lok listened to Jesus' story about the master who left on a journey, entrusting his servants with different sums of money, each according to his ability. The one who received five talents put those talents to work and earned five more. The servant receiving two talents saw a similar return. "But the man who had received the one talent went off, dug a hole in the ground and hid his master's money" (verse 18).

Lok heard that "after a long time the master of those servants returned and settled accounts with them" (verse 19). The two who had doubled their trust funds received praise and proportional rewards from their master. But the one who had only buried his master's money was rebuked for not even depositing the funds with the bankers for simple interest.

Markku read on in the chapter to where Jesus described the end-time judgment:

> "When the Son of Man comes in his glory, and all the angels with him, he will sit on his throne in heavenly glory. All the nations will be gathered before him, and he will separate the people one from another as a shepherd separates the sheep from the goats. He will put the sheep on his right and the goats on his left."
>
> verses 31–33

The missionary explained to Lok the need for people to repent from sin and prepare to face God in eternity by practicing a living faith here on earth. What especially captured Lok's attention was Markku's description of Jesus Christ as King and Judge at the end of the age.

For years growing up he had studied the Veda, the Hindu scriptures, and well remembered a passage describing a judge and redeemer said to appear at the end time with a balance in his hand

and the authority to send people to their eternal destinies. Lok knew that although Hinduism acknowledges millions of gods and goddesses, all named, the Veda gives no name for this particular ruler. As a result Hindus generally look on him as extraordinary, higher than all other gods.

When Lok heard the biblical description of Jesus, he instantly connected it to the passage from the Veda. All his life he had wondered about this unnamed redeemer and judge, and when he recognized Him in the chapter Markku read, he felt as though he had been introduced to an old friend.

With a summary of the Gospel of grace, Markku asked Lok if he wanted to pray and devote his life to Jesus Christ. Lok nodded. And suddenly, as the others bowed their heads and closed their eyes, the fear of God fell on him. He realized that this invisible King of the universe stood in the room and heard their prayers.

Lok confessed his sin and accepted Christ as Savior. Then Markku and Satoshi, the Japanese missionary, gave him a Nepali-language Bible.

Outside the rainstorm still raged. Satoshi and his wife, who lived nearby, left for home, while the Vortilainens offered to put up Lok for the night.

That night, sleeping in a third-floor rooftop bedroom, Lok dreamed of Jesus in the midst of a storm. Lok and a few friends were climbing a snowy mountain while floodwaters filled the valley below. The mountain pelted them with snowballs while the rising flood blocked their return.

"Lok, you've led us to a terrible place," his friends fumed. "Between the snow and the flood, we're going to die."

Lok, suddenly inspired, answered his friends, "Hey, I just heard about Jesus today. Let's pray to Jesus—maybe He'll save us."

And in his dream he took his friends' hands as they closed their eyes to pray. When they looked up, the sky shone clear and Jesus stood before them in blazing light. The floodwaters began to recede.

Lok woke up and started reading from his new Nepali Bible. The seed had been planted and was already bearing fruit.

But Lok continued to teach *tae kwon do* classes, and a few months later, when his missionary mentors were forced to leave the country under charges of proselytizing, his spiritual growth took a back seat.

Then in December 1984, following a life-threatening motorcycle accident, Lok had another dream in which Jesus appeared to him. He made a renewed commitment to Christ, followed this time by miraculous healing and a radical change of life.

Lok's father kicked him out of the house and he began preaching the Gospel all over his city of Pokhara, Nepal. He made many converts, was thrown into prison, preached to the other inmates and was thrown *out* of prison when too many of them converted. Other signs and wonders followed. In 1989 he planted Kathmandu Bethel Church in his country's capital. It quickly grew to more than a hundred members, and within five years numbered more than a thousand. The same year he established Kathmandu Bible College and Theological Seminary to train others for full-time ministry.

Today Lok has planted seven satellite churches and more than twenty house fellowships in different parts of Nepal. He has a vision for discipling the whole nation through new congregations of believers.

Who knows what might have happened to the teenage gangster if a man with an umbrella had not shown up at the right moment to escort Lok to his date with destiny?

Angels, Angels, Everywhere

The Bible contains hundreds of references to angels, seraphs, cherubs and other spirit beings, which often interact with humankind. An angelic visitation, either biblical or contemporary, constitutes a more specialized kind of dream or vision, in which someone sees and perhaps hears a spirit creature of otherworldly form and appearance.

Alternatively angels can appear in the guise of human beings, revealing their true identity only through improbable circumstances or actions that defy the laws of nature, such as appearing or disappearing. Even Jesus Himself—or "the angel of the Lord" in Old Testament terminology—may enter someone's circumstances briefly, disguised in human form, and reveal truth about Himself, causing that person to turn from sin, seek further knowledge of the Gospel or come to faith.

Genesis 18 and 19 tell the story of Abraham entertaining three visitors—evidently two angels and the Lord Himself. Abraham and his wife Sarah prepared a meal for them and the Lord delivered an important message. Then the two "men" headed for the city of Sodom to warn Abraham's nephew Lot that God planned to destroy the city, while Abraham pleaded with the Lord to spare it.

Genesis 19 specifically refers to the two men as angels, while the narrative continues to describe them walking, talking, eating and interacting with human beings. Clearly these messengers of God came determined to save Lot and his family from the impending judgment:

> With the coming of dawn, the angels urged Lot, saying, "Hurry! Take your wife and your two daughters who are here, or you will be swept away when the city is punished."
> When he hesitated, the men grasped his hand and the hands of his wife and of his two daughters and led them safely out of the city, for the LORD was merciful to them.
>
> verses 15–16

In dispatching the angels, the Lord showed His mercy even in sending a pair of them—enough hands to grab each member of Lot's family.

The New Testament acknowledges the ongoing interaction of angelic beings in our lives with an exhortation to hospitality: "Do not forget to entertain strangers, for by so doing some people have entertained angels without knowing it" (Hebrews 13:2). The reverse is also possible. In the case of Lok Mani Bhandari, an angel evidently hosted him—ever so briefly—in the shelter of his umbrella.

The Angel and the Dentist

"Fanny Cruz Pimentel!"
Her mother's voice roused the twelve-year-old from her thoughts.

"Yes, Mamá, I'm here." She scrambled to help with the dinner chores.

Trouble was, Fanny could not be sure she really *had* been here. Just then she had seen another one of those strange visions, almost an out-of-body experience.

Why do these things keep happening to me? she wondered.

Since her youngest years Fanny had been sensitive to the spiritual realm. In her native Dominican Republic, superstition mixed easily with nominal Roman Catholicism. But Fanny's mystical awareness was unusual. Sometimes special knowledge came to her through dreams and visions. At other times, while she was engrossed in an activity, she saw herself in a different place, observing people and events. Then, before long, she came back to her surroundings to carry on as before.

These supernatural experiences always left Fanny struggling with powerful emotions. On the one hand they frightened her because she had no control over them. Yet receiving revelations of unknown and future events bore a fascinating allure. People sometimes asked her about the things she saw and heard in her visions. Her abilities set her apart.

Her parents, Fanny knew, kept a watchful eye on their precocious oldest daughter. The dark-haired beauty often wondered if God—whoever He was—had a special destiny for her. Her upper-middle-class home life in the capital city of Santo Domingo afforded her excellent educational opportunities, and she supposed she had been given her spiritual sensitivity for a reason, too.

She well remembered her first experience, at age five, of spiritual reality. Her Catholic grandmother had fallen ill, and every day for a month Fanny's mother had sent her to keep her granny company. Because Fanny had started reading at age three, her grandmother asked her to read the Bible aloud. Beginning in the book of Exodus, Fanny found herself reveling day after day in the exploits of Moses and God's deliverance of the people of Israel.

Later they got to the passage in Deuteronomy 34 describing the death of Moses. Fanny felt so grieved she began to cry. Her grandma had dozed off, so Fanny set the Bible down and slipped quietly outside. It was about dusk. As she watched the day dying, she cried out for the God of Moses to take her life and use her.

Since then powerful forces seemed to pull at Fanny from different directions. Frequently she dreamed that an evil man sneaked up and was trying to entice her with an object like a coin. She always refused, but he would bare his teeth at her menacingly.

Now, in 1976, working with her mother on dinner, Fanny sighed at the memories. *There's no telling what my next dream or vision might be like. I wonder what all these things mean?*

She did not have long to wait for the next one. That very night after she went to bed, the twelve-year-old had a dream unlike any before.

As she slept, a figure in white came to Fanny's bedroom, asking, "Do you want to see the source of power for the whole universe?"

The excited girl said yes.

The angelic messenger took her by the hand and the two flew together. Higher and faster, beyond the earth and planets and stars—Fanny had never felt such joy.

Then the angel directed the girl's attention to an enormous cube of dazzling colors—colors so unusual they would remain painted on her memory years later, although she would never be able to describe them in words. In the center of the cube Fanny saw a regal King with long, white hair and a face that shone like a blinding searchlight. In front of Him lay a long, crystal table. Beyond that several old men—Fanny counted 24 of them—bowed on their faces, each offering a crown to the One on the throne.

"Here it is," her angel companion told her. "This is the center of the universe and the source of its power."

Speechless and breathless, Fanny could only gaze with wonder until, moments later, she awoke, certain she had seen the God of creation. Seven years would pass before she discovered her dream scene described in Revelation 4 and 21.

As a teenager Fanny continued to search for truth. But she did not find in the pictures and statues at her Catholic church the God she longed for. Nor did she hear a clear presentation of the Gospel.

Sometimes late in the tropical night she would wander outdoors while the city slept and call out to her unknown God: "God, I know You are there somewhere—can You hear me?"

No voice answered, but Fanny gleaned unexplained strength and comfort from those moments.

At the same time she began dabbling in activities where her mystical abilities found full flower. She became drawn to Ouija boards, New Age teachings, crystals and more. But something in her heart, despite her proficiency in these activities, kept her uncomfortable and nudged her beyond them in her spiritual walk. After four or five years she destroyed all her occult and magic items.

At nineteen Fanny had already finished college and was working in the Ministry of Tourism. Her turning point came with a terrible toothache and a trip to Dr. Aura Rodriguez, a dentist contracted by the employee insurance program of the bank where her mother worked. It was Thursday, July 28, 1983.

Although Fanny had never met this dentist, the older woman seemed to take unusual interest in her. Before beginning, Dr. Rodriguez prayed. Then, as she worked in Fanny's mouth, she shared her story.

"I used to have breast cancer," she confided, "but God healed me. I have been cancer-free for years now. Do you know what the Bible says about God's love and power and how we can know Him personally?"

Dr. Rodriguez' captive audience could do little more than gurgle short responses as the dentist explained the Gospel from beginning to end. She stopped often to read Scripture passages that documented what she was saying. For three hours she carried on, with patients biding time in the waiting room.

When she finished working, she asked Fanny, "Would you like to commit your life to Jesus Christ right now?"

Fanny weighed what she had heard. "Wow, it sounds so good— almost too good and too simple to be true. I don't know if I can believe it all. But if it *is* true, I do want it. I want that relationship with Him."

The two prayed together as Fanny asked the Lord into her life.

Afterward the dentist told her, "I really felt directed by God to spend all that time with you, even though other patients were waiting, because I sensed the Lord wanted to reach you today."

As she left the dental office that July afternoon, Fanny felt as though her life had changed, although she did not know exactly how.

Four days later, on Monday, August 1, a clear and persistent internal voice repeated, *Read the Bible. Read the Bible.*

Finally she dug through a dusty box and found an old copy of Scripture. At 8 P.M. she began reading in the Gospel of Matthew. For six or seven hours she read, wept and confessed her sins as the Holy Spirit convicted her. At last, in the middle of the night, she went to sleep in peace, knowing she had found the God she had been searching for all her life.

Fanny continued to have occasional dreams and visions of supernatural origin. Now, however, she could discern when they came from God and when the devil was harassing her. Through divinely arranged circumstances, she moved to Italy as director of the Dominican government's Office of Tourism in Milan. Other miracles followed as the Lord guided her to meet and marry Giovanni Basta and establish a Christian ministry, Visione Italia (now based in Naples).

The Lord indeed had a special destiny for Fanny's life. She recognizes now that God protected her during her years in mysticism and New Age. Her first experience of God at age five and her dream with the angel at age twelve served as touchstones of truth through the thickets of spirituality, until her dentist pointed her to the Word of God.

Angels Show Seekers the Way

In the early years after Jesus' resurrection, a sincere seeker of God named Cornelius, a centurion of the Italian Regiment, received an unexpected revelation during his regular afternoon prayer time.

One day at about three in the afternoon he had a vision. He distinctly saw an angel of God, who came to him and said, "Cornelius!"

Cornelius stared at him in fear. "What is it, Lord?" he asked.

The angel answered, "Your prayers and gifts to the poor have come up as a memorial offering before God. Now send men to Joppa to bring back a man named Simon who is called Peter. He is staying with Simon the tanner, whose house is by the sea."

Acts 10:3–6

Cornelius sent for Peter. At last he, his family and close friends heard the good news about Jesus—anointed by God, crucified and raised from the dead to provide the only way to the Father. Peter told the centurion,

"He is the one whom God appointed as judge of the living and the dead. All the prophets testify about him that everyone who believes in him receives forgiveness of sins through his name."

verses 42–43

Peter had required his own vision—repeated three times—before he could be sure God wanted him to go to the home of this Gentile. But when he did, the Holy Spirit fell noticeably on all who heard the message, and the first community of Gentile converts received baptism.

Like Cornelius, young Fanny Cruz Pimentel had been seeking and praying to God with limited understanding. Fanny's dream of the angel was less directive than the vision Cornelius received, but it gave her a reference to the truth until her dentist shared Jesus with her. And Fanny, like Cornelius, needed additional communication of the Gospel after the angelic appearance (as usual in instances of power evangelism) in order to come to faith in Christ.

Angels took a key role at the birth of Jesus in pointing the shepherds to Him. As the herdsmen watched their sheep during the dark night, "an angel of the Lord appeared to them" in such radiance they were terrified (see Luke 2:9). But the angel's words brought "good news of great joy" (verse 10). The heavenly messenger gave specific instructions about who the Messiah was and how to find Him. The shepherds found the Christ Child and began to spread the word. Later they returned to their flocks "glorifying and praising God for all the things they had heard and seen, which were just as they had been told" (verse 20).

Hebrews 1:14 describes angels as "ministering spirits sent to serve those who will inherit salvation." Perhaps the future tense indicates that God sends angels not only to believers—those who look forward to the fullness of face-to-face communion with God—but also to "not-yet" believers still journeying toward their eternal destiny in Christ.

Who's in the Driver's Seat?

With a rumble of shifting gears, the 65-foot truck-and-trailer tanker eased onto Interstate 5 at Oceanside, California. Her tanks empty after dumping a load of gasoline at the Marine Corps' Camp Pendleton, Linda Kangrga headed north on the freeway to pick up her "going-home" load in Orange County on the day before Father's Day, June 19, 1993. The ocean breeze through the open window stirred her long, blonde hair under her trademark Western-style black hat with a wide silver band. She had turned her life over to Christ just two weeks before.

When she got her rig up to speed, the 33-year-old moved into the number 3 lane, third to the right of the center divider. Fiddling with the radio knob, Linda's fingers searched for some snappy tunes to while away the afternoon drive. Then, just a couple of miles up the highway, a late-model black Jaguar veered in front of her and cut her off.

Instantly her mood turned foul. She slammed on her brakes and had to downshift.

"Idiot!" she yelled aloud. "Don't you know how dangerous that is?"

Two can play that game, she seethed.

With the highway open, she swerved left into the number 2 lane (a serious offense for big rigs), roared ahead of the couple in the Jaguar, cut back in front and hit the brakes.

The moment she stepped on her brake pedal, she remembered her newfound faith and a vise-grip of conviction squeezed her heart.

Sucking in her breath, she confessed, "Lord, I'm sorry, I'm sorry! Please forgive me—that was wrong. I could have endangered that couple's lives."

Ever since a divine and miraculous intervention in her life two weeks earlier, Linda's inner spirit felt exceptionally sensitive to the Holy Spirit. She could not get away with anything anymore. Easy as it would be to fall back into old patterns, she could sense the Lord giving her powerful guidance almost daily. Like a doe teaching a wobbly-legged young fawn to walk, God was showing her how to keep in step with Christ while surviving in a stressful world.

The Jaguar pulled out from behind her and sped on, fading into the traffic ahead. Just then Linda noticed in her left side mirror two helmeted motorcyclists on Honda Goldwing touring bikes.

Oh, my gosh, she shuddered. *Those guys must have seen the whole thing. God, have mercy.*

About ten minutes later she reached the San Onofre Inspection Station and truck scales. While Border Patrol agents stopped four lanes of auto traffic and visually checked for immigration violations, big rigs bypassed the backup by pulling into the scales on the right. On Saturdays, however, the scales were closed, so trucks simply slowed as they drove through the empty lane and continued on their way.

Linda eased her tanker into the lane behind a forty-foot refrigerated box truck. Suddenly she saw a California Highway Patrol officer step from behind a partition. He looked for a moment at the driver of the box truck and waved him on. Then he pointed at Linda and signaled her with an angry jerk of his thumb to pull aside into an inspection bay.

As she maneuvered into the bay, the officer went back behind the partition and returned in his patrol car, drawing up right in front of her. At the same time another CHP cruiser came around the scale house and parked behind her truck, trapping her.

Now Linda felt her blood run cold. *O Lord, no! They're going to arrest me for reckless driving!*

The officer in front strode over and yanked open the driver's door of Linda's cab.

"Do you want to tell me what's going on?" he demanded.

Linda tried to keep her voice steady while her heart pounded. "What do you mean, sir?"

"You were screwing around on the freeway—some black car. You want to tell me what happened back there?"

As calmly as she could, and without lying, Linda answered, "Well, I did have an encounter with a black Jag. I made a lane change but the Jag took off. I don't know where they are."

"Well, just a minute."

The CHP officer turned and motioned. Out from behind the partition came the two Honda motorcyclists.

Linda turned clammy. *Why, I didn't notice them passing me! Now they've got two witnesses against me, and they're going to make me pay for my stupid mistake—maybe cost me my job. Lord, help!*

One of the pair, a lumberjack-sized man probably in his forties, pulled his bike over to Linda's door.

The cyclist looked up at Linda, staring dumbfounded as his jaw went slack.

"Where—where's the guy?" he finally sputtered.

"Pardon me?" Linda asked.

"Where's the guy who was driving this truck? What happened to him? You must have stopped and let him out back there."

"No, sir," replied Linda, puzzled. "I'm the only one driving this truck, and I don't carry any riders. Look inside my cab—I've got a toolbox on the floor and my daypack on the other seat. If you'd like to see my daily log book, or look at my tattle tale, I'll show you—I'm the only driver and I didn't stop back there."

Linda knew that her tachometer chart—the "tattle tale"—would show that her speed had never dropped close to zero at any point between Camp Pendleton and the San Onofre scales.

The biker still shook his head in disbelief, as though to erase Linda's image from before his eyes.

"No, there was a man driving this truck," he insisted. "A man with gray hair and a long, gray beard."

What! Linda's mind spun in astonishment, as a fearful awe began to creep over her. *No way! With my window down, there's no way he could miss my black hat.*

The CHP officer frowned at the motorcyclist, then looked back at Linda. Shaking his head, he muttered something Linda could not believe she heard correctly.

"Excuse me?" she asked.

"Well, you're not a forty-foot box trailer anyway," he repeated.

Too bizarre! Linda thought. *Someone thought I was driving a reefer? How could anyone mistake a tanker for a box van?*

The shroud of confusion proved too much for the officer. He turned to the cyclist.

"O.K., that's all we'll need, thank you," he said, dismissing him.

When the two bikers drove off, the officer addressed Linda with a different tone.

"I'm sorry, ma'am," he said courteously. "There must have been some mistake. Have a nice day now."

"Thank you, sir," Linda replied meekly as he shut her door. Then, recalling the current holiday weekend, she called out her window, "Happy Father's Day."

Quivering inside and out, Linda steered her rig slowly through the bay and headed back to the interstate. No sooner had she merged into traffic from the bypass on-ramp, her hand still clutching the gearshift, than the tears began to flow. She could not explain what had happened, but whatever the two men saw, she felt convinced that the Lord sat in her driver's seat. Her heavenly Father was with her in the cab.

It was like He covered me, Linda marveled, *so they saw Him and not me.*

The more she pondered God's grace in sovereignly sparing her from well-deserved punishment, the more she bawled aloud, her mascara streaking in wavy black rivulets down her cheeks.

How could I not love and serve You with my whole life? she prayed. *Please teach me to tame my temper and learn patience. I want to be like You, Lord. Today I give myself to You again.*

Linda sensed the warmth of God's love surrounding her and drying her tears. And as she pulled into the refinery to fill up with her going-home load, she glanced toward the blue sky with a soft smile.

"Happy Father's Day, Dad. I love You."

Angels Help Minister God's Grace

"God's kindness is meant to lead you to repentance," declares the apostle Paul in Romans 2:4 (RSV). For weeks Linda Kangrga lived this verse as God revealed Himself and His love in wonderful, mighty ways, keeping her walking in awestruck humility until she made a permanent break with her old lifestyle. (We will meet Linda again in the next chapter.)

It is impossible to say for sure exactly what happened that afternoon on Interstate 5, but this episode suggests that when God opens someone's eyes to a vision of a heavenly being, the one who makes a spiritual turnaround need not be the one who had the vision. The men on the Honda Goldwings probably scratched their heads for days without realizing the significance of what they saw. But their testimony brought Linda back to the foot of the cross.

In one of the most extraordinary stories in the Old Testament, the prophet Balaam escaped death when his donkey saw an angel.

Balaam had saddled his donkey and set out on a journey that displeased God, so the angel of the Lord came to stand in his way on the road. Balaam saw nothing while the donkey turned aside twice from the vision. The third time the beast lay down under him and refused to go on. Mystified and angered by the animal's behavior, Balaam beat her. Then, as unremarkably as if it happened every day, the two carried on a conversation.

Then the LORD opened the donkey's mouth, and she said to Balaam, "What have I done to you to make you beat me these three times?"

Balaam answered the donkey, "You have made a fool of me! If I had a sword in my hand, I would kill you right now."

The donkey said to Balaam, "Am I not your own donkey, which you have always ridden, to this day? Have I been in the habit of doing this to you?"

"No," he said.

Then the LORD opened Balaam's eyes, and he saw the angel of the LORD standing in the road with his sword drawn. So he bowed low and fell facedown.

The angel of the LORD asked him, "Why have you beaten your donkey these three times? I have come here to oppose you because your path is a reckless one before me. The donkey saw me and turned away from me these three times. If she had not turned away, I would certainly have killed you by now, but I would have spared her."

Numbers 22:28–33

Then Balaam confessed his sin and received guidance from God regarding his journey.

In the New Testament Philip encountered an angel whose instructions put him in the right place at the right time for a divine appointment. After the apostle's ministry in Samaria, "An angel of the Lord said to Philip, 'Go south to the road—the desert road—that goes down from Jerusalem to Gaza'" (Acts 8:26). On the way Philip met an Ethiopian eunuch, an important official in the court of the Ethiopian queen, heading home to his country. As the man sat in his chariot reading prophetic Scriptures, he invited Philip to explain the meaning of what he was reading and its fulfillment.

Then, miraculously, they found some water on this desert road. When the eunuch confessed his faith in Jesus as the promised Messiah, Philip baptized him, and immediately the Spirit of God carried the apostle away. Apparently Philip's angel encounter took place solely for the conversion of this one man—a man of influence who would bring the Good News back to the continent of Africa.

Fear and Wonder in Shibuya Station

Tokyo cityscape rolled by outside the train as Helen Knight held her daughter's hand. She hoped five-year-old Joy would not notice her anxiety. After almost five years in Japan with The Evangelical Alliance Mission (TEAM), Helen, 30, still felt the frequent sting and loneliness of culture shock. This afternoon, moreover, had brought devastating news from her doctor.

From the Knights' mission station in Choshi on the easternmost edge of Chiba prefecture, Helen and her daughter had caught an early train that morning to make the long trip west to Tokyo. In

April 1962 a trip like this took close to five hours. No wonder she rarely left town.

As a wife, mother, missionary, language student and home-school teacher for Joy and eight-year-old Philip, Helen shouldered the daily stress of her demanding roles. Her home in Atlanta some-times seemed as distant as the moon. She and her husband, Brant-ley, had come to Choshi in 1959 after two years of language school—the only foreigners in a city of about 90,000. No one nearby spoke English well enough for her to talk with and Helen was not yet proficient in Japanese. As she had grown increasingly weak, thin and tired, her spreading pain had forced her to seek a doctor's help. Now he had just told her he suspected cancer.

To make the most of their time on the long train ride, Helen had brought along Joy and her kindergarten curriculum. Then, after spending all afternoon at the doctor's office, the two headed to Shibuya Station to catch the Yamanote Line encircling down-town Tokyo. Helen knew they needed to get the next train to make their connections for the long-distance ride home to Choshi.

It was about 6 P.M. when the pair stepped out at Shibuya Sta-tion. The commuter rush hour seemed to transmogrify the nor-mally polite and proper Japanese. Everywhere throngs of busi-nessmen pushed their way forward. Helen, unfamiliar with Shibuya Station, took Joy by the hand and threaded through the crowd toward the track where they needed to catch their transfer.

Because of where their train had just let them off, Helen and Joy ended up at the front end of the Yamanote Line train, where the track curved away from the platform, leaving a gap of many inches. Helen heard loudspeakers droning on but could not under-stand the message. Much later she would learn what the voice was saying: "Watch your step. There's a gap. Be careful."

The arriving train disgorged its exiting passengers. By now the mass of people surging toward the train doors had caught up mother and daughter like pebbles in the path of an avalanche. As they neared the train doors, Helen felt a heavy tug on her left arm as Joy lost her balance. In a moment her little daughter dangled help-lessly between the platform and the train.

Helen's weak arm could not lift Joy, and she realized in terror that she herself was about to go down.

Lord Jesus, please save her! came the cry of Helen's heart.

Immediately a tall, broad-shouldered Japanese man pushed out of the crowd on her left and scooped Joy up. With the five-year-old in his arms, he boarded the train, Helen right after them. The doors closed behind her, the train began to move and the man set Joy down safely between them.

Riders jammed the car but Helen bowed her head toward the man in gratitude.

"*Arigato gozaimashita,*" she murmured.

When she lifted her head, the man had disappeared. Not only that, but the crowd seemed to have filled in the place where he stood.

Helen's mind reeled. *He couldn't have gotten off! And there's no place for him to go in this packed car!*

She glanced around. Not a single man nearby resembled her daughter's rescuer.

Although she had been taught not to show public emotion in Japan, Helen broke out in hushed weeping. Immediately she thought of Psalm 34:7 (KJV): "The angel of the LORD encampeth round about them that fear him, and delivereth them."

She could only pray, *Thank You, Jesus, for saving Joy!*

Helen arrived home late that evening feeling awed and a little afraid, helpless yet protected, baffled but utterly grateful. The children went to bed right away, and in the quiet Helen shared with Brantley the heights and the depths of her day, letting her tears flow freely.

She did not share her experience with another soul, but Helen knew it had changed her. Slowly she opened up her knapsack of fears and concerns and began to commit each one to the Lord. Even when she felt completely alone, she held onto the assurance that God Himself was with her, in control and able to help and protect.

Two or three weeks later Helen checked into a Tokyo hospital for surgery. Doctors discovered not cancer but endometriosis. In June 1962 the Knight family returned to the United States for a scheduled furlough. And a year later in August, the Lord blessed Helen and Brantley with their third child, a miracle baby.

When the Knights returned to Japan in 1964, they wanted their older children to be able to commute to school in Tokyo. Their new mission location? Shibuya. Helen and Joy had hoped never to see Shibuya Station again! But as they prayed, the Lord helped them remember not their terror but His miraculous intervention in that place. Helen's experience in Shibuya Station had given her the confidence and courage she needed for many more years of ministry in Japan.

But God had still more fruit in mind—eternal fruit.

In 1973, after another home assignment, TEAM sent the Knights to the city of Niiza, northwest of Tokyo in Saitama prefecture. Helen and Brantley began teaching a Japanese-language Bible class every Thursday morning at the church with 25 or 30 Japanese women—some new believers, some seekers.

One Thursday in the spring of 1975, as Helen led the class, the Lord brought the train station episode to her mind. For thirteen years she had kept quiet. Now God seemed to be nudging her that this was the time to share it. She felt a little awkward. *How are they going to understand something I can't explain myself?* she wondered. But she plunged ahead.

As she recounted the supernatural event, Helen noticed a woman we will call Mrs. Suzuki, whose eyes filled with tears as she listened. Mrs. Suzuki, a Buddhist in her early thirties, had attended the Bible class off and on during the past year but resisted making a commitment to Christ.

When Helen finished her testimony, Mrs. Suzuki spoke up.

"Helen, when I was a very young girl, I, too, was pushed from a train platform," she said, dabbing at her eyes. "I fell flat on my face next to the nearest rail. The train was on its way and no one had time to rescue me, and I was paralyzed with fear. But the train came and left and passed over my little body with almost no harm." She looked at Helen eagerly. "Do you think your God saved my life that day?"

"I am sure of it," Helen replied with confidence. "He loves you and sent His Son, Jesus, to die for you. He protected your life that day, and now He wants to save your soul."

Helen's story of the angel in Shibuya Station was instrumental in turning Mrs. Suzuki's life around. She began attending Bible class regularly, and in June 1975 gave her heart to the Lord. A year later she was baptized. Now she serves as an officer in her local church.

Helen rejoiced at the glorious work of God. Through this experience He had not only calmed her fears and bolstered her faith but brought a precious Japanese woman into relationship with Jesus Christ. No doubt the angels in heaven praised God for prompting Helen with the courage to share her story at just the time it would make an eternal impact on one of her listeners.

Incognito yet Distinctive

Many passages throughout Scripture show God sending angels to protect, comfort, warn or encourage human beings, especially the weak, lost or helpless. While the Bible indicates that these celestial beings minister on our behalf, they are clearly God's agents, not ours. Nowhere does the Bible suggest that we as His children pray to angels or ask (let alone command) them to go or do as we desire. Yet our heavenly Father invites us to bring all our requests before Him and gives us freedom to ask Him to send angels where needed.

When angels—or "the angel of the Lord"—appear in human form, observers do not usually distinguish them at first. They look similar to ordinary men or women, culturally appropriate to the setting in ethnicity and dress. Yet often there is something different about them that leaves a deep impression—intense, piercing eyes, perhaps, a melodic voice or a warmth of love that leaves people yearning for more. Helen Knight's angel in Shibuya Station could have been any Japanese businessman commuting home after his workday, except that his unusual height and broad-shouldered build, perfect for rescuing Joy, set him apart from the crowd.

After Jesus' resurrection, He went undercover to link up with two travelers walking to the village of Emmaus outside Jerusalem.

The men shared their grief at the recent crucifixion of the One they hoped would redeem Israel, yet they did not recognize Him walking with them. As they journeyed, Jesus carefully explained the prophetic Scriptures that pointed to the Messiah and the suffering He would endure. When they arrived at the village, the men, hungry for more, begged their companion to stay on with them.

At last, during the evening meal, they discerned His identity:

> When he was at the table with them, he took bread, gave thanks, broke it and began to give it to them. Then their eyes were opened and they recognized him, and he disappeared from their sight.
>
> Luke 24:30–31

They also acknowledged that even on the road they had noticed something unusual about Him. "They asked each other, 'Were not our hearts burning within us while he talked with us on the road and opened the Scriptures to us?'" (verse 32). Jesus' appearance and teaching brought two doubting, despairing disciples back to faith in their living Lord.

Does God really have a role for angels in world evangelization? Consider this passage from Revelation:

> Then I saw another angel flying in midair, and he had the eternal gospel to proclaim to those who live on the earth—to every nation, tribe, language and people. He said in a loud voice, "Fear God and give him glory, because the hour of his judgment has come. Worship him who made the heavens, the earth, the sea and the springs of water."
>
> Revelation 14:6–7

No matter what form they take or what functions they perform, celestial beings advance the cause of Christ and His Kingdom. And as Christians labor alongside these messengers of God, people around the world come to worship and glorify the King of all creation.

6

"Miraculous Signs and Wonders"

Stories of Miracles

Delegates to the Soviet Lausanne Congress in October 1990 milled through the lobby of the Hotel Ismailova in suburban Moscow, mixing with tourists and locals in a hum of noise and activity. Among the crowd was John Robb, director of the Unreached Peoples Program for MARC (Missions Advanced Research and Communication Center), based in Monrovia, California.

The breathtaking transformation of Eastern Europe during the previous year and a half had set heads spinning as the pace of democratization zoomed into hyperdrive. To hold a Congress for the Soviet Union, bringing together 1,300 Christian leaders from all over the vast country to plan for its evangelization, would have seemed world-class fantasy not many years before. Who could have known that in less than twelve months the Soviet Union would cease to exist?

John traveled extensively for MARC, a division of World Vision International, giving seminars on unreached peoples and strategies for establishing the Kingdom of God among these groups. But the idea of training Christian leaders in Russia was as new to John as almost anyone. Now, as he approached the Hotel Ismailova staff to make room arrangements for his two-day unreached peoples seminar starting the next morning, he was well aware of the hotel employees' limited proficiency in English.

Am I going to be able to tell them what I need? he wondered.

His wavy hair, boyish smile and twinkling eyes behind wire-frame glasses complemented his friendly disposition, but none of these attributes would help with Russian vocabulary.

As John struggled to communicate, a dark-haired man of about 35 stepped out from the lobby crowd and offered to interpret. He was a medical doctor, John learned. Quickly Dr. M. settled everything with the hotel staff, and the two continued to talk as they went to check out the seminar location.

"I really appreciate your help," John said as they began setting up the room. Then he noticed a major problem. "Oh, no—what am I going to do for a screen?"

He had planned to use an overhead projector to display transparencies against the wall, but the room was painted dark green.

"I've got an idea," Dr. M. suggested. "My infirmary is nearby. I'll get a white sheet we can hang on the wall with medical tape."

The scheme worked. Finally, the room ready, John turned to his new friend.

"Dr. M., you've been so kind. Can I buy you a cup of coffee, just to say thanks?"

Over steaming brew in the hotel coffee shop, they got better acquainted. John learned that the bachelor doctor was an Azerbaijani from the southern Caucasus region of the Soviet Union and a Muslim.

"I grew up in Baku where I've still got family," he said. "I came to Moscow for my medical training, and now I share an apartment here with my brother. There are probably sixty thousand Azerbaijanis in the Moscow area."

John explained the purpose of the Lausanne Congress, then asked his companion, "Have you heard about Jesus?"

"Uh, yeah," Dr. M. answered, wrinkling his brow. "He was a Japanese, wasn't He?"

John could only pause in silence as he gathered his thoughts. *Why, here's an educated doctor who doesn't know the first thing about Jesus!*

When he found his voice, John shared with Dr. M. about the Person and work of Christ. Then he remembered a booklet in his briefcase. A few days earlier, near the beginning of the Congress, Russian Christians had given him literature to distribute to anyone he met. Everywhere people hungry for spiritual reality took the tracts, booklets, Gospels and pamphlets. By now John had given it all away—all except one booklet that the believers told him was designed for Muslims.

"Here's a little booklet, Dr. M., that I'd like you to have. It's written especially for Muslims and explains about Jesus. Take a look through it, and if you want to know more, call me in the morning." John smiled as he gave this prescription to the doctor.

The next morning the phone in John's hotel room rang early.

"I'd like to come to your seminar," said Dr. M.

John gulped. *A Muslim in my unreached peoples seminar? When we're going to be talking about outreach to Muslims and others?* He mumbled something in response.

"Excuse me?"

"Uh, um—all right, come ahead," John finally answered.

Dr. M. did attend, and when the time came for participants to split into discussion groups from different areas, the doctor ended up with the Christian leaders strategizing to reach Muslims from the Caucasus region. As the discussions continued, John heard thunderous laughter roll out of that corner of the room. Later one of the leaders filled John in. It turned out Dr. M. was giving cheerful advice on how to evangelize Muslims like himself.

A couple of days later the Congress concluded. John was packing his bags and preparing to leave for the airport, when Dr. M. dropped by his hotel room unexpectedly. He brought John a friendly greeting card with his address and some books about Russia highlighting various things for visitors to see and do.

John was glad to see the doctor again and thanked his friend warmly. But the gifts put him in a spot. He had given away the last of his Christian literature. All his California souvenirs were gone, too. Yet receiving Dr. M.'s tokens without presenting something in return could appear disastrously rude in a country that cherished the cultural importance of exchanging gifts. What should he do?

Stalling for time, John thumbed through one of Dr. M.'s books while his churning thoughts tried to dig up a gift idea. A cry arose from his heart: *O Lord, what I'd give for a Russian New Testament right now!*

No sooner had the thought formed when a knock came on the door.

"Pardon me," John said to Dr. M. as he went to answer.

On the other side of the doorway stood two Russian men next to a trolley cart piled high with Russian New Testaments. John stared at them like a walleyed pike.

Are they angels? he wondered in awe.

One of them handed him a volume, and he took it as though in slow motion.

"Who are you?" he asked finally.

"We're Gideons."

John almost laughed with relief.

Then the volunteers with the Bible distribution society told him in broken English that only a month before, Soviet President Mikhail Gorbachev had approved a law lifting restrictions against freedom of religion.

"We've just received permission to distribute New Testaments to every room in this hotel," they explained.

John thanked them gratefully, then turned and presented the book to his Muslim doctor friend. Dr. M. accepted it with gratitude and stashed it in his briefcase. Then the two said their good-byes.

Three months later Dr. M. wrote to John in California.

"This book you gave me is the best book I have ever read," he raved. "It's my friend and constant companion. I've read it and reread it."

The men kept in touch. And eight months later, when John returned to Russia in June 1991 to give unreached peoples seminars in other parts of the country, Dr. M. took him to dinner one night.

Over Azerbaijani food at the Baku Restaurant in Moscow, Dr. M. leaned forward and told John quietly, "I have given my heart to Jesus Christ as my Savior. I've put my faith in Him."

More good news followed. John visited or passed through Moscow six more times over the next four years, sharing dinner with Dr. M. and encouraging him in his faith. Soon Dr. M. led his brother to the Lord, then his father and grandfather back home in Azerbaijan. He attended different church fellowships in Moscow and began meeting with other Azerbaijani doctors in a seekers' Bible study. In addition he published a tract for his patients in both Russian and the Azerbaijani language that reprinted from the Bible some healing narratives of Christ.

John never did secure another Russian New Testament to leave in his hotel room in place of the one he had given Dr. M. But he wrote a grateful letter to the Gideons recounting the story of how a New Testament presented by two of their workers appeared miraculously at the exact time needed and played a starring role in the salvation of a young Muslim doctor in Moscow.

Miracle or Coincidence: Having Eyes to See

Was it a miracle for Gideons—even in Moscow—to come to John's hotel room with New Testaments? By itself, no. But to show up at the precise moment John expressed to God his desperate need and wish for one? Many people with "eyes to see" or "ears to hear" (as Jesus put it) would conclude that the timing, too perfect to be coincidental, has all the fingerprints of divine intervention.

Miracles may include a wide variety of events that stretch the bounds of probability. Often it is the timing rather than the nature of the event that makes it miraculously improbable. Divine appointments, miracles involving nature and circumstances that defy mere coincidence often fall into this category.

When Jesus called the first disciples at the Sea of Galilee, He asked Simon Peter to take his boat into deep water and let down the nets for a catch. The fisherman protested that he and his partners had already spent the whole night hard at work without catching a thing. Nevertheless they went ahead and followed Jesus' suggestion.

> When they had done so, they caught such a large number of fish that their nets began to break. So they signaled their partners in the other boat to come and help them, and they came and filled both boats so full that they began to sink.
>
> Luke 5:6–7

Did this seem like a miracle to men who made their living catching fish? Witness their reactions:

> When Simon Peter saw this, he fell at Jesus' knees and said, "Go away from me, Lord; I am a sinful man!" For he and all his companions were astonished at the catch of fish they had taken, and so were James and John, the sons of Zebedee, Simon's partners.
>   Then Jesus said to Simon, "Don't be afraid; from now on you will catch men." So they pulled their boats up on shore, left everything and followed him.
>
> verses 8–11

Perception of miracles depends heavily on a person's worldview. Our culturally and educationally patterned understandings of reality and the way the world works form a mental framework or point of view by which we organize our lives. New data that fit our mental grid get integrated into it. But when information finds no place to fit, most often we reject the new information rather than rearrange our grid to accommodate it.

Someone with an entirely naturalistic worldview who does not believe in miracles never will see one, no matter how much documentation or evidence is provided. This person's mental grid does not allow for miracles, so he or she must explain away evidence to the contrary.

In his book *How to Have a Healing Ministry in Any Church* (Regal, 1988), C. Peter Wagner writes,

Convincing a skeptic is a thankless effort. Jesus Himself would not perform a miracle to convince skeptics because He knew it wouldn't do any good. Because they did not believe, they would not be able to see what Jesus did. In a true sense, believing is seeing.

page 144

Could this help explain why reports of miracles come more often out of non-Western cultures? People whose worldviews allow for the possibility of divine intervention in the earthly realm—or people who have had their worldviews rearranged through a so-called paradigm shift—will see things others simply cannot see.

This is good news for missionaries and evangelists working among cultures open to signs and wonders. When God orchestrates unusual events, people in such cultures are more likely to recognize a higher power at work. Christians ministering among them must then be ready to interpret the sign, its meaning and source.

The next story highlights a nature miracle that went recognized but uninterpreted until believers came to explain its divine message.

In the Wind and Fire

On Sunday, July 31, 1994, heavy rains swept through many parts of Cambodia. Storms and flooding destroyed crops and homes. But out of the sky that night in one small mountain village came a phenomenon that brought residents to faith in the living God.

About eighty miles southwest of Phnom Penh in the Elephant Mountains, Buddhist priests had been rebuilding their temple on one of the peaks of that range, near the village of Pech Nil. The road over the mountains from the capital to the port city of Kompong Som snakes through a steep pass, and in past decades several cars making the tortuous journey had plunged off the side. Now "spirit houses" or small shrines dotted the edge of the cliff marking the spots where people had attempted to appease the spirits of the dead drivers.

Christians in Phnom Penh had prayed for months about the forces of darkness they believed controlled the area. Sophal Ung, with his wife, Deborah, and Nan Khorn helped pastor a group of believers who sensed that a high-ranking demon called that territory home. Witchcraft, idolatry and other perverse practices flourished like germs on an open wound. No house church or fellowship existed there. The believers began to pray for a breakthrough.

The Buddhists, meanwhile, forged ahead with their building project. They moved the statues and idols out of their dilapidated temple into a small structure nearby and began to rebuild a new temple on the old site. In Cambodian style they laid the floor and upright framing posts, then put on the roof covering before adding the walls. By July 31 the work neared completion, and they began to place some of the idols in the new temple.

While rains pounded the area, five Buddhist priests staying at the temple got ready to retire for the night. Suddenly they heard a deafening rumble, like the sound of a dozen or more army tanks shaking the ground with a thunderous roar—and coming their way. They scrambled for the door and saw a ball of fire aimed straight at their temple from out of the sky above an adjacent mountain peak.

"Look out!" someone yelled.

Four of the priests escaped out the door, but the last one remained inside when the fireball struck with a mighty crash. It seemed to bring with it a powerful whirlwind. The fire did not burn, but the wind picked up the temple and hurled it fifty yards, where it and the idols inside shattered into rubble. The priest inside felt himself flying with the building, but when it smashed he suffered no injuries. In fact, he testified later, he felt a strange sense of peace and joy. The air around him felt cool and refreshing.

People from the village of Pech Nil also saw the ball of fire hit the temple. When villagers began gathering the next morning to figure out what had happened, they discovered that many of them had felt the same unusual joy as the flying priest.

Puzzled murmurs spread from neighbor to neighbor: "What's going on? Our temple has been destroyed, but we're not particularly anxious or upset about it."

Sometime later, when floodwaters receded in the valleys and the roads through the passes reopened, word began to circulate about the celestial phenomenon in the Elephant Mountains. In early September 1994 a television crew from a CNN affiliate in Phnom Penh interviewed the Buddhist priests about their experience. The combination of wind and fire had so astonished them, they explained, that they concluded it was a sign from heaven. But they did not know which spirit or enlightened being had sent them a message.

When Sophal and Deborah Ung and Nan Khorn heard the story, they knew the Lord had answered their prayers for a breakthrough. With a small group from the church they traveled to Pech Nil and met with the Buddhist priests. They listened to the account of the man trapped in the temple when the wind had picked it up.

"Do you understand what this means?" Nan asked him.

"No, I've never heard of anything like this," the priest replied. "But I feel good about it—somehow my life was saved."

Nan, Sophal and Deborah jumped headfirst into this opening for the Gospel. They read passages from the Bible about God's love and care for people and His desire that all be saved. They also pointed out that the Lord hates idolatry. When people worship created things instead of the Creator, according to Romans 1, God pours out His wrath.

"He showed His judgment on sin through the fireball and the whirlwind that destroyed the temple and the idols," Nan told the priest. "Yet in wrath God remembers mercy. He spared you personally from harm. The cool, refreshing air, your peaceful lack of fear and the joy in the village all point to His concern for people and how He wants to have a relationship with you."

Nan cited 2 Peter 3:9: "[God] is patient with you, not wanting anyone to perish, but everyone to come to repentance."

Nan and Sophal went on to identify Jesus as God's greatest gift of love to humankind, the only One who can bring God's salvation to men and women.

"Do you believe God sent Jesus to earth to die for our sins and rise from the dead?" they asked. "And that He sent these signs from heaven to bring you this message?"

"Oh, I believe! I believe!" the Buddhist priest responded. "All along I felt this was a message from the spiritual realm, but until you came I didn't know who had spoken. I've been waiting to learn the name, and now I know—it's Jesus."

The believers prayed with the priest as he gave his life to the one true God and His Son, Jesus Christ.

As Nan, Sophal and Deborah continued sharing in the village, they discovered unusual responsiveness to the Gospel. Deborah spoke with several Buddhist nuns, some of whom came to faith in Jesus. And over the coming months the believers worked to establish a home fellowship in the isolated area.

During Jesus' earthly ministry the unbelieving Pharisees asked Him for a sign from heaven, and He refused because of their hard hearts. But in a little village in a remote corner of Cambodia in 1994, a sign from heaven came unbidden, and the Lord Jesus found hearts there ready to receive Him.

Judgment and Mercy

On the Day of Pentecost following Jesus' ascension, two nature miracles, or "sense phenomena," accompanied the preaching in various languages that led to an immediate ingathering of three thousand new believers.

When the day of Pentecost came, they were all together in one place. Suddenly a sound like the blowing of a violent wind came from heaven and filled the whole house where they were sitting. They saw what seemed to be tongues of fire that separated and came to rest on each of them.

Acts 2:1–3

The fire that did not consume and the sudden, violent sound of wind contributed to the extraordinary scene that day, which attracted thousands of baffled spectators.

The whirlwind and fireball at Pech Nil, in contrast to Pentecost, came as a sign of divine judgment rather than divine anointing, according to the interpretation Nan Khorn gave the Cambodian phenomena. Yet in both cases observers discerned the hand of God in a miraculous display of His power in the earthly realm, and people came to salvation.

Nan Khorn pointed out to the Buddhist priest that in the midst of God's judgment He also showed His mercy. God does not delight in punishing sinners, Ezekiel 33:11 indicates: "I take no pleasure in the death of the wicked, but rather that they turn from their ways and live." In every instance His ultimate goal is to redeem men and women from sin and bring them into an eternal life relationship with Himself. As James 2:13 says, "Mercy triumphs over judgment!"

A simple but profound story of God's mercy in miraculous timing and circumstance comes from Jack McAlister, founder of World Prayer Network and for 33 years president of World Literature Crusade. During one of their Every Home Crusades in India, staff workers walked or bicycled six million miles to deliver Gospel literature to each home in the nation. Every home in India received two booklets: *Are You Happy?* for adults and *He Wants to Be Your Friend* for children.

About 1976 a young Indian university graduate, despondent over his lack of employment opportunities, stood on a chair with a rope around his neck preparing to commit suicide, when he noticed that the chair was a little crooked. He got down to straighten it, to ensure the success of his effort to kill himself. But there, under one of the legs of the chair, he found a copy of the Every Home Crusade's *Are You Happy?* booklet.

He stared at the title in disbelief. "Am I happy? I'm about to commit suicide!"

Nevertheless he read the message. Then he gave his heart to Jesus. Later he joined the Every Home Crusade staff as a Pioneer Crusader, walking personally to every home in eight thousand Indian villages to deliver the good news of Christ that had saved and changed his life.

Jesus' first miracle on earth demonstrated the mercy of God in what might seem a dumbfounding way: He saved face for an embarrassed host who had run out of wine for his party. As the apostle John tells the story, the water in six stone jars, each holding twenty to thirty gallons, turned to wine and rescued the day for the master of ceremonies at a wedding. "This, the first of his miraculous signs, Jesus performed at Cana in Galilee. He thus revealed his glory, and his disciples put their faith in him" (John 2:11).

Read on for a contemporary story from Galilee in the Holy Land.

God Speaks My Language

The Israelites' crossing of the Jordan River, when the Lord held back the waters so they could enter the Promised Land on dry ground, was unquestionably more miraculous than a tour bus rumbling over the Allenby Bridge. But the Israelites could hardly have been more excited than Reigh Lang was on February 19, 1980.

Months earlier, when Reigh's church had put out a flyer announcing a Holy Land tour, his spirit leaped instantly at the opportunity. He had no doubt the Lord meant him to go. An intimate group of about 25 people signed up for the pilgrimage, many of them leaders from the two sponsoring churches, then known as Calvary Chapel Yorba Linda and Calvary Chapel Whittier, sister congregations in Southern California.

Reigh, a 51-year-old bachelor at the time, had made a spiritual turnaround just over a year before. Although he had known about the Lord while growing up, he had become a professional backslider over the years. Now the gray-haired special agent in the security department of the Southern California Gas Company burned with passion for Jesus, fired up with living a life dedicated to serving Him.

The tour spent two days each in Cairo, Egypt and Amman, Jordan, then headed across the Jordan River to Israel for about a week and a half. This trip represented the first visit to the Holy Land for most of the travelers, so anticipation ran high.

After a thorough customs check on the West Bank, the group transferred to an Israeli tour bus and met their new guide, Shalom, a tall Jewish man in his forties with a dark mustache and bright eyes. An Argentine immigrant to Israel, Shalom spoke several languages, held multiple degrees in history and knew both Old and New Testaments well, putting him in demand as a guide.

As the bus cruised south along the Dead Sea toward En-Gedi and Masada, someone with a guitar began leading worship and praise songs. The group from Calvary Chapel Whittier had learned some Jewish songs that the Yorba Linda people picked up quickly, and Shalom seemed sincerely moved that these Christians would take such joy singing choruses with Hebrew words and verses from the Old Testament.

One favorite chorus—"*Baruch hashem Adonai, baruch hashem Adonai*" ("Praise the name of the Lord"), with verses from Psalm 98—turned into a kind of theme song as the group continued their musical worship throughout the tour. It also became a call and response whenever something good happened.

"*Baruch hashem!*" ("Praise the name!") someone would call out.

"*Baruch hashem!*" Shalom would answer, reverencing the Lord's name, as good Jews do, by not speaking it aloud.

Reigh Lang was flying on a spiritual high, especially after his rebaptism in the Jordan. With a hotel room to himself, he often enjoyed time in the evenings to pray and reflect on his pilgrimage. As he meditated, the words of the first chapter of the Gospel of John played over and over in his mind. For about three weeks several verses and sentences from that chapter had cycled through his thoughts like a song that keeps coming back with each new dawn: "In the beginning was the Word, and the Word was with God, and the Word was God. . . ."

At Caesarea Philippi in the far north of Israel, where the group stayed overnight at a kibbutz, the tour leaders planned an outdoor worship service for Sunday morning, February 24. Everyone, including Shalom, gathered in a lovely, tree-shaded area by a waterfall, one of the headwaters of the Jordan River at the foot of Mount Hermon. As they sat on rocks, John McClure, pastor of Calvary Chapel Whittier, led the service at this historic place where Jesus' disciple, Simon Peter, had made his confession of faith: "You are the Christ, the Son of the living God" (Matthew 16:16).

The group entered a time of prayer, with several people voicing praises and petitions one after another. Reigh, deep in concentration, felt urged by the Holy Spirit to share the words percolating in his heart. Without paying much attention to what others had said, he spoke out a short message, perhaps half a minute, based on truths from the first chapter of John.

"And there's victory in the Word through Jesus," he concluded.

At the end of the service, people began chatting as they prepared to leave. Reigh saw Shalom go to talk with someone. Heading back to the bus, Reigh had just found a seat when, a few moments later, Shalom followed him in.

"Reigh, I didn't know you understood Hebrew," the guide said.

"I don't," Reigh replied. "Why do you ask?"

Shalom's bright eyes took on a dazed look.

"During the prayer time," he answered slowly, "Len Cerny spoke right before you. He prayed in perfect Hebrew. Then what you said in English was the direct translation of his words." The guide bit his lip. "I just talked with Len. He says he doesn't speak Hebrew either."

Reigh felt almost as confused as Shalom.

Later, conferring with Len, Reigh learned that his psychologist friend had prayed aloud in what he believed to be a heavenly tongue or prayer language, unknown to him. Then, when Reigh had spoken up, Len had assumed he was giving the interpretation of the tongue through a gift or anointing of the Holy Spirit.

"As far as I knew," Reigh explained to Len, "I was just expressing words from John 1 that have been running through my mind for the last three weeks. This is astonishing, isn't it?"

Indeed, their guide seemed touched—almost like a changed man.

Other tour members learned the news as the story began to circulate and they saw the impact on Shalom. At least one listener confirmed that the tongue in which Len had spoken had sounded like a Semitic language.

In the coming days several members of the tour group had opportunity to talk with Shalom. As they discussed passages from the Old and New Testaments, including references to Jesus as the Messiah, Shalom received their words with great openness.

When they returned to Jerusalem, Shalom directed the tour bus off the beaten track—to his mother's home.

"I want my mother to meet you special people and hear you sing your favorite Jewish song," he said.

With gusto the group serenaded the little grandma: *"Baruch hashem Adonai! Baruch hashem Adonai!"*

At the end of the trip, the Californians pooled funds to give Shalom a special gift. Some of them found a silversmith's shop in the Hasidic section of Jaffa, the old district in the southern part of Tel Aviv, where they bought a ring for their guide and friend. They had it inscribed inside with the date of their tour and the initials *BH* for *baruch hashem*.

On an outdoor plaza in Jaffa, with a view of the blue-green Mediterranean and the wide beaches of Tel Aviv stretching north, the group presented their gift to Shalom. When he saw it and read the inscription, he blinked back tears.

"Thank you, friends," he managed. "I have felt so much love and warmth and acceptance from you all. I will never forget you."

When their plane lifted off from David Ben-Gurion Airport outside Tel Aviv, Reigh Lang said another prayer for Shalom. He understood that Shalom's position as a well-known tour guide precluded him from expressing faith openly in Jesus as Messiah. But Reigh had no doubt that the man's heart and soul had been profoundly touched. The engraved silver ring, Reigh felt sure, would always remind Shalom of the love of their group—and the day at Caesarea Philippi when God spoke his language.

Language Miracles

In addition to the miraculous sound of wind and appearance of fire at Pentecost, the major event that attracted onlookers' attention was a language miracle that God worked through the Jewish believers.

All of them were filled with the Holy Spirit and began to speak in other tongues as the Spirit enabled them.

Now there were staying in Jerusalem God-fearing Jews from every nation under heaven. When they heard this sound, a crowd came together in bewilderment, because each one heard them speaking in his own language. Utterly amazed, they asked: "Are not all these men who are speaking Galileans? Then how is it that each of us

hears them in his own native language? . . . We hear them declaring the wonders of God in our own tongues!"

Acts 2:4–8, 11

Each disciple, like Len Cerny, probably had no idea what language he was speaking, and perhaps did not even understand himself. But tour guide Shalom, unlike the listeners in first-century
Jerusalem, got a double-barreled miracle when he heard his own
language from a speaker foreign to the tongue, then a translation
from another speaker just as foreign.

The miraculous tongues at Pentecost quickly drew a crowd for
Peter's first sermon. And few preachers have enjoyed such results:
"Those who accepted his message were baptized, and about three
thousand were added to their number that day" (2:41).

God again used miracles to attract attention to the spoken Word
of God when Philip proclaimed the Gospel in Samaria.

When the crowds heard Philip and saw the miraculous signs he
did, they all paid close attention to what he said. With shrieks, evil
spirits came out of many, and many paralytics and cripples were
healed. So there was great joy in that city. . . .
When they believed Philip as he preached the good news of the
kingdom of God and the name of Jesus Christ, they were baptized,
both men and women.

Acts 8:6–8, 12

Signs and wonders, as always, can open the door for the Gospel
but cannot themselves save anyone. Effective evangelism requires
communication of "the good news of the kingdom of God and the
name of Jesus Christ." With a language miracle, interestingly, the
supernatural sign and the communication of truth about God can
occur simultaneously.

"Meet Me on the Hill"

I introduced Linda Kangrga in the previous chapter without
describing her background in the church or her wilderness journey through the lost world of drugs. Years of intercession by her

family and others had seen only temporary breaks in the shifting cloud patterns of confusion, paranoia and depression.

Linda had grown up in a Christian family in Glendale, California, the youngest of three children. Always a bit of a rebel, she accepted the Lord as a youngster through the Sunday school program at Glendale Presbyterian Church, but began hanging out in her teen years with friends who yearned to look cool and be independent. By high school she was drifting spiritually. Soon afterward she sank into a quagmire of cigarettes, drugs and impetuous behavior.

Linda's interest in engines and the outdoors made her a natural for the trucking industry. From her first trucking job—home delivery of bottled water—she graduated to larger rigs, including double tanker trucks that carried the water from mountain springs to the bottling plant. Her scope of friends narrowed to fellow truckers, many of whom prowled the dark and slimy underside of life. After her marriage fell apart, Linda began tumbling further into an abyss of drug-induced paranoia.

Then on June 6, 1993, God sovereignly intervened in the life of Linda (nee Novak) Kangrga, my younger sister.

* * * * *

Linda and her trucker friends sometimes laughed at how they could work all week behind the wheel of a big rig and then get a charge out of spending their day off at a car or truck show. Sunday, June 6, 1993, was no exception. Rain had fallen overnight, threatening to cancel the exhibition of classic cars, roadsters, T-buckets and more. But by morning the gray clouds had wrung themselves dry and the "Fontana Days" car show carried on.

Linda did not want to miss this one, hosted by her hometown of Fontana, California. Early that morning the 33-year-old blonde drove her black '55 Chevy sedan delivery to the show site on a nearby grassy ballfield where freshly laid straw helped soak up the mud. With her came her live-in friend and co-worker, Dean Berg, a tall, quiet fellow about 25 years older, with the tanned and deeply lined face of one who had spent many years bucking bales onto the back of a hay truck. During her fifteen years in the trucking business, Linda had handled a variety of rigs, but now they both drove tankers, hauling gasoline, diesel and jet fuel. Linda's 65-foot Peterbilt was her pride and joy.

Car shows normally offered an opportunity to kick back and hang out with friends for the day. But on this day Linda had trouble relaxing. Having spent extra time working that week, her body felt exhausted, yet her agitated mind and emotions would not let her rest.

Linda had become involved, like a number of truckers, with cocaine and methamphetamine ("speed," "crystal meth") as a way to keep alert during long hours on the road, even though after years of use their effect no longer seemed like riding a tiger so much as getting bitten by one. Still, something else kept bothering her—something she could not quite put her finger on. She shook a cigarette out of her pack of Kools and lit up, trying to dispel nervous energy. Dean, undoubtedly noticing her anxiety, gave her extra space.

At the end of the car show around four o'clock, some of their friends wanted to go bowling. Linda and Dean took the '55 home and drove to the lanes in her everyday Camaro. But when they got out of the car, Linda felt more restless than ever. The clouds had lightened into a layer of white cotton, just beginning to pull apart into snatches of blue. Linda looked north toward the Cajon Pass between the San Gabriel and San Bernardino Mountains and saw a sunburst coming through the clouds, shining like a spotlight on a patch of hillside.

"Hey, Dean, why don't we go for a drive instead of bowling?" she asked her friend. "It's a beautiful day now, and I really need to get out of town for a while."

She knew Dean sensed something peculiar, but he did not object, so they said good-bye to their friends inside the bowling alley, got back into the Camaro and hit the road, heading north on Sierra Avenue. As Linda drove she kept her eyes fixed on the sunburst ahead of her. Something in the mountains was drawing her like a magnet. It felt almost like a pull to go home.

Turning off onto Devore Road, Linda took the gently winding two-lane route toward Glen Helen Regional Park. The name reminded her of her childhood hometown of Glendale fifty miles west.

If I can't go back to Glendale, maybe I can go to Glen Helen, she mused.

But on the way through the foothills she began to feel ill, so when they reached the park she and Dean got out to catch some fresh air, stroll around and enjoy the scenery. On the crisp breeze, washed clean, wafted the fragrance of rain and wet grass. Linda felt refreshed.

After a while they climbed back into the car and started down the hill again. But no sooner had Linda taken the first curve in the road than nausea returned full-force.

"Man, what's going on?" she wondered aloud. "You know I don't usually get carsick, especially when I'm driving."

Devore Road afforded almost no place to pull over to the side, but Linda found a turnout where she could park. She shut down the engine and told Dean, "I just need to walk this off or something."

Dean, with quiet patience, said little, but seemed to understand that whatever was going on, Linda had to deal with it herself. He stayed in the car when Linda stepped out.

As she turned to her right, she spotted a little sign: CHRISTIAN CONFERENCE CENTER. Long-dormant memories stirred of camps she had attended while growing up at Glendale Presbyterian Church. Then she noticed that the turnout where she had parked accessed a tiny dirt road leading up the hill. She followed it about 150 yards to the top of a knoll. A hundred yards farther down the road she could see a small building, but she seemed to have the grounds to herself.

From the plateau on the knoll, a magnificent view stretched off in all directions. Colors shone with special brilliance in the clean air. Linda drank it in, feeling revived.

Well, I'm better now, she decided.

She turned to go back down the hill and instantly felt sick again, her stomach curdling like sour milk.

Good grief, what's going on?

Linda returned to the view and breathed deeply until the nausea passed in another few moments. But when she tried again to leave, her digestive upset kicked in once more.

Now her mind stewed, too, spiced with a generous helping of guilt. She had been messing with dope off and on since just after high school. And the drugs in her system from recent days, she realized, on top of inadequate food intake, were no doubt contributing to her distress.

She sensed that God knew this, too.

After waiting for the latest wave to pass, she made a third attempt to go back to the car. Again the sickness hit her as soon as she turned around.

In desperation Linda looked to the skies and cried aloud, "Lord, if there's something You want to say, please tell me! Please show me that You love me and that You care. What is it You want to tell me?"

Almost in tears, Linda dropped to her knees near a small tree. The moment her knees hit the dirt, her belt buckle broke off and fell to the ground. Startled, she picked it up to examine it. She had worn the silver buckle with the Peterbilt logo virtually every day for as long as she could remember.

How in the world did this just break? she puzzled. *It's German sterling silver!* She turned it over to see the broken back clasp. *Is this my message from God?*

As she pondered what it meant, Linda decided there could be two messages.

A belt is something that binds you, she reflected. *It goes around your body and keeps you tied up. That's like the drugs.*

Her heart kindled with a spark of hope. *Has God just broken the ties that bind?*

In addition, the Peterbilt logo on the buckle she wore every day reminded her that for years her job had come first in her life. Her Peterbilt truck represented her identity, and pride and devotion to it had sped the demise of her marriage a few years back.

Staring at the broken belt buckle, she sensed God telling her, *I'm going to release you from both of those bondages—the drugs and the idolatry of your truck.*

In shock and awe that the Lord would give her this kind of visible, tangible sign, Linda knew unmistakably what she had to do. Gathering her courage, she dug a hole with her hands in the dirt beneath the tree and set her beloved belt buckle in the hollow. She also removed her leather belt from its loops, rolled it into a spiral and set it beside the buckle. Then she buried both of them, piling the hole high with dirt and placing a rock on top.

She stood up, every nerve alive with electricity. *Dear Jesus, please accept this sign of my recommitment to You as Lord and Savior.*

If she wanted to keep her freedom, she knew, she had to leave the symbols of her bondage there on the hill—walk away, not look back, not think about them. Linda gazed out again at the spectacular view, then turned her face to walk straight down the hill, feeling fine. As she came down the road she sensed God's glory all around and knew she was changed.

Dean, still sitting in the car, stared at her as she approached, even though her absence had spanned only about twenty minutes. She got in behind the wheel of the Camaro and took a deep breath before trying to explain what had happened.

"Well, you look different," Dean affirmed when she had finished. "When you walked back to the car, you looked like Moses coming down off the hill—you know, in that Cecil B. De Mille movie *The Ten Commandments.*"

"Wow, maybe it *is* like that," Linda responded, still trembling. "I know I met with the Lord on that hill."

Linda drove back to Fontana in a cloud of awe, her body tired but her spirit more alive than ever.

Back in her apartment, with her mind turning over and over, she pulled out a cigarette absentmindedly and lit it. In that instant terror gripped her as though she had lit the fuse to a stick of dynamite. Her spirit lurched back, crying, *Aaagh! I can't smoke!*

And she sensed a patient voice chide her gently, *Look, I just met with you out there, and now you're going to do this?*

Immediately Linda snuffed out the cigarette, crushed her pack of Kools and threw them away. That day, after several years of smoking, she quit cold turkey—and suffered no trace of nicotine cravings.

In the days to come, when Linda's party buddies came around and she refused their drugs, they demanded to know what had happened to her. She told them the story down to the last detail, after which they sat back mumbling in bafflement.

Only the grace of God, Linda knew, had brought her back home. She found buried in her old Bible a bookmark that said, "Every day is a gift from God and how you live it is your gift to Him." This motto seared itself onto her consciousness as the Lord revealed Himself in many miraculous ways over the coming weeks—including sparing her the consequences of her reckless driving (as we read in the last chapter) by the appearance of the man in the driver's seat with the long, gray beard. This series of supernatural events, stunning her with fresh demonstrations of God's love and power, trained her and built up her faith until she had broken from past bondages.

Linda learned about the power of God to live one day at a time in a challenging environment. Christ reminded her that His sacrifice on the cross and deliverance called for a similar laying down of her life, according to His words in Luke 9:23: "If anyone would come after me, he must deny himself and take up his cross daily and follow me." Taking up her cross, she learned, meant following Him up the road to Calvary, climbing that hill to the place where complete self-sacrifice is the only appropriate response.

Now, when the Lord wants to draw Linda into deeper commitment in some aspect of her spiritual life, He has only to whisper in her ear, *Come away, My beloved. Meet Me on the hill.*

Recognizing the Source of Power

To anyone who has lived through similar bondage, Linda Kangrga's instantaneous deliverance from drugs and cigarettes would likely qualify as a miracle.

Researchers point to nicotine as the most addictive drug, even more habit-forming than cocaine. An Associated Press article printed in *The Los Angeles Times* on December 23, 1994, began, "Only about 8% of American adults who try to quit smoking actually succeed" (p. A4). And may we guess how many of those eight-percent successes, using any means including "nicotine patches, counseling, hypnosis or the cold turkey method," suffered no withdrawal pangs? If Linda had taken part in the 1993 survey cited in the article, she might have been the only one!

Linda's experience led her back to the family of God partly because she already knew the Gospel message. When the Lord began speaking to her heart and convicting her, her background enabled her to recognize the supernatural intervention as coming from God, the Father of the Lord Jesus Christ.

Notice, in contrast, what happened in Lystra on the first missionary journey of Paul and Barnabas. Paul declared a miraculous healing over a man lame from birth, who then jumped up and walked for the first time.

> When the crowd saw what Paul had done, they shouted in the Lycaonian language, "The gods have come down to us in human form!" Barnabas they called Zeus, and Paul they called Hermes because he was the chief speaker. The priest of Zeus, whose temple was just outside the city, brought bulls and wreaths to the city gates because he and the crowd wanted to offer sacrifices to them.
>
> Acts 14:11–13

The supernatural sign prompted an instantaneous response of worship, but here the confused crowd misunderstood the source of the power until the apostles explained their own humanity, in contrast to almighty God.

Clear communication of the Gospel of Christ, then, must go hand-in-hand with any ministry in signs and wonders. Even so, miracles do not guarantee that faith and salvation will follow. On the heels of supernatural events that included the resuscitation of Lazarus, John 12:37 says, "Even after Jesus had done all these miraculous signs in their presence, they still would not believe in him." Only the Holy Spirit working in someone's heart can birth saving faith:

> When the kindness and love of God our Savior appeared, he saved us, not because of righteous things we had done, but because of his mercy. He saved us through the washing of rebirth and renewal by

the Holy Spirit, whom he poured out on us generously through
Jesus Christ our Savior, so that, having been justified by his grace,
we might become heirs having the hope of eternal life.

Titus 3:4–7

Our persistent intercession for others, even through years of
unresponsiveness, can help open a way for the Holy Spirit to flow
into their lives—perhaps in miraculous ways.

Out of the Wreckage

"Hey, thanks, Michael. Why don't you go on home now? You
look dead-tired."

Michael's friend had no idea how close to literally true his words
would come.

Thirty-two-year-old Michael Koh adjusted his glasses as he
rubbed his eyes. Every night for the past week he had spent long
hours overseeing the deliverance team at the evening rallies of
international evangelist Reinhard Bonkke in Kuala Lumpur, capital of Malaysia. Several churches in the area had collaborated to
staff the rallies with nearly one thousand counselors, of whom
twenty had specific training in deliverance—many of these from
the church Michael pastored.

This Sunday night closed out the campaign, but by the time
Michael eased into his Toyota Corona and headed for home down
the highway to Petaling Jaya, a nearby western suburb, the clock
hands had crept past midnight into early Monday, November 20,
1989. Fighting a fever as well as drowsiness, Michael's mind drifted
back to the message God had given him when he had awakened
that morning praying. It seemed so long ago now! During the morning service of his 600-member church, Vision Valley Centre,
Michael had repeated the message to the congregation.

"The Lord is indicating that some very heavy activity in the
spiritual realm is coming," he had told them, "and there will be an
intense battle from today onward. For some of us, our lives will
never be the same out of this."

Michael drove on down the highway, normally well traveled but almost deserted at 12:30 A.M. Just as he neared a construction site, he fell asleep at the wheel. His right foot sagged down on the accelerator, and the Toyota plowed straight into a large stationary crane with a sickening crunch of twisting metal.

The front end of the car seemed to fold in on him. The steering wheel hit his chest and broke, while glass and metal tore at his face. In an instant it was over. Now fully awake and conscious, Michael felt a burning pain radiate from his right upper leg. What alarmed him most was that he could see absolutely nothing. His right eye was filled with glass from his eyeglasses, crushed and ground into the cornea. His left eye—well, Michael could not quite tell even where it was. His whole face, in fact, seemed to have been ripped into a bloody mess.

In the deathly quiet Michael heard a voice that made his skin crawl, not quite audible but just as clear.

So you think God is a loving Father? the diabolic voice cackled. *What do you have to say about this, then? It's just as you said—your life will never be the same.*

From somewhere inside his spirit, Michael pulled out words that challenged even him at that moment.

"I know that it's especially in a situation like this that God will show just how loving He is," he murmured aloud in a rebuke of the devil's lies.

About ten minutes passed. Michael heard a car slow down and pull over. Then a voice: "Oh, my God!" And the car sped off again, leaving him in silence.

After perhaps ten more minutes, another vehicle pulled over. Michael heard only low, unfriendly mumbles. He could not tell what they were doing.

Just then a third car stopped. More voices: "Hey, get away from him! Beat it, you guys!"

Two new voices addressed him with concern.

"Those guys were about to try to rip you off or something," one explained. "They probably thought you were dead."

Somehow his rescuers pretzeled him out of the mangled Toyota, flagged down a passing van and removed seats in the back of the van to lay Michael on the floor. Still he could see nothing. Ten or fifteen minutes later they arrived at the emergency room entrance of a hospital in Petaling Jaya, where Michael learned the horrifying truth.

"Doctor! This guy's eyeball is hanging out!" an orderly hollered.

All the sounds of the emergency room came through extra clearly to Michael's sight-deprived brain. As the ER personnel scrambled about him, he heard every gasp, gag and groan: "Poor guy." "Poor fellow." "No way this guy's going to see again." "How gruesome." "Dang, this guy's messed up." "Ugh, I'm going to vomit."

The doctors stabilized the broken femur in Michael's right leg and gave him a tetanus jab. Amazingly Michael had suffered no serious chest injuries from the broken steering wheel. But an eye specialist on call came in and spelled out the facts for him.

"Your face has been severely lacerated," she said, "and this eye"— referring to the left one—"is completely smashed. Don't expect ever to see from it again."

The medical team pushed the eyeball into its socket and began sewing up the side of Michael's face with 42 stitches. Because they feared brain damage, the doctors could not risk giving Michael any anesthesia.

Throughout, Michael remained conscious and tried to pray. He had asked someone to notify his church staff, and knew they would be interceding even then.

At one point he felt a strong sense of the Lord's presence. Distinctly he heard whispered words: *I'm going to heal you.*

The eye specialist and her assistants hovered over him for a few hours, cleaning out as much glass from his eyes as possible and setting the loose eyeball back into place. She was still stitching him together about 4 A.M. when Michael spoke up suddenly, his voice urgent and excited.

"Doctor, I can see something! I can see from both eyes! It's blurry, but I can see!"

"There's no way. It's not possible. You've got some phantom neurological activity, maybe—that's all."

"But I can really see!" he insisted. "Test me out!"

She held her hand close in front of Michael's face. "How many fingers am I holding up?"

Michael looked carefully through a hazy blur.

"One, two, three, four—yeah, four. Praise God! I can see!" he shouted again.

The room began to buzz with the news while the doctor shook her head and finally conceded, "Yeah—praise God, I guess. I don't know how it's possible."

When she finished stitching, the medical team dressed his wounds, wrapping bandages around Michael's head, including his eyes. They transferred him to a ward and began arrangements to set his leg in traction later that same Monday.

Sometime around midday a nurse came to change Michael's dressings. When she finished unwinding the bandages around his head, he almost gasped for joy.

"My Lord, I can see a lot more clearly! O God, praise You! It's almost like my normal, uncorrected vision!"

No one could find any explanation.

A team from orthopedic surgery drilled a nail into Michael's knee in preparation for traction, when a member of Michael's church, a medical specialist, came to the hospital. He made arrangements quickly to transfer Michael to another hospital in the city equipped to perform a more advanced operation. That evening in the new hospital, surgeons opened Michael's thigh and inserted a pin into his leg through the marrow, holding the femur together where it had made a clean break.

Michael remained in the hospital for a month. Another surgeon performed plastic surgery on Michael's face, taking more than two hundred stitches in the process.

Over time his skin healed well enough that a casual observer would not immediately notice the scars behind his glasses. And his new glasses needed a less powerful prescription for correction than the old pair. Tests about four weeks later indicated that his eyesight was better than before.

During that hospital stay an old friend came to visit. Six or eight years ago "David" had attended a church Michael had planted in

Kuantan, across Peninsular Malaysia on the east coast. But he had decided not to pursue the Christian life.

"Hey, Michael!" David greeted him. "I heard you were laid up. How're you doing?"

"What are you doing in town?" Michael answered. "Good to see you!"

The two talked for quite a while as Michael described his accident and what God had done in healing him.

"The eye specialists say it's miraculous—they've never seen anything like this happen. I give all the glory to God."

David listened intently, blinked back tears and looked down, shaking his head.

"Man, I need to get right with God," he blurted out. "The Lord is calling me back—I know it. You know, I've been involved in gangs, even leading one of them. But nothing satisfies. I need God in my life and the kind of power and love you're describing."

David prayed with Michael by the hospital bed and gave his heart to the Lord.

Several other Malaysian friends came to Christ, too, when they heard the testimony of Michael's miraculous healing.

And God had even bigger things in mind.

About a week before Christmas 1989, Michael went home from the hospital. On Christmas Day he attended a special morning service and greeted his church family for the first time since the accident. The guest speaker, Ken Newton from Australia, a friend of about four years, had just concluded the service when the Lord gave him a prophetic message for Michael.

In front of the congregation, Ken shared what he had heard: "Within a very short time after this accident, God is going to use this to expand His Kingdom, and you are going to be out of Malaysia soon. The Lord says He is going to use you to raise up people who will know God, display strength and do exploits."

Just after the start of the new year, Michael returned to work at the church. He got around easily on crutches with the pin in his leg—maybe too easily. Twice the metal pin worked its way out the back of his hip, and he had to return briefly to the hospital where doctors knocked it back in with a mallet. Eventually they removed the pin because the bone was healing so quickly, although Michael remained on crutches for six months or so.

In June 1990 Michael prepared to fly to the United States for his annual summer course work at Fuller Seminary in Pasadena— advanced training that would help him with church growth and church planting in Malaysia. Before he left, his prayer partners gathered to intercede for him. Several received similar impressions from the Holy Spirit: "You will meet a group of people you've never known before. But you will not go to them—they'll come to you. They will hear about what God has done in your life with this miracle, and they will want to learn from you and be mentored."

As Michael studied in his cubbyhole apartment in a Fuller housing complex, he kept in touch by phone with his prayer partners back home. During each call one of them would ask, "Have you met this group of people yet?" Michael's repeated answer: "No, not yet."

Hitching around campus on his crutches, Michael attracted friendly inquiries about what had happened. One woman he chatted with, Jennie Genske, called him later to see if they could get together for a breakfast meeting. Michael agreed, but they did not set a specific day. Meanwhile, a couple of weeks passed and one of his Malaysian prayer partners phoned again.

"Have you met this group of people?"

"No, not yet."

"Well," said the intercessor, "I have a feeling you're going to meet them very, very soon."

The two finished their conversation and Michael hung up the phone. With his hand still grasping the warm receiver, the phone rang again. It was Jennie Genske with a proposal.

"I've got some friends I think would be very interested to get to know you. We'll be free during Labor Day weekend. Do you think you could come do a day of teaching with us?"

Although Michael had yet to meet any of the others, including Jennie's husband, he agreed.

About a dozen people gathered the first weekend of September for a morning and afternoon of teaching. The mostly twenty- and thirtysomething college graduates and business people bonded in a special way as the Holy Spirit moved in their midst.

Michael returned to Malaysia shortly afterward, but by January 1991 the network of friends decided to continue meeting informally for fellowship in one another's homes. Following Michael's summer study that year, the group began to see themselves more as a new church plant. By summer 1992 the network had a definite identity, although the membership evolved a bit. Michael met his future bride while in the States, and in the fall of 1992 Cindy joined him in Malaysia for the last six months of their engagement. They married in April 1993, relocated permanently to Pasadena and launched Vision Christian Fellowship in May 1993 with about thirty members.

Ken Newton's prophecy, three and a half years after its Christmas Day reception, had largely found fulfillment. Although at the time Michael had dreamed only of building the Church in Malaysia, the Lord had led him out of that country altogether. Many who joined the new church or heard Michael speak gave their lives to Christ after an initial invitation to "come see someone who's been miraculously healed from a terrible accident." Less than a year after its founding, the Pasadena church grew to over one hundred and began initiating new fellowships.

Your life will never be the same. The Lord's word to Michael on the morning before his accident still echoes in his memory. It has proved true for himself as well as scores of others.

Miracles of Healing

Some biblical stories of healing are so dramatic, unexpected or medically unexplainable that the text calls them miracles. Jesus' second miraculous sign occurred during another visit to the village of Cana in Galilee, the same site where He turned water into wine. This second miracle took the form of a dramatic healing of a young man on his deathbed in a town several miles distant.

There was a certain royal official whose son lay sick at Capernaum. When this man heard that Jesus had arrived in Galilee from Judea, he went to him and begged him to come and heal his son, who was close to death.

"Unless you people see miraculous signs and wonders," Jesus told him, "you will never believe."

The royal official said, "Sir, come down before my child dies."

Jesus replied, "You may go. Your son will live."

The man took Jesus at his word and departed. While he was still on the way, his servants met him with the news that his boy was living. When he inquired as to the time when his son got better, they said to him, "The fever left him yesterday at the seventh hour."

Then the father realized that this was the exact time at which Jesus had said to him, "Your son will live." So he and all his household believed.

John 4:46–53

St. Augustine (354–430), bishop of the town of Hippo Regius on the north coast of Africa, devoted a chapter in his major work *The City of God* to the documentation of contemporary miracles— many of these healing miracles with which he personally was familiar. He confessed his frustration at having to limit his chapter to about twenty incidents and neglect many others in order to return to his main theme.

Actually, if I kept merely to miracles of healing and omitted all others, and if I told only those wrought by this one martyr, the glorious St. Stephen, and if I limited myself to those that happened here at Hippo and Calama, I should have to fill several volumes and, even then, I could do no more than tell those cases that have been officially recorded and attested for public reading in our churches.

Book 22, chapter 8

Near the end of this chapter Augustine concluded, "It is a simple fact, then, that there is no lack of miracles even in our day. And the God who works the miracles we read of in the Scripture uses any means and manner He chooses."

Michael Koh's miracle of healing gave him a powerful testimony that brought many to faith in Christ.

But signs and wonders had already played a significant role in his ministry. Several years earlier, toward the beginning of his church-planting work, the Lord had used Michael as an intercessor in a miracle that was perhaps even more extraordinary. That story belongs in the next chapter.

7

"Women Received Their Dead Raised to Life"

Stories of Extraordinary Miracles

Michael Koh's semi-conscious mind teetered in the fragile balance between waking and sleep. An extended time of prayer had dragged late into the night, and the friend he was praying with (a young new believer) had already drifted into dreamland.

Lying on a mat in the meeting hall of a storefront church in Kuantan, West Malaysia, Michael felt the stress of the church-planting challenge he shouldered. Born in Singapore of ethnic Chinese parents, raised on the west coast of Peninsular (West) Malaysia with six years of schooling in England, graduated from the University of Malaya with a degree in English literature, Michael, not yet 24, had already helped pioneer one new church. But Kuantan, on the east coast, presented the young church planter with particularly stony soil.

The area, heavily Muslim, embraced widespread animism and occult practices. Few evangelical churches grew to any size. In 1981

Michael's Kuantan Christian Fellowship counted only about eighteen members after approximately a year in existence.

As sleep overtook intercession for spiritual breakthrough, Michael fell into a dream state and imagined he saw his church pass before his eyes. He spotted one of the new converts, just a month old in Christ, a 42-year-old everyone called Auntie Khoo. The Chinese-speaking woman suffered chronic asthma and had almost died several times. As Michael watched, a dark, hooded figure crept toward her. Intuitively he perceived it as a spirit of death—a high-ranking demonic power.

Somehow Michael sensed that if he could defeat this evil wraith, a breakthrough would follow, bringing many people to deliverance in Christ. In his spirit he challenged the dark being and saw it turn toward him. As it approached he felt a wave of oppression wash over him, paralyzing his muscles and vocal chords.

Unable to move or cry out, Michael could only rebuke the figure spirit to spirit. Silently he declared over and over, *I rebuke you, you spirit of death, in the name of Jesus!*

Finally the menacing creature seemed to shrink back and Michael found his voice. From his semi-conscious state he shouted aloud, "I break your power, in Jesus' name!"

Immediately the specter dissolved, and both he and his friend lurched awake.

"Pastor Michael, are you all right?" his friend asked from a nearby mat. "When I was asleep a second ago, I felt so overcome with fear—I couldn't move or speak. But when I heard you call out, everything just lifted and the oppression broke."

"I was experiencing the same kind of thing," Michael responded. And he told his friend about the vision and what he sensed it meant.

One evening about a week later Michael was leading a Bible study training session for a small group of potential leaders when the church phone rang. One of Auntie Khoo's daughters (who, with her sister, had given her life to Jesus only a couple of weeks before her mother) was on the line.

"Please, could someone come take us to the hospital? Mom is having a very bad asthma attack."

One of the men left to help them while the study group prayed for Auntie Khoo, then carried on.

About 9:30 P.M. the phone rang again. The believer who had driven the women to the hospital was reporting dire news.

"Pastor Michael, it's really bad. Auntie Khoo collapsed and they put her in the intensive care unit. It looks like she may not make it."

Michael and another brother from the church dropped everything and headed out. As they sped ten or twelve minutes across town, one thought churned through Michael's mind: *I'm still new in ministry—I've never done a funeral before! God, You can't let this happen!*

Then, like a flashbulb popping, he remembered his strange dream of the week before. By the time they reached the hospital, an aggressive faith had arisen in him.

Rushing to intensive care, they found the other man from the church with Auntie Khoo's daughters, Bee Leng and Bee Lian, standing outside the unit. But the attending physician, Dr. Y., came out and blocked their way.

"Don't even think about going in there," he warned them. "She already stopped breathing ten minutes ago and now her heart has stopped, too. It's too late." He grew more agitated. "Why didn't you bring her in earlier? What were you trying to do, faith healing?"

Michael looked at the doctor, a Chinese man in his late thirties whom Michael had met after first arriving in Kuantan. A nominal Christian, he exhibited cynicism toward anything supernatural, yet tonight Michael sensed unusual anxiety and defensiveness. Much later he learned the doctor had given Auntie Khoo the wrong injection, which had hastened her death.

Dr. Y. went back into the ICU, and the believers huddled outside the door to pray. A window in the door afforded a view of medical personnel scurrying here and there. As Michael led, the group prayed every way they knew—in English and in tongues, with petitions to God and rebukes to Satan's henchmen. For the second time in a week, Michael broke the power of a spirit of death with the authority of Jesus Christ.

Almost fifteen minutes passed. Then someone gasped. Through the window in the door they saw Auntie Khoo sit bolt upright in bed and appear to say something. In a flurry of activity, hospital staff surrounded her.

Sometime later Dr. Y. stepped out into the hall, flushed but subdued. He glanced from face to face in the prayer circle.

"It's a miracle," he said finally. "For over 24 minutes she stopped breathing, with no heartbeat most of that time. Then without warning she sat up and asked for a drink of water. I don't see any asthma symptoms now. There's no explanation for it, but she seems perfectly well."

Michael and the men from his fellowship raised their voices in praise, while Bee Leng and Bee Lian hugged each other and cried.

A day later Auntie Khoo was transferred out of intensive care into the ward for observation, where Michael and her daughters visited with her. The younger women translated from Chinese for Michael, who spoke only English and Malay, while Auntie Khoo described what she experienced while her lifeless body lay in the ICU.

"I saw myself in a very beautiful place," she said, "with an incredible array of colors all over. A Man—I'm sure it was Jesus—came and spoke to me. Everywhere a bright and warm light was shining. It was so wonderful and beautiful, more than anything I've ever seen before. I didn't want to leave."

While they talked, Dr. Y. entered the ward on his rounds.

"You're a real miracle woman," he affirmed to Auntie Khoo.

Michael marveled as the doctor checked his patient. Never had he perceived such an open, positive attitude from Dr. Y.

Before he left the physician turned to him. "Say, Michael, what time is your worship service?"

Sure enough, Dr. and Mrs. Y. visited Kuantan Christian Fellowship that week. And within days the story of Auntie Khoo swept through the city and an explosion of people showed up in their meetings. An incipient Chinese-speaking group for which Michael had been training leaders grew within a few weeks to about 35.

The church entered a season of extraordinary healings and miracles. Almost every week God boggled minds through powerful answers to prayer. With so many people in that region of the east coast focused on practical needs like health, employment, financial or scholastic success, Michael saw the Lord meet people in the trenches to touch their lives where they hurt the most.

God also gave Michael a prophetic message as he interceded for Kuantan. The Lord showed him that six or eight key people in the city—a national soccer player, for instance, the biggest developer, a high-ranking Freemason, a prominent doctor and past presidents of the Rotary Club—would become believers and join Kuantan Christian Fellowship. Within about a year and a half every one of them came to faith in Jesus Christ and took on positions of leadership in the church.

From the small but faithful band Michael led at the time of Auntie Khoo's miracle, the church mushroomed to more than one hundred members over the next twelve to eighteen months, about 85% of them new converts. With trained leaders in place, Michael turned the church over to others when God called him to continue church planting elsewhere.

Michael saw a recognizable pattern emerge. Kuantan Christian Fellowship, which quickly grew past two hundred, followed the same model starting sister congregations in other cities. Before moving into full-fledged ministry, a team of intercessors prayed for many days or weeks to identify the spiritual forces of darkness ruling in a city. They lifted the people of the city to God in continuous intercession and bound the demonic spirits they discerned through the authority of Christ. When they sensed a breakthrough in the spiritual realm, the evangelism began. Through door-to-door campaigns and large rallies, nonbelievers had opportunity to witness and experience the power of God in answer to prayer for healing and practical needs. Over and over the church planters saw the Holy Spirit open many hearts to salvation within a short time.

Michael went on to plant five more churches, including his current congregation in Pasadena, California, where God moved him after his own miraculous healing (recounted in the previous chapter). Until Auntie Khoo's peaceful homegoing to her Lord in July 1995, she remained at the church in Kuantan, a living witness to the One who said, "I am the resurrection and the life. He who believes in me will live, even though he dies; and whoever lives and believes in me will never die" (John 11:25–26).

Extraordinary Miracles

Jesus made the declaration just quoted before He raised Lazarus from the dead—probably the most famous biblical story of resuscitation. The power of this kind of miracle to generate faith in Christ scarcely has equal.

The Gospel of John describes the effect of the miracle on the mourners who had come to comfort Lazarus' sisters, Mary and Martha, four days after their brother was entombed: "Many of the Jews who had come to visit Mary, and had seen what Jesus did, put their faith in him" (11:45). The testimony spread, and not long afterward the two sisters and Lazarus co-hosted a dinner in Jesus' honor.

> A large crowd of Jews found out that Jesus was there and came, not only because of him but also to see Lazarus, whom he had raised from the dead. So the chief priests made plans to kill Lazarus as well, for on account of him many of the Jews were going over to Jesus and putting their faith in him.
>
> John 12:9–11

Even in Old Testament times God raised a number of people from the dead, using such incidents to point people to the true Lord Jehovah and beyond to the promised Messiah. The writer of the book of Hebrews lists an honor roll of Old Testament characters whose faith merited commendation. In a summary of the exploits and experiences of several "who through faith conquered kingdoms, administered justice, and gained what was promised" (11:33), the writer attests that "women received back their dead, raised to life again" (verse 35).

The term *extraordinary miracles*, found in Acts 19:11, is in itself remarkable. Does it imply that some events weigh in as simply "ordinary miracles"? Dare we expect any signs and wonders to occur so commonly that people no longer perceive them as exceptionally unusual? Yes or no, all God's miracles, great and small, glorify Him and deserve our deepest thanks and praise.

Luke seems to imply, in the context of Acts 19, that extraordinary miracles can include healing or deliverance that takes place through material agents such as handkerchiefs, outside the presence of someone spiritually gifted to mediate miracles:

> God did extraordinary miracles through Paul, so that even handkerchiefs and aprons that had touched him were taken to the sick, and their illnesses were cured and the evil spirits left them.
>
> verses 11–12

C. Peter Wagner writes in his book *Blazing the Way* (Regal, 1995) of a story he heard from William Kumuyi, pastor of the Deeper Life Bible Church in Lagos, Nigeria, and head of a large African church-planting movement. In November 1993 Kumuyi spoke at Fuller Seminary's annual Church Growth Lectures. Here is his story from Nigeria, as Wagner tells it:

> Part of the usual weekly program in all of the 4,500 Deeper Life Bible Churches is a Thursday-night miracle meeting. On one of those nights, the pastor of an outlying church felt led to invite all those who had sick people at home to hold up their handkerchiefs, and he prayed a blessing of God's healing power upon them. They were to return home, place the handkerchief on the sick person and pray for healing in Jesus' name. He was unaware that the chief of a nearby Muslim village was visiting his church that night—the first time he had ever attended a Christian service. Although the Muslim did not have sick people in his home, he also held up his handkerchief and received the blessing.
>
> Soon after the chief had returned to his village, a nine-year-old girl died and he went to her home to attend the wake just before the burial. While there, he suddenly remembered the handkerchief, retrieved it, placed it on the corpse and prayed that she would be healed in Jesus' name. Then God did an obviously

"unusual" miracle and raised the girl from the dead! The chief called an immediate ad hoc meeting with the village elders who had witnessed what had happened, then turned around and declared to his people: "For many years we have been serving Mohammed; but from this moment on our village will be a village of Jesus!" Needless to say, a Deeper Life Bible Church is now thriving in the village.

page 166

Does this sort of thing seem superstitious? Some people who accept the use of anointing oil in prayer for healing may draw the line at holy water, prayer cloths, salt or other agents sometimes employed to administer the blessing of God. Yet each of these items has a scriptural precedent. Could other items, by extension, serve the same purpose, should God so will? I heard one woman, a prophetically gifted international speaker, describe what happened a few years ago on a particularly anointed ministry trip when a woman she was chatting with admired her earrings. Impulsively the speaker took them off and gave them to her friend. Moved by this generosity, the woman put on the speaker's earrings and immediately fell over under the power of the Holy Spirit.

Even some of the most broad-minded believers squirm at stories from the pre-Reformation days of Christianity, when relics such as bones of martyrs were credited with a role in various healings and miracles. Without question, some fraud and abuses took place when relic-sellers, motivated by greed and profit, took advantage of an atmosphere of superstition. But should we write off all such reports?

Incredibly, this kind of story has biblical precedent, too. A single verse tells what happened one spring during a Moabite raid on Israel:

> Once while some Israelites were burying a man, suddenly they saw a band of raiders; so they threw the man's body into Elisha's tomb. When the body touched Elisha's bones, the man came to life and stood up on his feet.
>
> 2 Kings 13:21

On the issue of material agents used in signs and wonders, perhaps all believers would agree on one truth: The power to heal, deliver or perform miracles does not rest in the medium itself, any more than it rests in the human minister. This kind of power belongs to God alone, and flows from Him whenever and through whatever means He chooses.

"It's Very Wonderful to Die!"

In chapter 3 we met Virgo Handojo, the young Indonesian delivered from demonic bondage through a prophetic word of knowledge, who later led a teenage girl to Christ after receiving a prophetic message about the Javanese daggers in her home. After his conversion in March 1979, Virgo, the oldest of eight children, began to pray for his family—parents, two brothers and five sisters. As ethnic Chinese Indonesians, Virgo's family observed Buddhist customs, burning incense and presenting food to ancestral spirits. They also mixed in Javanese animistic beliefs. His parents opened their home to groups that practiced spirit-channeling and Ouija séances.

When Virgo gave his life to Christ, a realization hit him: *I know now that if I die, I will go to heaven to be with the Lord. But what about my family?*

His parents allowed him to use their home for Bible study meetings but stood back from any involvement themselves.

"You know," he told his mother, "when I joined the Kundalini black magic group, I never asked you to join with me. But this is different. Now I have a relationship with Jesus Christ that I want you to have, too. Jesus gives us the only way to heaven after we die."

But his mother brushed aside his appeal.

One day Virgo returned home while a Bible study was in progress and noticed a verse someone had written in felt pen on a white board: "Believe in the Lord Jesus, and you will be saved—you and your household" (Acts 16:31). The words came alive in his spirit, along with a strong assurance that his family members would put their faith in Christ.

Virgo continued to pray and fast for them. Then one day while he was out of town, the Lord answered his prayer in a remarkable way.

* * * * *

The warm, humid air of tropical Indonesia wafted through the family home in Semarang, central Java. Sri Wahyuni felt troubled. On this early morning in June 1979, her oldest son, Virgo Handojo, had already set out for Salatiga to enroll at the university there, an all-day process. Her second son lived and studied at a university in Jakarta, while her husband, Andi Santoso, and her six other children—a third son and five daughters—had not yet left the house for the day.

As Sri cleaned up the kitchen, her daughter Tina approached her. For weeks Tina, going on eighteen, had suffered excruciating headaches.

"Mommy, my head is hurting again," she confessed.

Sri looked at her daughter with sad eyes. "Tina, let me tell you what I planned to do this morning."

When the family faced an unresolvable problem, one of the parents often went to a witchcraft practitioner who consulted spirit beings for guidance—advising clients, for instance, what combination of herbal medicine would bring the desired result. Tina's father had already made one attempt to confer with the shaman, but after he got his motorcycle out, a sudden downpour of heavy rain had prevented him from leaving. This morning Sri planned to go herself.

"I know Virgo would be against it," she told her daughter, "so I didn't tell him. But I'm concerned about you, Tina. I don't want to see you suffer."

Sri began to cry, and went to lie down on her bed while Tina followed and continued to talk with her. About 8 A.M. Sri, without warning, fell unconscious. In alarm Tina shook her mother but got no response. Then, terrified, she ran for her father.

"Daddy, come quick! Mommy's collapsed!"

Andi dashed into the bedroom and tried to wake his wife, to no avail. Soon the other sisters and the third brother, Boen, gathered around the bed, fighting panic.

"Quick, call the doctor!" Andi cried to his son.

With no 911 instant telephone emergency service—indeed, no phone at all—Boen rushed off first to get an uncle who lived nearby (following the Indonesian pattern of family precedence). As Sri's brother and closest blood relative, he could then take her to the hospital.

Meanwhile Sri lay lifeless while terror and trauma swirled around her. In a few minutes Boen returned to the house with his uncle.

Suddenly a voice came from Sri's body. The family saw her lips move but heard a dignified man's voice, as if they were witnessing some surreal ventriloquist act. Andi, the children and their uncle knelt around the bed, stupefied, and listened as the authoritative male speaker carried on a conversation with Sri in her own voice—two voices from one body.

"It's time for you to get right with God," boomed the male voice. "You need to go to church and believe on the Lord Jesus Christ."

Sri's voice answered, "What do we have to do?"

"You all need to go to church and give your hearts to Christ, to live lives pleasing to Him," came the authoritative response.

Great wails arose as the family cried out, confessing their sins and pledging to turn to Jesus as Savior. "Please, God, we will go to church and follow You. Just let us have our mother back."

As the conversation in Sri's body continued, God affirmed His love for the family and reassured them that their small acts of kindness had not gone unnoticed.

"You have a good wife, very dedicated and selfless," the voice said at one point. "She never complained when your neighbor built a wall so close to your house that the air could hardly come in your windows. I remember these things."

Some time later Sri opened her eyes and sat up. In her own voice, but with a dreamy, otherworldly tone, she said to her husband,

"I've just met with the Lord. I have to go back to Him. Please take good care of the children."

She hugged her brother, her husband and each child in turn, then collapsed again on the bed, out cold.

Once more the family raised loud cries of lamentation, pleading for God in His mercy to forgive their sins and bring back their mother.

Finally, about 2 P.M., Sri Wahyuni awoke as though reviving from a coma. With another round of cries and hugs, Sri drew her family close and composed herself enough to recount her adventures.

"This sounds incredible, I know, but I really believe I met with God," she began. "He came and took me to heaven, and I saw Jesus standing in a green robe with a big cross. I've never felt the kind of happiness I felt at that moment—no sickness, no confusion, everything so clear and free and joyful. Honestly," she continued, "it's very wonderful to die!"

Her family gaped in astonishment as Sri went on.

"Jesus and I had a long conversation. Eventually I said, 'Lord, I would like to stay here with You, but I'm only 44 and I have children to raise. Little Liana is not quite nine years old. Would You allow me to go back to the world and raise my children, and then I'll come back here with You?' Jesus told me, 'All right. If you return to the world, will you promise to deny yourself and bear your cross and follow Me?' I said, 'O.K., Lord, I promise.'

"And then," said Sri, finishing her story, "I saw Jesus pass by with the cross, and felt myself coming down like into a basket. The next thing I knew I was back here on the bed alive in my body."

A jumble of voices filled the air as the family wept, prayed and gave gratitude to God.

When Virgo returned home about five in the afternoon, his family members were sitting talking around his mother's bed, their eyes red and swollen.

"What's happened?" he blurted, glancing from one to another.

"Mommy almost died today!" Tina told him. "And the Lord Jesus came! We have to go to church!"

"Yes, I met Jesus in heaven," his mother explained, repeating her story.

His father and brother each told their versions as well.

When Virgo heard what Jesus had said to his mother, he exclaimed, "Why, those words come straight out of the Bible! 'Deny yourself, take up your cross and follow Me.' You've never read the Bible. How could you know—"

Wonder settled over Virgo and the others as they recognized another evidence of the miraculous hand of God.

Virgo's family did go to church with him and every one of them became a Christian. His brother in Jakarta heard the story, too, although he came to Christ through a different circumstance. Tina's headaches, stress-related, dissipated after she completed important school exams.

Now Sri Wahyuni testifies that since that day, her outlook has changed completely and she has never feared dying. When she promised to deny her own self-sufficiency, take up her cross and follow Christ, she received full assurance that when her earthly body finally quits for good, she will find herself in the glorious presence of her Lord.

Prayer and Bodily Miracles

As Virgo Handojo has pondered why God intervened supernaturally in his and his family's lives, he traces a spiritual thread back to his grandfather who, for 25 or 30 years, prayed daily for his family. Virgo recalls from childhood that the older man always seemed to want to pray. At meals, at bedtime, at every activity, his grandfather urged, "Family, let's pray. Come pray." His faithful intercession, Virgo believes, played a major role in how the Holy Spirit broke through in mighty ways to bring each one of his family members into the Kingdom of God.

Prayer also figured prominently in the miracle of Pentecost, when the early Church was born. After Jesus' ascension the disciples met in an upper room in Jerusalem. "They all joined together constantly in prayer . . . " (Acts 1:14). For ten days they raised concerted, united and continual prayer until the Day of Pentecost. Only then did the Holy Spirit descend in power, filling each of them and drawing three thousand to believe in the Gospel, receive baptism and join in fellowship with the disciples.

Sri Wahyuni's conversion experience can be classified without doubt as extraordinary. Yet the Bible tells about someone who had not simply an out-of-body experience but a miracle of supernatural transportation, in which his body suddenly moved from one region to another. We already reviewed the story of the apostle Philip, one of the first cross-cultural missionaries, who preached to the Ethiopian eunuch on the road to Gaza and baptized him after he declared his faith. Then,

> When they came up out of the water, the Spirit of the Lord suddenly took Philip away, and the eunuch did not see him again, but went on his way rejoicing. Philip, however, appeared at Azotus [Ashdod] and traveled about, preaching the gospel in all the towns until he reached Caesarea.
>
> Acts 8:39–40

What happened to Philip's body when "the Spirit of the Lord suddenly took [him] away"? The Bible does not explain. But Philip found himself twenty or thirty miles distant in a town near the coast, where he began sharing the Gospel again. Presumably the Lord needed him there at that moment for the sake of those ready to receive the message of Christ.

Gravity and other laws of nature seem immutable to the modern scientific mind, overcome only by higher natural laws—the way the laws of aerodynamics governing a jet engine temporarily supersede the force of gravity pulling that plane toward earth. Yet above all the natural laws of the universe stands the Creator of those laws. Although He generally chooses to operate according to the principles He established to govern the world, God has not stepped back passively from His creation and forsworn further involvement. The Lord, still sovereign over all He has made, can at any time set aside the laws of nature when doing so serves His higher purposes.

Nor do mechanical failures stand in God's way, as the next story illustrates.

The Healing of the Windmill

The windmill was on the fritz again.

How many times has that thing broken down? wondered Randy Nelson.

Randy and his wife, Edie, had been serving as missionaries to the nomadic Turkana for more than nine years, following the Holy Spirit-inspired dream of Nangodia, the former diviner, about a foreigner bringing a message from God (which we read about in chapter 4).

In this barren desert region in northwestern Kenya, water was liquid gold. The windmill, about two hundred yards from the Nelsons' home at the little settlement of Lorengalup, usually pumped about 625 gallons of groundwater per day, enough for almost a hundred people plus two or three herds of goats or camels. Now, in the early fall of 1989, the flow had petered out once again.

A few days before, the Turkana women who hauled water to their huts every day in plastic jerry cans atop their heads had noticed the water level dropping in the covered cement tank next to the windmill. Water normally flowed up from the 125-foot pump shaft through a length of two-inch galvanized pipe into the storage tank. But when Randy took the lid off the tank, he saw just a trickle dribbling from the pipe. Before he could figure out what was wrong, the water stopped completely.

Randy radioed a missionary colleague, Bob Chapman, to come help replace the suction cup gaskets inside the pump, a procedure they had performed several times before. Bob, a medical doctor, lived with his wife about four hours away. Getting at the cylindrical pump required pulling up the pump drive rod, using pipe wrenches to unscrew each of its six twenty-foot lengths of pipe one at a time.

But replacement cup gaskets failed to solve the problem: Still no water bubbled out. Randy and Bob hoisted up the drive rod again and discovered some wear on the inner working part of the pump. Time to call in extra help and equipment.

With the water in the tank dwindling alarmingly, Randy radioed Mike Harries, the Kenyan contractor who had built the windmill in early 1980 with partial funding from World Vision. The radio crackled as he made connections with Mike's home in Thika, a city outside Nairobi, 460 miles south by road.

"Mike, I need your help," Randy pleaded.

Mike agreed to come. A bush pilot, he flew to Lorengalup in his small plane with a mechanic and a large hand-driven winch, landing on a dry lakebed about half a mile from the Nelsons.

The four men used the winch to pull up the heavy pipe casing that enclosed the drive rod and through which water traveled to the surface. The brass pump housing attached to the end of the casing appeared in good order. But when they fit the pump, with its new suction cups, inside the casing, they discovered the problem.

"Good grief, look at this," Mike said, holding up the pieces. "The drive unit has worn down the inside of the casing—probably through sand action. You can see daylight between the suction cups and the pipe casing."

Everyone took a look. Sure enough, about a quarter inch of space between the gaskets and the casing gapped open.

"No wonder the windmill went dry," continued Mike. "The pump couldn't get any kind of seal. Even with oversized gaskets it's not going to work. The whole pump will have to be replaced."

Randy and the others discussed options. Mike agreed to fly home and send a new pump from Thika. To preserve the working parts of the underground system of the windmill, the men put everything back together, broken pump and all, so it would be in order when Randy and Bob installed the new pump by themselves later on. Bob then drove to Nairobi, where he needed to meet and accompany a heart patient being airlifted to the United States for specialized medical attention.

For two days the windmill ran dry. But after Mike got home to Thika, he radioed Randy back with bad news: "I can't locate the pump you need here."

Randy and Edie decided to drive to Nairobi and see what they could find in the capital city. Only a day or two's supply of water remained in the tank. When that ran out, the Turkana women would have to hike six miles to fill their jerry cans at the nearest hand-dug waterhole in the dry bed of the Turkwel River.

Before leaving, Randy climbed the thirty-foot-tall metal support frame of the windmill to shut down the fiberglass blades, because more damage could result from letting the mechanism continue to pump dry. He folded the tail of the windmill to lock the blades and prevent them from spinning, securing them with an attached metal chain.

Then the Nelsons loaded up their four-wheel-drive Jeep Cherokee with supplies for the journey, as well as their two sons—Robbie, about two months shy of his eighth birthday, and five-year-old David. As they pulled away from the Lorengalup settlement, they waved good-bye to Nangodia and a few of the forty-some members of his extended family outside their cluster of palm-leaf huts.

"It's hard to believe we've been in Turkana almost ten years," Edie commented to her husband as the dust kicked up behind their Jeep.

Since the first fourteen baptisms of Nangodia and his immediate family in December 1979, a few hundred Turkana in that area had come to know Jesus as Savior, most of them through Nangodia's testimony. The fellowship groups continued to grow in numbers as well as spiritual maturity. The previous spring in 1989, Charles Kraft, professor at Fuller Seminary's School of World Mission, had come to Nairobi to teach a seminar for missionaries and local leaders on prayer for divine healing. Randy and Edie had followed up by training the Turkana believers in how to pray for the sick and injured according to a biblical model.

When the Nelsons arrived in Nairobi, Randy scouted everywhere, without success, for a new windmill pump. He finally called Bob Chapman in the U.S. and commissioned him to locate and bring back a pump about a week and a half later when the doctor finished obtaining treatment for the patient in his care. Then, without the new pump, the Nelsons made the long journey back to Lorengalup.

In the distance across the barren desert, the family could spot the shining white of the blades atop the windmill and knew they were approaching home—a welcome sight after ten days away. When they got closer, however, what Randy saw disturbed him.

The tail of the windmill spread out fully unfolded and the blades spun like a pinwheel in the breeze.

"Some kids must have fiddled with the chain shutting the blades," Randy fretted. "I hope there isn't more damage to the works."

"That surprises me," Edie said. "You know you're about the only one willing to climb the support tower."

As they pulled up to their home, a young Turkana man named Ikadukan came running over to the Jeep. He greeted the family warmly, then gushed the news: "The windmill—it's pumping water again!"

The Nelsons stared at their good friend with honest skepticism.

"A couple of days after you left," he went on, "about a dozen women decided to pray for the windmill, just as you've been teaching us to pray for the sick. They figured if God can heal bodies, why not a broken windmill?"

Randy and Edie listened with growing awe as Ikadukan recounted the story.

The Turkana women, led by Ata Ekal, a tall, older woman and a strong Christian, had surrounded the windmill structure and, following their biblical training, laid their hands on it as they prayed for its repair. After an intense season of intercession, including many songs of worship, they sat down in the shade of a hut about forty yards away to rest before more prayer.

Within two hours a sudden, strong wind arose (called, ironically, a "dust devil"). Not unusual in the Turkana region, a large, localized dust devil might gust up a couple of times a week somewhere in the area. But this one spun out of nowhere and struck the windmill squarely. Somehow the metal chain broke, the tail unfolded into the wind and the blades began to twirl with abandon. Someone went to check the water storage tank and discovered fresh water now pouring out of the pipe. The women rejoiced and praised God for His dramatic answer to their prayers of faith.

After the Nelsons unloaded their Jeep, Randy went to the windmill to see for himself. Perplexed at how a broken pump that did not seal could possibly pull water out of the ground, Randy conceded that there might be some mechanical explanation beyond his knowledge. But the sudden wind, directed straight at the wind-mill—strategically timed right after the women's unusual prayer—strong enough to break a metal chain? And all of that just to free the blades to operate a broken pump? Randy shook his head.

He shook it again after he saw the water flowing into the tank and climbed the tower to inspect the broken chain.

The windmill continued pumping water over the next few days, gradually tapering off in volume. Just about the time Bob Chapman arrived with the new pump around a week later, the flow stopped. The two of them then worked a full day to complete the installation, using the winch left by Mike Harries.

The story of the miraculous functioning of the windmill got incorporated into the testimonies of the Turkana believers, and as a result more Turkana came to trust in this powerful, loving God who answers prayer for personal needs. The incident deepened Ata Ekal's faith and she became one of the main evangelists of the Turkana church. Today the region hosts well over a thousand nomadic Turkana believers, most of whom have heard how the God who rules the universe has no trouble healing a windmill.

Multiplying Matter and Suspending Gravity

One spring day at the Sea of Galilee, Jesus performed two extra-ordinary miracles, the first in the afternoon and the second overnight. Both defied natural explanation and both drew people to confess faith in Christ.

The story of the five loaves and two fish that fed five thousand men, besides women and children, is recorded in all four Gospel accounts. Jesus, out of compassion for the hungry throng crowd-ing around Him late in the day and far from village vendors, asked His disciples to find food for them all. Andrew located just one boy "with five small barley loaves and two small fish, but how far will they go among so many?" (John 6:9).

After Jesus had the crowd sit down in orderly groups on the grass,

[He] then took the loaves, gave thanks, and distributed to those who were seated as much as they wanted. He did the same with the fish.

When they had all had enough to eat, he said to his disciples, "Gather the pieces that are left over. Let nothing be wasted." So they gathered them and filled twelve baskets with the pieces of the five barley loaves left over by those who had eaten.

After the people saw the miraculous sign that Jesus did, they began to say, "Surely this is the Prophet who is to come into the world."

verses 11–14

Right after the meal, Jesus sent His disciples across the lake in a boat, while He stayed to dismiss the crowd and pray alone in the hills. For several hours after dark the disciples, many of them experienced fishermen, strained at the oars and fought a headwind to pull three or three and a half miles from shore. Matthew's version tells the story this way:

During the fourth watch of the night [3 A.M. to dawn] Jesus went out to them, walking on the lake. When the disciples saw him walking on the lake, they were terrified. "It's a ghost," they said, and cried out in fear.

But Jesus immediately said to them: "Take courage! It is I. Don't be afraid."

"Lord, if it's you," Peter replied, "tell me to come to you on the water."

"Come," he said.

Then Peter got down out of the boat, walked on the water and came toward Jesus. But when he saw the wind, he was afraid and, beginning to sink, cried out, "Lord, save me!"

Immediately Jesus reached out his hand and caught him. "You of little faith," he said, "why did you doubt?"

And when they climbed into the boat, the wind died down. Then those who were in the boat worshiped him, saying, "Truly you are the Son of God."

Matthew 14:25–33

The first incident suggests that the hungry crowd enjoyed the miracle as passive beneficiaries. Even the disciples could not muster faith that the boy's meager lunch would stretch far. Yet the Lord sovereignly worked a wonder in multiplying natural matter.

The second incident shows Jesus suspending the laws of gravity, and when brash Peter stuck his neck out, he walked on water, too. But here Peter's faith evidently determined whether he sank or stayed afloat.

Whether a miracle comes at the initiative of God or as an outgrowth of our faith, both incidents illustrate the only appropriate response—an attitude of humble worship that proclaims, "Truly You are the Son of God!"

Up the River without a Coffin

A great wail arose from the little bamboo home on stilts over the damp Mekong River floodplain. As Jun Mon lifted her voice in anguish, neighbors from the other one-room homes nearby began to cluster at her door. The sound of her cry told them all they needed to know: Her husband, Khev Choen, was dead.

For three years Khev Choen had grown steadily sicker. The neighbors in this slum district outside Phnom Penh, Cambodia, had seen how crushing fatigue and weight loss sapped more and more of Khev's strength. About a year earlier he had become virtually bedridden, and for the past couple of months he had lain in his home completely paralyzed. Two or three days ago, Jun Mon knew the end was near when his skeletal body—about forty years old but looking more like seventy—slipped into unconsciousness.

And about 6 P.M. on this late November day in 1993, Jun Mon saw Khev stop breathing once and for all. Herbal medicine and a witch doctor's advice—all she could afford—had done nothing to help her husband.

Choked with grief, Jun Mon let her tears flow as the neighbors tried to comfort the widow and her children. Just two weeks before, a ray of hope had entered her life when a small group from a Christian house church came through her neighborhood. Jun Mon remembered the day they saw her sitting outside her tumbledown home, the picture of despair.

"What's the matter?" they had asked.

"My husband is very sick," she brooded. "He's going to die soon."

A young woman named Theavy Ser led the group in praying for Jun Mon. They shared the Gospel with her, and she eagerly embraced the hope of eternal life through Jesus Christ. Jun Mon's sister also turned to the Lord through their witness. The Bible they gave her fed deep longings.

But now death had come for Khev Choen.

As word spread through the neighborhood, a Buddhist priest arrived about eight in the evening with two of his monks. Intimately familiar with the harsh realities of death in the slums, the priest checked the body carefully to determine that all signs of life had fled. He performed the usual ritual, then turned to the widow.

"So very sorry," he murmured, eyes averted. "Tomorrow morning we will return to prepare for the cremation. We'll have to take some of your wooden floor boards to make a coffin, a box for the cremation."

Jun Mon sighed. Already the floor and roof of her home suffered yawning gaps.

After the Buddhists left, neighbors continued to come and sit with Jun Mon. Theavy Ser showed up to offer comfort as well.

As time passed, the group began to thin. Theavy felt prompted to pray with Jun Mon and her sister. Theavy pointed out passages in the Bible proclaiming Christ's victory and power over death and the grave. Jun Mon sensed faith beginning to stir.

About midnight Theavy left for home. Jun Mon's sister agreed to stay with her through the night.

In the stillness Jun Mon read the Bible by candlelight, drinking in the scenes of Jesus' miraculous signs. Kneeling near her husband's stiffening body, she held her Bible before her in both hands and began to pray.

"Lord Jesus, my hope is in You now. Outside of You I have no hope—my husband is dead. But if You can heal my husband, I will serve You the rest of my life. I will do whatever You ask me to do."

For three hours Jun Mon, joined by her sister, wept and pleaded with God in prayer.

Suddenly, about three in the morning, Khev Choen sat bolt upright shouting, "I'm alive! I'm alive!"

Terror hit the women, despite their faith.

Khev stood up on legs that had not held his weight in months and patted his body. "Yes, I'm here! I'm alive! My stomach—oh, I'm so hungry!"

"Khev!" Jun Mon cried, overcome with joy and wonder. "Of course you're hungry—you haven't eaten since you fell into a coma a few days ago."

She nearly danced to the kitchen area where she ladled out a bowl of rice soup from a big kettle. Her husband gulped down two bowlfuls. When he finished, he set the bowl aside.

"Am I ever glad to be here," he said. "You won't believe what happened to me."

Khev's wife and sister-in-law huddled close as he told his story.

Some time before—evidently when Jun Mon noticed he had stopped breathing—Khev Choen became aware of two men dressed in black approaching his bed. They escorted him out of the house, and the three began to walk down the road. Darkness hovered all around, although Khev could make out a procession carrying a coffin and marching toward a wide river.

They reached the riverbank, and Khev watched as the marchers dumped the coffin into the water. An unseen force drew the coffin across to the far shore, and then a kind of lift pulled the coffin up onto the bank.

From his side of the river Khev could see an imposing man on the other bank sitting at a table with two enormous books. Khev did not remember the man giving an explanation, but somehow he understood. One book contained the names of people who had already died. In the other, the man turned to a blank page and picked up something like a giant hot iron. When he pressed the iron across the page of the book, there appeared the names of people about to die.

As Khev watched from his side of the river, he heard a deep voice boom toward him like a mountain echo. "Choen, why are you here?"

Khev answered, "Well, I—I'm dead."

"Where's your coffin?" the booming voice asked.

"I don't have any coffin."

"You don't have a coffin? Well, then, go back home."

Slowly Khev turned away, and realized his two escorts in black had disappeared. He followed the road back toward home, and his steps and spirit lightened as he went.

Hey, I'm free! he thought. *I've got another chance!*

Just then he came to a fork in the road and stopped. One path was shrouded in darkness, the other bathed in brilliant light. As Khev studied them, he heard a gaggle of voices muttering softly behind him: "Which way is he going to . . . ? Wait, let's see. . . . Will he choose the dark or the light? Which one?"

Well, if I'm really free now, Khev figured, *I'm not going to choose the dark. I choose light.*

He took one step into the path of light, when suddenly he heard a door slam behind him.

"That bang was the last thing I remember before I sat up and found myself back here," he told the women.

Jun Mon shook her head with astonishment. Just having her husband alive and well stretched her brain as much as she could handle. Then she could contain herself no longer. Without thought for the time, she ran outside and began knocking on doors. "My husband is alive! Hallelujah!"

Her close friend and neighbor came out, groggy with sleep. "Alive? Alive!"

The two began jumping with excitement, and she joined Jun Mon in shouting, "Hallelujah!"

A few other neighbors stirred and began gathering at Khev Choen's house to see for themselves. Around six o'clock, as the rest of the neighborhood started to wake, Khev decided to get some fresh air for the first time in about a year. As he walked down the road, he saw gaping mouths and glassy-eyed faces. He heard doors slam and people calling to family members, "Khev Choen's ghost is haunting us!"

Later that morning Theavy Ser and some church members visited the Choen home to offer help to Jun Mon. When they saw Khev alive, their praises rocked the neighborhood.

"This is the resurrection power of God!" Theavy exclaimed.

She and the others shared with Khev the identity of Jesus Christ as Savior, Lord, Judge and King. He knew immediately that Jesus had restored his life, and committed himself to Him.

·

Not surprisingly, the little home fellowship Theavy Ser had planted began to mushroom. Within a few months the cell group grew from four to 32, packing out the home where it met. In May 1994 Mony Mok, a Cambodian pastor from Long Beach, California, visited the area and videotaped Khev Choen's testimony. With a modest love gift that Mony had brought from the United States, local believers began to build a new home for Khev and his wife. It soon became the gathering place for another house church.

Khev Choen, now strong and healthy, lives each day as a walking testimony to the grace and power of God.

Lifting Up the Name of the Lord

God can perform extraordinary miracles of resuscitating dead nonbelievers to bring them, and probably others, to salvation in Christ. He can also raise up dead or dying believers for the purpose of causing those who see or hear of their powerful testimony to devote their lives to the Lord.

The story of Jesus raising the son of the widow in Nain illustrates both the compassion of the Lord, which motivates His supernatural intervention in human lives, and the proper response of awe and praise:

> Jesus went to a town called Nain, and his disciples and a large crowd went along with him. As he approached the town gate, a dead person was being carried out—the only son of his mother, and she was a widow. And a large crowd from the town was with her. When the Lord saw her, his heart went out to her and he said, "Don't cry."
>
> Then he went up and touched the coffin, and those carrying it stood still. He said, "Young man, I say to you, get up!" The dead man sat up and began to talk, and Jesus gave him back to his mother.
>
> They were all filled with awe and praised God. "A great prophet has appeared among us," they said. "God has come to help his people." This news about Jesus spread throughout Judea and the surrounding country.
>
> Luke 7:11–17

Not many years later, Peter's resuscitation of Dorcas (called Tabitha) generated a testimony that electrified a whole city, bringing people to faith in Christ. After being summoned by Tabitha's mourners,

> Peter sent them all out of the room; then he got down on his knees and prayed. Turning toward the dead woman, he said, "Tabitha, get up." She opened her eyes, and seeing Peter she sat up. He took her by the hand and helped her to her feet. Then he called the believers and the widows and presented her to them alive. This became known all over Joppa, and many people believed in the Lord.
>
> Acts 9:40–42

Sometimes modern-day tales of extraordinary miracles, including suspension of the laws of time and space, can be difficult to swallow, especially if they seem pointless in the eternal scheme of things. But God may want us to take part in bringing about the point He has in mind. When we unabashedly recount some amazing thing the Lord has done, crediting Him alone with all the glory, one of our listeners may be moved by the Holy Spirit to seek out this omnipotent God and make Him Lord and King.

"Everything God does has a purpose," says Pastor Mony Mok, reflecting on Khev Choen's story. "Every miracle needs to return praise and honor to Him. He doesn't do signs and wonders for no reason, but for the praise of His glory. When these things happen, our job is to lift up His name."

8

"We Wrestle Not against Flesh and Blood"

Stories of Spiritual Warfare

"O.K., let's roll!"

With all luggage and bodies stowed, the busload of high school students and their adult counselors pulled out and headed for the autobahn. Their two-day bus ride from Heidelberg, Germany, would lay over in Budapest, Hungary, before reaching its destination: Turda, Romania, a town of about ten thousand people just south of Cluj.

Don Creasman sat back and took a deep breath. Friday, April 3, 1992—at last they were on their way for the nine-day trip. The 35-year-old father of three served as director of Heidelberg's "Club Beyond," working with Military Community Youth Ministries, a branch of Youth for Christ and Young Life. The Club ministered to teenage sons and daughters of the overseas U.S. military community in Heidelberg. Their group would join others from Germany, Italy and Spain—a total of 190 high-schoolers and fifty adults converging on a boys' orphanage in Turda for "Project Romania '92."

As an outreach ministry, Club Beyond and its partners touched the lives of many teens who did not yet know Christ. Don figured probably half the kids on this trip came from non-Christian family backgrounds. He said another silent prayer that the young people would benefit as much from this service project as the orphanage, where they planned to help with remodeling, plumbing and a daily children's Bible program.

Miles of countryside and cityscape scrolled by on each side as the bus rumbled east. As Don covered a yawn, he heard snatches of conversation from the seat behind him.

". . . tarot cards. . . ."

He twisted sideways enough to see seventeen-year-old Brian laying out cards and telling the fortunes of a couple of other kids. He watched for a moment as Brian, through thick glasses, studied the cards he had turned up and interpreted their meaning for his listeners. Then Don faced forward again.

Major trouble, he stewed. *How do I gently put a stop to this?*

Don liked the softspoken, articulate high school junior and sensed that Brian liked him. But he often wondered what attracted the teenager to Club Beyond. Brian's home life lacked any Christian influence, and he had told Don once, "I don't see why the Bible should be revered more than any other book." Yet the Club seemed to scratch an itch of some kind: Brian had signed up early for the Romania trip and paid in advance.

At the next rest stop, about twenty minutes down the road, Don drew Brian aside in the crisp spring air before they reboarded the bus.

"Brian, I noticed you telling some fortunes with tarot cards back there," he began. "Is that something you're into?"

"Yeah, I play around with it," Brian answered, shifting his six-foot-two frame. "I've got a fair amount of occult and New Age stuff at home. It's pretty cool, the power you can tap into."

Don swallowed. "Well, Brian, you know this trip is sponsored by a Christian group. I'd appreciate it if you would put the cards away for the rest of the time."

"Aw, if you say so." Brian ran a hand through his blond hair. "You know, I'm not even sure why I came on this trip, really."

"I think I know why," said Don. "I think God's after you!"

In response Brian only rolled his eyes.

When the group arrived in Turda on Saturday, temporary chaos reigned as 240 teenagers and adults began staking out sleeping quarters in the public school adjacent to the orphanage. Chairs and desks were moved into the hallways while army cots were lined up in the classrooms. About eighteen guys, including Brian and Don, shared a room.

Framing the participants' daily work at the orphanage were morning meetings and evening praise services at the Romanian Baptist church nearby. Through the worship and sharing times, sponsors hoped that teens not yet part of the family of God would catch the bigger picture of Christ's love and self-sacrifice.

On Tuesday night the praise service took an unexpected turn. With about one hundred Romanians looking on from the balcony, the 240 guests enjoyed energetic and enthusiastic worship in song. Then the leader of the meeting asked the young people, "Would anyone like to share about what's been going on with you?"

One after another, teens stood to praise God for His work in their lives. The Spirit of God began moving. Powerful emotions crested and some kids broke into tears, while all over the room prayer arose spontaneously.

The planned message that evening never materialized, but the Lord spoke to many hearts. Don later learned that the Romanian church members had arrived two hours beforehand to pray for the service.

During "cabin time" that night in their makeshift classroom dormitory, Don's group talked about what had happened. One of the guys announced that he had just committed his life to Christ. But when Brian's turn came, he shared—as he had the night before—about the energy of the life force and auras and expanded consciousness. Don's muscles tensed as he felt confusion creep into the room like a cockroach under cover of darkness.

O Lord, protect the fragile new faith of these kids! he prayed silently.

The next night the Holy Spirit touched more lives. During cabin sharing, a new believer told the rest of Don's young charges that at the evening praise service he had led one of his smoking buddies to Christ. The atmosphere in the group sparked with excitement—until Brian spoke.

"I had an out-of-body experience during the service tonight," he said. "Through astral projection I saw myself drawn to a brilliant light that radiated power. I think it was a Christ manifestation."

After lights-out, Don lay on his cot wrestling with surges of anger. Despite his fondness for Brian, this New Age talk infuriated him. He could see it undermining the work of the Holy Spirit in the other kids' lives. Then, in a flash, Don realized he was not dealing with simple interpersonal conflict. This was spiritual warfare!

At 7:30 the next morning, Don snagged two other staff men in the school hallway outside their sleeping quarters.

"I want you guys to agree with me in prayer," he said, explaining the situation about Brian. Then the three of them huddled in the hall, their arms about one another's shoulders, while Don led in prayer using 2 Corinthians 10:3–5.

"Lord, we know we're not fighting a human enemy here. In the name of Jesus we take up our spiritual authority to bind the spirits of darkness in Brian and demolish the strongholds over his mind. We cast down every argument and pretension that sets itself up against the knowledge of God, and in Jesus' name we command every thought of Brian's to become obedient to Christ. Lord Jesus, we claim him for You through Your blood shed on the cross."

A sense of peace and confidence washed over Don. And he noticed two extraordinary developments: That very day Brian stopped any further mention of New Age concepts. And later that day Brian came to him and expressed interest in learning more about Jesus.

On Friday night some members of the group went out to a restaurant before the final evening service. As they neared the end of the meal, Don saw his young friend Brian enter the restaurant and sidle over to his table.

"Don, can you take a walk with me?" he asked.

The two headed out into the night, their jackets buttoned against the brisk air. Brian said little as they walked five minutes to a knoll overlooking the city to the north. For a moment they gazed in silence.

"Don, I wanted you to be the first to know," Brian declared. "I stood right here ten minutes ago and gave my life to Jesus Christ."

Joy flowed between them as they joined the jubilee of the angels in heaven.

The closing praise service that night became a victory celebration as well. Before bed Don gave Brian some follow-up material to help him understand his commitment.

The next morning everyone shared good-byes all around and boarded buses for home. On the two-day drive back to Heidelberg, Don and other counselors had plenty of time to talk with Brian. Don made sure he knew that a relationship with Jesus focused not on acquiring His power but on becoming like Him in character.

Brian seemed to receive their words with openness. But he confessed that he confronted a dilemma—what to do with all his occult books and paraphernalia.

"I've got a lot of money in them," he confided. "It's a pretty good-sized collection."

The Lord, they responded, would direct him what to do.

Two days after their return to Heidelberg, Don asked Brian about the books.

"I trashed them all, Don," he told him.

He began reading the Bible instead from cover to cover, and attended chapel services and a Bible study regularly. In June he repainted the walls of his bedroom at home from black to blue.

Brian experienced both triumphs and setbacks as he struggled to deal with the temptations, accusations and deceptions of the kingdom of darkness. Don continued to disciple and pray with him. After Brian's graduation he left for college in the United States, and kept contact with Don during holiday trips home. Now an InterVarsity Christian Fellowship group at his school helps him maintain his freedom in Christ.

As much as anyone, Brian knows the reality of the powers of darkness. But now he wields the weapons of the Spirit, which ". . . have divine power to demolish strongholds" (2 Corinthians 10:4).

The Spoils of Victory—Human Souls

Many breakthroughs like this one occur after believers recognize what they are up against. Don Creasman might have continued witnessing and explaining biblical truth to Brian to no effect, but he realized Brian was held captive by enemy forces using him for their own purposes. Spiritual conflict never takes place on the human level alone. "For we wrestle not against flesh and blood, but against principalities, against powers, against the rulers of the darkness of this world, against spiritual wickedness in high places" (Ephesians 6:12, KJV).

Humans are precious to God; we are made in His image and intended to glorify Him. The more human beings Satan can take captive, the more he can keep God from receiving the full glory He deserves. Wherever people exist, therefore, the devil sends in troops to wage war. The spoils of victory for which Satan lusts are human souls.

Every soul "rescued . . . from the dominion of darkness and brought . . . into the kingdom of the Son" (Colossians 1:13) represents a triumph for God and a defeat for the devil. As we recognize the spiritual battle taking place in the heavenlies whenever we engage in missions and evangelism, we can stay alert to counter-strategies and begin to target our prayers with the focused intensity of a laser. Successful military generals study their opponents not out of unhealthy fascination but with the wise desire to avoid traps. Foresight in spiritual warfare arms us for victory ". . . in order that Satan might not outwit us. For we are not unaware of his schemes" (2 Corinthians 2:11).

Praying according to Scripture, as Don did, releases the power of the Word of God over the people we intercede for. In Ephesians 6:17 Paul lists as part of our spiritual armor "the sword of the Spirit, which is the word of God." Hebrews 4:12 says that the word of God is living and active. Sharper than any double-edged sword, it penetrates even to dividing soul and spirit, joints and marrow; it judges the thoughts and attitudes of the heart.

Wielding the Word of God in prayer for others effects powerful changes in the spiritual realm. For Brian the turnaround took place almost immediately after the intercession.

Brian and Don also knew that Satan could regain the ground he had lost in this battle if Brian did not destroy the occult items that gave the devil a foothold in his life. Brian's response was costly, mirroring the events in Ephesus when the apostle Paul preached in that ancient center of power and magic.

Many of those who believed now came and openly confessed their evil deeds. A number who had practiced sorcery brought their scrolls together and burned them publicly. When they calculated the value of the scrolls, the total came to fifty thousand drachmas. In this way the word of the Lord spread widely and grew in power.

Acts 19:18–20

Sometimes the defeat of the devil through deliverance takes place so dramatically and publicly that many witnesses turn to God at the demonstration of His power. Here is one such story from Sri Lanka.

Demonization and Deliverance in Trincomalee

Thousands already sat clustered together and many more streamed in to find a place on the grassy field.

Looks like another good crowd tonight, Ranjit DeSilva noted.

As president of Lanka Bible College in Kandy, Sri Lanka, Ranjit had brought about 25 students with him to assist evangelist Christopher Daniel at his campaign in Trincomalee, on the east coast of this island nation in the Indian Ocean.

About eight thousand primarily Hindu Tamils had attended each evening of their weeklong outreach in August 1972, and each evening a few hundred indicated decisions for Christ. Ranjit then led morning meetings for the new believers, as many as could come, in a rented town hall.

As he looked out on the growing Wednesday night crowd, he said another prayer for the local churches and pastors who would follow up the converts and try to get them planted into new home fellowships.

Ranjit and Christopher sat on the platform with several pastors from the city as the evening program began in musical worship. A rope about twenty feet away cordoned off the four-foot-high platform and sound equipment they had set up. Ranjit felt his stomach growl and thought about dinner later that night. As one of the campaign's preachers, he spent the daytime fasting with prayer for the evening meetings. He knew from experience that through fasting God often releases additional spiritual power to break strongholds of darkness.

Chris Daniel stood up to give the message, preaching in Tamil. He had covered a couple of points when a commotion at the front of the crowd arrested everyone's attention. A woman in her early thirties, fire in her eyes and obscenities in her mouth, leaped into the cordoned area around the platform.

"I curse your God and I curse your message!" she screamed with ear-shattering decibels. "May you all be damned to hell!"

Ranjit and several pastors sitting with him stood up and joined Christopher in rebuking the demons controlling the woman. "In the name of Jesus Christ, we command you to be silent and come out of her!"

But her fury raged on. She shrieked and shook violently until her long, black hair flew out of its bun and began whipping around her face.

Suddenly she stood still, breathing deeply. With a dark and determined look in her eye, she walked directly to the platform.

Oh, my word, she's going to try to topple the stage and knock us to the ground! Ranjit thought in alarm. He had seen demonized people with the strength of ten beefy men wreak superhuman destruction in similar situations.

But the woman turned the tables in an unexpected way. When she reached the platform she quietly laid her head down on the edge of it at the pastors' feet.

What now? Ranjit wondered. *Is the demon submitting itself to the higher power of Christ in us?*

Wrong again. With one hand, fingers together straight and stiff, the woman began to make slashing motions across her neck. An eerie wail cut through the air. "Give me blood, or we won't go— give me blood, or we won't go."

Ranjit recoiled. He knew that witch doctors in Sri Lanka often required a blood sacrifice to cast out evil spirits. Sufferers usually brought a goat or chicken to be killed before release would come.

Refusing this demonic demand, the pastors again rebuked the evil forces holding the woman in bondage.

"In Jesus' name we bind the spirits of darkness," proclaimed Christopher at the microphone. "Jesus shed His blood once for all time to deliver us from the kingdom of Satan."

Then Chris began to command specific demons to depart under the authority of Jesus. With prophetic words of knowledge, he called out four evil spirits one by one. When he named the fourth, the woman suddenly collapsed onto the ground in a motionless heap.

The crowd, deathly still and silent throughout this drama, gasped audibly. Ranjit feared they thought she had died. Several women from the evangelistic team hurried over to assist her. Revived, she stood to her feet, calm and in sound mind, but flushed with embarrassment when she saw all eyes turned on her. Quickly she tied up her hair and allowed herself to be led to one side for private counsel.

"Glory to God!" Christopher declared to the crowd. "This is the power of the Jesus we're preaching about—power to save and deliver from evil. You have seen the miracle right now in front of your eyes, the demonic stronghold broken." With divine anointing he continued, "How many of you are ready to give your lives to Christ?"

All over the grassy field, hands sprouted like winter rye. Ranjit guessed that of the crowd of some eight thousand, perhaps seven thousand were indicating a decision. Christopher explained what it meant to receive Jesus as Savior and Lord, and asked those willing to take that step to repeat the sinner's prayer after him.

The counseling team, overwhelmed, scrambled to gather in the harvest ripening around them everywhere. The woman herself prayed to receive Christ.

Many more new believers attended Ranjit's Bible study the next morning. The news surged through the city, and the next night perhaps ten thousand people packed the area for the evening meeting. At the invitation, the number of people who raised a hand to pray and accept Christ grew from hundreds to thousands.

What a breakthrough! Ranjit exulted.

On Friday morning, only two days after the dramatic display, Ranjit noticed the same young woman among the group who came for Bible training. Afterward she approached him and a few of the other leaders.

"I need help," she confessed, trembling with fear. "The witch doctor at my temple came to me yesterday and threatened me. He said if I don't quit this new religion, he'll tell the demons to come back. He said that as a Hindu I shouldn't even have gone to your meeting."

"Don't be afraid," Ranjit told her. "The power of Christ is greater than any other power."

He and some team members prayed over the woman, asking God to protect her from all evil with the covering of Christ's blood, which had paid for her sins.

On Saturday evening, the close of the campaign, Ranjit and Christopher asked the woman to give her testimony from the platform. She did so, describing the previous bondage in her life and how God had delivered and brought her to salvation in Jesus Christ. Many more that night responded to the Gospel.

Ranjit and Christopher left Trincomalee almost sheepishly. They felt they had midwifed the birth of a ten-ton elephant and then saluted the new mom at the door with a cheery good-bye. The city pastors, unprepared for such progeny, gathered what new believers they could and started several house churches. But Trincomalee did not even have meeting halls big enough to contain the crop of converts. No doubt much of the harvest was lost.

Yet without question the Spirit of God moved on countless lives that week. Many members of the family of God in Trincomalee, Sri Lanka, now trace their salvation to the time when a visible sign of God's victory over the forces of darkness powerfully underlined the message of the Gospel of Jesus Christ. The campaign that week echoed the ministry of both word and power described in Mark 16:20: "The disciples went out and preached everywhere, and the Lord worked with them and confirmed his word by the signs that accompanied it."

Clear Communication and Preparation Needed

As early as the second century A.D., Irenaeus (c. 130–c. 202), bishop of Lyons in southern France, wrote about conversions taking place as a result of deliverance from demons:

> For some do certainly and truly drive out devils, so that those who have thus been cleansed from evil spirits frequently both believe [in Christ], and join themselves to the church.
>
> *Against Heresies,* II.32.4

Yet deliverance breeds controversy. Even Jesus faced opposition when He ministered to demonized people.

> They brought him a demon-possessed man who was blind and mute, and Jesus healed him, so that he could both talk and see. All the people were astonished and said, "Could this be the Son of David?"
> But when the Pharisees heard this, they said, "It is only by Beelzebub, the prince of demons, that this fellow drives out demons."
>
> Matthew 12:22–24

Jesus' successful spiritual warfare led some observers to incipient faith, and others (perhaps not eyewitnesses) to blasphemy. Those with resistant hearts saw in Jesus' encounter with the demons the operation of evil. Jesus described such people in Matthew 13:13:

"Though seeing, they do not see; though hearing, they do not hear or understand."

No miraculous sign, particularly any kind of spiritual warfare, will universally convince people of who Jesus is. But those who minister in supernatural power can reduce misunderstanding by emphasizing biblical truth. Because the woman's deliverance in Trincomalee took place in the midst of an evangelistic campaign, the witnesses could understand in context the source of superior power. Consistently exalting the name of Jesus through both word and deed points people to Him: "I, when I am lifted up from the earth, will draw all men to myself" (John 12:32).

Sometimes the testimony of truth and power draws so many people so quickly that the Body of Christ gets taken by surprise. The account from Sri Lanka points out the potential hazard of engaging in power evangelism without preparation for the response. Particularly in a large-group setting, demonstrations of God's supernatural power can result in unprecedented, unanticipated openness to the Gospel.

"And that's the sad thing about the crusade ministry," Ranjit DeSilva reflects. "You see the impact, you see these tremendous miracles that shake the whole place, and then the Church doesn't have the structure to contain the work of God."

When each member of the Body is ready, equipped and working together with others in the full range of needed roles, the Lord's missionary army will make the greatest advances for the Kingdom of God. Front-line troops must wield their weapons of the Spirit skillfully, while medics bind up the wounded and minister to the captives freed from prisoner-of-war camps. Under the direction and training of our Commander-in-Chief, the Lord Jesus Christ, all God's people can work in cooperation, prepared to gain significant spiritual victories.

How Does Your Garden Grow?

In a one-room wood-frame office just down the path from his small Samo long house, deep in a remote corner of the Papua New

Guinea rain forest, Dan Shaw worked through some Scripture translations in the Samo language.

We first met Dan, a self-described Baptist boy from Tucson, in chapter 2. Through a reluctant prayer he mediated God's healing of Hogwanobiayo, the older man from Kwobi, a Samo village of one hundred people among the six hundred Samo in the Western Province. But this story begins about two years before that breakthrough.

Immersed in concentration in his work for Wycliffe Bible Translators, Dan almost did not notice someone approaching until the visitor charged into his office.

"You've got to come see my garden!" announced the young man with the big smile. "I'm planting my garden today and I want you to see it."

Dan gazed at Tiyani, a typical Samo in his early twenties, about five feet four with chocolate brown skin and wiry black hair.

Well, this is interesting, he thought. *I never associated Tiyani with enthusiasm over plantain gardens—unless he happens to be going out beyond the fringes into the forest with a young lady!*

"Tiyani, by this date I've seen only about a thousand Samo gardens," Dan answered. "What's the point here?"

"Well, you've got to come," Tiyani insisted. "I want you to come."

So they went.

While they made the fifteen-minute walk to the garden plot, Dan thought back to Tiyani's initiation rite—one of the first events he had witnessed after he and his wife, Karen, joined the Kwobi village culture four years earlier. As the son of the village headman, Tiyani oozed the good-natured conceit and self-importance of youth. Dan found him charming and brilliant, a valuable help in translation work whenever he could pin him down to spend some time with him. But often after a few days working with Dan, Tiyani would laugh it off, head for the forest and not show up again for weeks.

Still, by this summer of 1973, Dan had translated significant portions of the Bible. Not many weeks remained before he and Karen would return to the United States for their first furlough.

The two men arrived at the area of the forest where Tiyani had cleared a plot of about fifty square yards. Some men and women from the village bustled about preparing to help plant. A huge stack of plantain shoots lay ready.

"Isn't it beautiful?" Tiyani crowed.

"It certainly is."

Because of the area's torrential rainfall, over two hundred inches per year, Dan knew the Samo planted their gardens under the protective canopy of tall trees until after they saw the crop take root and begin to grow. Then they cut down the surrounding trees to open the garden to the sunlight. Dan was also familiar with the Samos' traditional planting rituals that took place once a plot was cleared and ready.

O.K., this all looks pretty normal, he thought. *Now comes the garden magic.*

To protect a garden from the ravages of the spirit world as well as the natural world, the Samo used two main kinds of garden magic. First they made a hole in the ground with a digging stick and dropped resin from a certain kind of tree into the hole, all the while chanting spells. In this way they hoped to protect the young roots from grubs and other underground vermin. Then they chewed special bark from the *nasi* tree and walked around the periphery of the garden spitting it out, chanting this time to protect the surface of the garden from destructive forces, including wild pigs, birds or evil spirits. Only after the garden magic did they plant.

"Well, I'm ready now," Tiyani told Dan ceremoniously. He picked up his digging stick and plunged it into the ground.

But instead of pulling it out, dropping in the resin and chanting spells, Tiyani lifted his head to the treetops.

"Dear God," he called out, "I want *You* to make my garden grow. I want You to protect my garden. You know the grubworms ate up my last garden. I'm hungry! I need good food. You protect my garden underground. And I don't want my crop destroyed by the pigs or cassowaries or evil spirits. You protect my garden on top."

As Tiyani prayed, Dan and the Samo who listened stood in shocked silence. No garden magic? Unheard of! Dan realized Tiyani had taken the traditional chants and turned them into a prayer to God.

When the young man finished, Dan found his voice. "Tiyani, this is remarkable. Where did you get this idea?"

"Well," he said, "from you."

Suddenly Dan turned anthropological.

"Wait a minute, now," he replied. "As an anthropologist and Christian missionary who takes culture seriously, I have never told you to pray for your garden. I've never suggested you need to do these kinds of things. I've been waiting for you to make that decision on your own. So you didn't get it from me. I've never said that."

"No," Tiyani admitted, "that's true. But I watch you." He leaned on his digging stick. "When you eat your food, you ask God to make it good for you. When you go into the forest with us, you pray and ask God's protection against any evil forces there. You do with prayer what we do with the camouflage."

Dan knew well how the Samo wore bark belts and stuffed leaves into their armbands and legbands to hide from evil spirits in the rain forest, literally disappearing before one another's eyes.

"We do our garden magic to make the crops grow," Tiyani continued, "but you pray and ask God to do this. So I've been watching you. I've also been reading this thing you call God's Book. Doesn't it say in Colossians chapter one that God made all things, including what we can see and what we cannot see?"

"Yeah, that's what it talks about."

"Well, we can't see things under the ground. We can't see the spiritual forces that could affect our gardens. But if God made these things, He must have authority over them. Why should I chant to try to connect with these forces God made if I can pray to God Himself? Why not go where the real power is?"

Speechless with astonishment, Dan could only marvel at how this young man had put it all together.

"You're amazing, Tiyani," he finally said. "You've understood God's message for your life and what it means for you, and you yourself have applied that to the reality of planting a garden. Incredible. God bless you."

Dan rejoiced at this breakthrough for the truth of God. But the real test, he knew, lay ahead. Would Tiyani's garden grow?

Shortly afterward the Shaws left on furlough. Over the coming months they prayed with intense urgency for Tiyani and his garden: "O Lord, please honor Tiyani's faith and make his garden grow well, for Your name's sake."

With the plantain's long growing cycle, up to eighteen months, Tiyani's harvest would come just before the Shaws' return to Papua New Guinea in early 1975—if the grubs and pigs did not destroy the crop first.

When they arrived back in Kwobi, Dan sought out his young friend. "Tiyani, tell me about your garden."

Tiyani smiled one of his famous ear-to-ear grins. "That was an unbelievable garden. It grew so well. I got more food from that garden than I could ever have imagined."

He went on to explain the impact on the other villagers of his unprecedented style of garden dedication. Dan understood that the other Samo who had witnessed his prayer did not express serious alarm or ridicule openly, partly because of Samo cultural patterns and partly out of respect for Tiyani's position as the headman's son. They did, however, take keen interest in seeing what happened to Tiyani's crop.

The strongest reactions had come, Tiyani told Dan, from those who knew nothing about what he had done. He explained how he enjoyed sharing his plantains and watching the others eat.

"These are wonderful plantains," they said. "What kind of magic did you do to make your garden grow?"

Tiyani laughed and told them, "I didn't do any magic."

Then his guests gasped and grabbed their stomachs. "Oh, no, this food has no essence! My stomach is empty!"—a typical Samo response to food that has gone unprotected or unblessed.

At this reaction Tiyani confronted his guests. "No way—that's not true. You feel your stomach. Keep your hand there. Now tell me honestly: Is your stomach empty?"

"No," they admitted.

"How does your stomach feel?"

"Satisfied."

Tiyani moved in for the knockout. "It was God who filled your stomach. I didn't do any magic—I asked God to make my garden grow. I put my trust in Him and He protected my garden and made it grow so well, as you've just tasted. God filled your stomach today."

The story of Tiyani's garden left a deep impression on many Samo villagers. And with the healing of Hogwanobiayo not long after, a large-scale spiritual turnaround began in the village. People came to understand the Word of God and recognize His power in their midst as they saw it manifested in practical ways.

The Power Encounter

Looking back on his twelve years working with the Samo, Dan Shaw sees Tiyani as one of the first Samo Christians and the first real pastor of his people. After his experience with his garden, villagers came often to ask Tiyani questions about Jesus Christ and the power of God. On other occasions he took bold stands against superstitious behavior and pointed to the Scriptures to back up his position. By declaring fearlessly the power of God over the lesser power of spirit beings, Tiyani helped to build up the Samo church as people began transferring their allegiance to the King of all creation.

Tiyani's decision to pray to God instead of perform garden magic is a low-key but prototypical example of a power encounter. In a power encounter, a believer in the God of the Bible takes a stand against false, demonic beliefs and practices, trusting in the power of the Lord to triumph visibly over the power of evil. Generally observers then acknowledge and bow to the supremacy of God.

The classic Old Testament example of a power encounter took place on Mount Carmel when Elijah confronted the prophets of Baal, a story recorded in 1 Kings 18:16–46. Because Israel and King Ahab had turned from God to the worship of Baal, Elijah summoned the people to a showdown. "How long will you waver between two opinions?" he demanded. "If the LORD is God, follow him; but if Baal is God, follow him" (see verse 21).

Elijah proposed that he and the prophets of Baal each choose a bull to sacrifice, lay it on an altar but not set it aflame. "Then you call on the name of your god, and I will call on the name of the LORD. The god who answers by fire—he is God" (verse 24).

For the better part of the day, the prophets of Baal cried out to their god in a frenzy of shouting, dancing and bloodletting. Elijah even taunted them to try harder to catch their sovereign's notice. "But there was no response, no one answered, no one paid attention" (verse 29).

Finally Elijah called the people near. He built an altar to God, arranged the wood and laid the other bull on it. He even dug a trench around the altar and, as the drought-stricken people watched aghast, ordered water poured on the offering and the wood, enough to run off and fill the trench.

> At the time of sacrifice, the prophet Elijah stepped forward and prayed: "O LORD, God of Abraham, Isaac and Israel, let it be known today that you are God in Israel and that I am your servant and have done all these things at your command. Answer me, O LORD, answer me, so these people will know that you, O LORD, are God, and that you are turning their hearts back again."
>
> Then the fire of the LORD fell and burned up the sacrifice, the wood, the stones and the soil, and also licked up the water in the trench.
>
> When all the people saw this, they fell prostrate and cried, "The LORD—he is God! The LORD—he is God!"
>
> verses 36–39

Power encounters can change hearts and lives dramatically for the Kingdom of God, but notice part of Elijah's prayer: "I . . . have done all these things at your command" (verse 36). Believers who set up power encounters out of their own zealous presumption put themselves in grave danger. Only with the anointing and clear direction of the Holy Spirit should believers enter this kind of spiritual warfare.

Tiyani did not face down the demonic powers directly. He simply took a stand for the truth of God's Word about the almighty Creator's dominion over all He has made. With a bold, public proclamation to the visible and invisible worlds, he declared his faith in the Lord's power to protect his garden, and left the results to God.

"Say to This Tree . . ."

Tsegaye Legesse crouched in the shade above the bank of the river Awash. Flicking at a fly, he watched as villagers descended the bank to the stream flowing through a gully twelve or fifteen feet lower. Children played while women fetched water from the brown current. Other adults crossed the river to their work in the fields beyond. And nearly every one of them, passing by, stopped to kiss the gnarled bark of a certain majestic tree at the river's edge.

More grand and imposing than the other trees nearby, the leafy giant, its trunk two to three feet in diameter, stood as the central focus of worship for the Oromo people in the district of Adama, some sixty or seventy miles southeast of Ethiopia's capital city of Addis Ababa. Tsegaye's spirit grieved to see their devotion to this towering sentinel. As Ethiopian manager of World Vision's Adama Project, an integrated development program with a Christian context, Tsegaye felt the idolatrous worship of this tree undercut efforts of the project staff to bring the Kingdom of God in all its facets to the community.

When the Adama Project began at the end of 1989, Tsegaye learned the tree had stood for generations, its root system fanned through the moist soil drinking in life and strength. The Oromo people in this region, animistic with a mix of folk Islam, ascribed divine stature to the tree and the spirit they believed inhabited it. Prayers and offerings to the branched behemoth helped ensure protection from disaster, they thought. They often brought an animal, usually a chicken, to slay at the base of the trunk as a blood sacrifice to the tree spirit.

The people's bondage and deception blanketed the area in spiritual darkness, which only added to the suffering and misery the Adama Project staff had come to address. Because the Oromo had no way to bring the water of the river gully up to the higher, arid plain of surrounding land, they faced crop failure and famine whenever a year of drought blew its hot breath across the parched ground. The approximately twenty Christians on staff, all Ethiopians from other parts of the country, began an ambitious irrigation project. Using gas-driven pumps, they aimed to draw water up into a system of canals that would accommodate several thousand needy people in the Adama district.

As work on the pumphouse and canal system continued, the Adama Project staff met daily at 5 A.M. for corporate prayer, lifting to the Lord their own needs and the needs of the community they served. Tsegaye and the others expressed their deepening concern about the Oromo worship of the tree god.

"I see this idolatry as a lead weight around the people's necks," Tsegaye said. He noted that the World Vision philosophy of holistic ministry incorporated the Gospel of Christ as the cornerstone of their assistance projects. "As long as people continue this demonic devotion to the tree, the whole process of transformation crucial to their health and development is threatened."

They asked God to show them how to pray. One promise of Jesus from the Gospel of Luke stood out to them in living color: "If you have faith as small as a mustard seed, you can say to this mulberry tree, 'Be uprooted and planted in the sea,' and it will obey you" (17:6). Claiming this promise in faith, the team began to pray aggressively that God would bring down the giant green idol.

As the believers worked and interacted with the community, the Oromo learned that they were praying about their tree by the river. Over the next six months people watched the leafy sentinel with growing suspense. Slowly it began to dry up. Foliage withered. Branches and roots shriveled.

Then one morning villagers going down to the river stopped in their tracks at the sight before them. The entire tree had torn out of the ground at the roots and toppled into the river, lying stricken like Goliath after his encounter with David. Every other tree remained healthy and standing.

Awestruck, people ran to tell the Christians, "Your God has done this! Your God has dried up the tree! It's because of the power of your prayers!"

As astonishment swept the community along with the news, the Oromo asked the believers of the project staff to explain more about their God. In the days and weeks that followed, about a hundred people received Jesus Christ as Lord and Savior.

With this event the Holy Spirit began stirring hearts to faith. When Tsegaye and the project staff first came to the Adama area, only 27 known Christians lived in the entire region. Less than three years after the tree died, more than 370 Oromo villagers had given their lives to Christ.

Tsegaye has no doubt the staff's warfare prayer initiated the spiritual power encounter over the idol tree, leading to a remarkable breakthrough in receptivity to the Gospel. At the same time he credits the staff's balanced approach to witness and ministry as the foundation for establishing the Kingdom of God in the community. Love and power work together, Tsegaye affirms. "The secret is the good fellowship, prayer and sharing among our own staff, which stimulate love for one another, and in turn cause non-Christians to trust us. It is the exemplary conduct of our staff that is making the difference."

By understanding and interweaving the whole spectrum of threads in the tapestry of God's Kingdom, the Ethiopians of the Adama Project saw tremendous fruit from their prayers and labors, to the glory of God.

Uprooting the Demonic

The encounter of Tsegaye Legesse and his colleagues with the spirit tree in Ethiopia, more than the story of Tiyani's garden, involved direct prayer against the powers of darkness holding the local people in bondage. Yet the Adama Project staff knew the limits of their authority under Christ and wisely did not cut down the tree themselves. By leaving the uprooting to God, they allowed the Oromo people to draw their own conclusion and acknowledge the Lord's superior power when He intervened sovereignly.

In the fourth century, St. Martin of Tours took a more confrontational stance against the pagan tree of a certain shrine. He purposed to cut it down, but the people there opposed him. Finally one of the pagans proposed a diabolical kind of power encounter. The people agreed to cut down their own tree if Martin would stand under it so as to be crushed by its fall. Martin accepted the arrangement.

His biographer, Sulpicius Severus, described the scene in chapter 13 of his *Life of St. Martin:*

> Since the tree leaned to one side, so that there was no doubt in what direction it would crash when cut, Martin was bound and placed at a point chosen by the peasants and where no one doubted the tree would fall. They themselves then began hewing down their own pine tree with joy and gladness. At a distance stood a crowd of wondering bystanders. Now, little by little, the pine began swaying and threatening ruin by its fall. From their distant stand the monks grew pale, and, as the peril came nearer, in their terror they lost all hope and faith, expecting nothing other than the death of Martin. But, he waited with steadfast confidence in the Lord. The pine cracked as it finally was cut through. It now began to fall, it now began to crash upon him, when he finally raised his hand and made the sign of salvation in its direction. The tree—and you would have likened its backward action to a tornado—crashed in just the opposite direction, so that it all but overwhelmed the peasants who, as they thought, had taken places of safety. The pagans, stupified [*sic*] by the miracle, raised a great shout to heaven, while the monks wept for joy; all joined in exalting the name of Christ. It is generally agreed that salvation came to that region on that day.

No one but the Holy Spirit of God can ordain these kinds of situations and sustain His people through them. Zechariah 4:6 reminds us of the true perspective: "'Not by might nor by power, but by my Spirit,' says the LORD Almighty."

The Line in the Sand

On February 2, 1991, a warm summer night in Montevideo, Uruguay, Alfredo Peña and his band of fifteen to twenty believers, mostly pastors like himself, headed for the beach. Tens of thousands already lined the shores for close to ten miles along the southern fringe of Uruguay's capital city, at the wide mouth of the Río de la Plata where it opens to the South Atlantic. But none of the beachgoers had in mind a carefree evening in the refreshing sea breezes. The pastors intended to take a bold—some said crazy—stand against the cult of Lemanjá.

As director of Uruguay's Every Home Crusade, Alfredo, about forty, carried a deep concern for spreading the truth of the Gospel message. In a country once strongly secular and apathetic toward spiritual issues, growing disillusionment had prompted a desperate search for deeper meaning. But instead of turning to Jesus Christ, many turned to spiritism and New Age thinking. Over the past five or ten years, Alfredo had seen the worship of Lemanjá mushroom, sucking in people from all ages and classes of society, particularly the young. Now up to 450,000 Uruguayans—one of every seven—participated in the Lemanjá cult and other religions of Afro-Brazilian origin, with the numbers increasing every year.

Her followers considered Lemanjá mother of the water and queen of the seas, with authority over the gods of storms, lightning and rain, harvest and hunting, as well as roads, iron and war. They believed their prayers to Lemanjá brought answers to the problems of daily life. Almost any night of the year devotees could be found on the seashore practicing their rituals, but the cult designated February for special worship and honor to their goddess. Public festivals on the first four days of the month drew 50,000 to 100,000 people who massed nightly all along the Montevideo beachfront. In addition, many boats offshore motored up and down the coast with practitioners praying to Lemanjá for a good fishing year.

Alfredo's little crew, prompted and emboldened by the Holy Spirit, decided to spend one of the festival nights at the main beach confronting people with the truth about Jesus Christ. They claimed an area on the sand, and with a small, portable loudspeaker began to sing and praise with all the volume they could muster: "Blessed be the name of the Lord. . . ."

All around them small groups of cultists, some headed by priests or leaders of the sect, performed their rituals. The sounds of song and dance echoed back and forth as Lemanjá devotees lifted their worship and petitions to their goddess, including prayers for blessing as well as cursing people. Some sacrificed animals or hens while others set out food, flowers or money as offerings. In the darkness thousands of flickering candle flames stretched for miles along the shoreline like a fiery serpent.

The pastors took turns preaching through the loudspeaker. "Jesus Christ, the Son of God, was sacrificed for us, and He is the only sacrifice for our sins that God accepts! Only the blood of Jesus, not the blood of animals, can forgive and cleanse us from sin! He died once for all the human race, and through His resurrection from the dead He alone can reconcile us to God!"

As Alfredo and his colleagues prayed together, they sensed God directing them to set up a power encounter between the Kingdom of light and the kingdom of darkness. They drew a wide line in the sand on the beach and petitioned the Lord among themselves: "Father, show Yourself strong in our midst, we pray. Let anyone crossing the line to our side be freed and saved by Your mighty power."

Their preaching and worship of Christ eventually attracted onlookers curious about this oddball group. The first person who wandered across the line in the sand suddenly fell to the ground, immobile. A couple of pastors picked him up, took him into their midst and began praying to deliver him from demonic bondage—not to overcome his will but to liberate him from the power of the enemy, so he could choose freely whom to serve. More people followed. Some line-crossers collapsed and lay still. Others who fell shook and cried out with manifestations of evil spirits. As the pastors ministered deliverance, they discovered that those who had dedicated themselves to Lemanjá, not just dabbled in the rituals, required more intercession to set them free.

That night, over the course of several hours, more than 75 people crossed the pastors' line. All of them fell to the ground. All received prayer for deliverance. And all came to salvation in Jesus Christ after the pastors shared the Gospel with them.

"Glory to God!" Alfredo exulted when the group finally left the beach to go home. He knew they had made little more than a scratch in the Lemanjá stronghold, but 75 souls had passed from darkness into light and received counsel on following up their decisions in one of the local fellowships of believers.

The leaders of the sect, however, did not take this new threat lightly. When they learned what had happened, they began to target the pastors with a campaign of intimidation. Over the next few years, as more pastors and laypeople joined in reenacting the power encounter during the annual festivals, Alfredo and other pastors received death threats. They discovered bloody sacrificed animals on the doorsteps of their churches and homes. Opponents on the beach hurled stones at them. Yet they carried on as they sensed the Lord directing them, and more people each year found freedom and new life in Christ.

In 1994, moreover, the believers raised the stakes.

That year over one hundred of them, mostly laypeople by now, gathered on the last of the major public festival days, February 4. Near their location on the main beach stood a new statue of Lemanjá. The priests of the cult had received not only permission but financing from the city government to erect the idol. Still the worshipers of Christ pressed forward.

They knew that each year at midnight of the last festival night, cultists on all the beaches placed sacrifices into the sea as offerings to Lemanjá. Flowers, food such as rice or corn, written petitions, money, animal parts including the legs of white hens—all were cast onto the waves, where the winds and currents and tides always took them out to sea. Whatever would not float of its own accord the devotees put into containers. On the deep waters where the goddess was thought to dwell, she supposedly received the offerings, then bestowed blessings on her worshipers.

During the final festival night of 1994, the band of Christians prayed publicly that God would reverse the direction of the ocean currents. "O Lord, don't let the sea receive their offerings! Let the people understand that Lemanjá cannot save, and that only You are worthy of worship!"

In the post-midnight hours most of the beachgoers began drifting home. Early the next morning, Christians and cultists tuned in to live media reports of an unprecedented event. Somehow the normal sea currents had changed and all the offerings to Lemanjá had washed back onto the beaches. Street children, the first to discover the debris littering the sand at dawn, picked through the items with eyes peeled especially for offerings of money.

Television interviews of the Lemanjá leaders left no doubt about their outrage.

"The evangelicals have done this!" they charged. "Their prayers against Lemanjá angered her and caused the sea to reject our offerings!"

The spiritual warfare between the forces of Lemanjá and the forces of Jesus Christ heated up like a furnace. Yet more cultists, after witnessing the tremendous demonstration of God's superiority over the waves and the principalities of the sea, visited the churches wanting to learn about the power of Christ. The pastors now believe that intensive church planting all over Uruguay will serve as the key strategy to break down the dominion of darkness and shine the light of the Gospel throughout the nation.

Alfredo Peña continues his ministry. The death threats keep coming. Some still think him crazy. But one thing he knows: For several hundred people since 1991, the power encounters on the beach paved the way for Jesus Christ to win the eternal victory of their salvation.

Keeping in Step with the Spirit

The success of the believers on the Montevideo beach probably hinged on two essentials. First, Alfredo and the other pastors sensed clear guidance from the Holy Spirit to engage in this activity; and second, they went not as Lone Rangers but as a united group. Unity boosts the effectiveness of prayer of any kind, but in the realm of spiritual warfare prayer, unity often proves indispensable. Just after Jesus' discussion about the disciples' authority to bind and loose, He taught them,

> "Again, I tell you that if two of you on earth agree about anything you ask for, it will be done for you by my Father in heaven. For where two or three come together in my name, there am I with them."
> Matthew 18:19–20

Occasionally a believer on the front lines, perhaps a missionary working among an unreached people group, will have no other Christian nearby with whom to join in prayer. In these cases the unmistakable direction of the Holy Spirit becomes even more essential.

James O. Fraser (1886–1938), who ministered often alone among the Lisu tribe of southwest China, never engaged in a head-on power encounter with the forces of darkness, but learned how to follow the Spirit's leading in praying warfare prayers for the advance of the Gospel.

When a key village near the Burma border rejected the Gospel message, Fraser retreated to pray through his discouragement in solitude and seek the Lord's will. God led him to 2 Chronicles 20, where King Jehoshaphat, in the face of formidable opposition, received this prophecy through Jahaziel:

> ". . . The battle is not yours, but God's. Tomorrow march down against them. . . . You will not have to fight this battle. Take up your positions; stand firm and see the deliverance the LORD will give you. . . . Do not be afraid; do not be discouraged. Go out to face them tomorrow, and the LORD will be with you."
>
> verses 15–17

In her biography of her father, Eileen Crossman writes that Fraser "was deeply stirred by this remarkable chapter and spent the next few hours in 'fighting prayer.' At about midnight he felt victory, as his journal recorded."

Crossman then quotes this journal entry:

> Seem distinctly led (he wrote) to fight against "principalities and powers" for Middle Village. Have faith for the conversion of that place, and pray as a kind of bugle-call for the hosts of heaven to come down and fight for me against the powers of darkness holding these two old men who are hindering their villages and perhaps three others from turning to Christ. Have a good time of fighting prayer, then sleep in much peace of mind.

Crossman goes on to note the result:

> Early next morning James retraced his steps to Middle Village. The people there seemed much more responsive. Eleven of the thirteen families wanted to become disciples of the Lord Jesus.

"Victory," he recorded, "just as expected—hardly striking a blow!"

On the next day twelve more families came to ask if they too could accept the message he had brought to them and become children of God. It seemed as if the tide had turned.

But James Fraser had another lesson to learn. The following night he prayed the same way for a second hostile hamlet nearby, with great faith that God would score another victory. The next morning, however, the villagers spurned him and his message. Even the traveling companion he brought with him from Middle Village, a new believer, turned against Fraser and renounced his faith. Crossman describes what happened next:

> Numb and broken, James quietly retreated to his little empty room. It seemed a total defeat and his spirits reached a new low. But here God showed His loving kindness. A great sense of peace came over James when he humbled himself in his prayers. He had begun to assume victory would be automatic; village after village would turn to Christ if he prayed the fighting prayer. He saw again that there was no room for cavalier faith in the work of God; it had the wrong kind of confidence.

His next journal entry follows:

> Find considerable peace (he wrote) in just leaving the whole matter of these villages in God's hands. But the rebuff of spirit has been very severe, and I shall walk more humbly before the Lord—yes, and before Satan too,—after this.
> *Mountain Rain*, Overseas Missionary Fellowship, 1982,
> pages 143–44

Those engaged in spiritual warfare soon learn there are no easy answers, stock solutions or fail-proof formulas. Only dynamic guidance from and obedience to the Holy Spirit will see battles won. Satan's real power necessitates our respect. Yet God's power, infinitely more vast, should fill us with both hope and humility. God wants us to depend on Him, not on our understanding or use of the authority He has given us. As we walk moment by moment in His will, He can and will give us specific instructions on where, when and how to engage in effective intercessory warfare that binds demonic spirits and frees people to come to Christ. "Since we live by the Spirit, let us keep in step with the Spirit" (Galatians 5:25).

9

"I Myself Will Drive Them Out"

Stories from the Muslim World

Bill Gray's wake-up call came early that Monday. In the first light of dawn on October 11, 1993, he and David Russett, roommates at Hotel Tirana in Tirana, Albania, began to stir. If the intercessors hoped to pray at one more site before their mid-morning bus left for the airport, they would need to hurry.

As part of a prayer journey team of 31 people from New Life Church in Colorado Springs, Colorado, they had spent the past week based in Tirana, the capital, interceding for the Albanian people. They gave special prayer emphasis to the Muslim population, then estimated at more than forty percent of the nation. The New Life team represented one of 270 prayer journey teams from around the world fanning out that October to pray on location in 62 countries of the "10/40 Window." The initiative, dubbed "Praying through the Window," focused on a geographical rectangle stretching roughly from 10 degrees to 40 degrees north latitude, and from West Africa through East Asia—an area containing the least-evangelized nations of the world.

On their last morning in the country, Bill, David and seven others from the New Life team wanted to pray at a Tirana hospital complex. Earlier God had arranged an unexpected contact with a bilingual American missionary working in Albania. Gus, in his mid-forties with thinning, light brown hair, ministered frequently at the hospital and would serve that morning as the group's translator.

"I've spent months gaining favor with the hospital staff," Gus warned them as they headed out, "but you never know when they might deny you entrance. And I've never gone to the hospital at this time of morning. There's no telling whether we'll be able to get in at all. And you already know," he went on, "it's risky to pray for Muslims in particular. Just be alert to any sign of problems."

Around the hospital complex and its several buildings, a wall enclosed the grounds. As they approached the main gate, they noticed a bustle of activity and men with television cameras on their shoulders. Cathy Kiepke and another woman from the prayer group ambled over to investigate.

"It's a crew from ABC News," Cathy reported to the others who joined them. "They're filming a story on some kind of mobile hospital unit, an airplane where patients are being taken for eye surgery and the Albanian doctors can get special training."

The prayer team and television team exchanged a few words, and when the American TV crew entered the hospital complex, the prayer warriors filed in right behind them like a caboose. As they passed through the main hall of the building that housed the eye unit, the intercessors noticed doctors and nurses standing on both sides, staring with stiff, unsmiling faces.

Do they know who we are? Bill wondered. *Are they going to kick us out?*

A couple of turns later, the cameras continued down the hall while the intercessors ducked to their right into a wing of the eye hospital. The prayer team never saw the TV crew again.

After they entered the first large room, Gus turned to the others.

"This is amazing!" he whispered. "I've never seen so many doctors and nurses here at the same time!"

Initially the intercessors huddled together, taking cues from Gus.
In this wing perhaps forty people of all ages were hospitalized, most
lying on beds that protruded like teeth from the side walls of two
large wards. Family members hovered near several of the patients.
Most knew Gus already.

"I have some friends here who would like to pray for you," he
told them. "Is that all right?"

Quietly the intercessors approached the beds, soon splitting into
groups of two or three so as to pray for more patients. Gus translated for the small group he accompanied, while the others simply smiled and projected an attitude of love as they prayed from
patient to patient, laying on hands and sometimes anointing with
oil. They received warm smiles in return, and many patients
squeezed the intercessors' hands or lifted arms for a hug.

Soon everyone wanted prayer. Patients beckoned pray-ers to
come over, while some family members sidled up and tugged on
arms, leading intercessors back to the beds of their loved ones. In
some cases Gus read portions of the Bible in Albanian or translated as team members read.

A few nurses and doctors in the ward watched the goings-on
with interest. Gus chatted with them, then hustled to gather the
intercessors in the center of the room.

"It's incredible!" he exclaimed. "The staff wants us to pray for
them, too."

As Bill moved to join the group, he marveled at their changed
expressions. *Are these really the same stony-faced people we saw at the
door?*

At the feet of the beds in the middle of the room, the prayer
team formed a circle around some long tables, joining hands with
the nurses, doctors and a few patients who got out of bed. Gus
explained that the group was going to pray. Then, one by one, the
intercessors spoke out with a prayer, a prophecy, a Scripture verse
or a song. Although Gus did not translate, the Albanians plainly
felt the power and presence of God. Tears flowed down nurses'
cheeks, while other upturned faces shone with wonder.

Afterward the intercessory team walked through a narrow section of the wing that had a few semi-private rooms on each side. In another large ward at the end of the wing, they ministered to several others.

Then, on their way back, Gus pulled Bill and David into one of the side rooms. "Come in here a minute—I'd like you to meet this guy."

In the tiny room lay two men, probably in their late fifties. Gus nodded toward the one in the bed on the right. "This man is a believer. I've talked and prayed with him many times and he's fully committed his life to Christ. But don't even go over to the guy on the left. He's a Muslim—almost completely blind—and he's always refused to have me pray for him."

Bill and David ministered briefly to the Christian, who started to weep, smiling through quiet tears of joy. Then, as the two said good-bye to him, Gus conversed in Albanian for a moment with the Muslim.

The intercessors were headed for the door when Gus called them back. "Wait a minute, guys. This man wants us to pray, too."

The men reentered the room, joined by Cathy Kiepke. One or two other women stood near the door looking on. The gray-haired Muslim, scruffy and wrinkled, lay still, his eyes nearly closed in slits. When he glanced up, the team could see a white film over one of his eyes.

Bill and David began to pray aloud, while Gus laid a hand on the man and Cathy stretched out hers. With authority they interceded for healing and salvation in the name of Jesus, asking God to reveal Himself. David quoted from Scripture.

As they prayed, the man broke down in tears. Cathy reported later that she was watching as the man's eyes started to enlarge. The white film cleared slowly from his eye until it disappeared.

By the end of the prayer the Muslim's eyes were completely open. Bill smiled and gave him a hug, sensing genuine appreciation as the man squeezed back. Then Bill raised a hand showing two fingers.

"Gus, ask him if he can see how many fingers I'm holding up."

Gus translated, and the man responded by holding up two of his own.

Bill took a couple of steps backward and repeated his sign. "Now how many?"

Two again, the man indicated.

The cramped room limited the experiment, but Bill stepped back as far as he could.

"Now how many?" he asked, holding up three fingers.

The man raised his hand—three.

The intercessors praised God aloud for touching the man with His healing power. More hugs, and the team turned to file out the door.

Then the man spoke up in Albanian, pointing to the sky. Gus told them afterward what he had said: "I now believe!"

As the group left the eye unit, staff and patients hugged and tugged at them as though to prevent them from leaving. The prayer team made a brief visit to the building that housed the cancer ward, where several others received a touch from the Lord. Then, the clock ticking, they raced to catch a ride back to their hotel, and then to the airport.

In all, the intercessors had spent only an hour or so on the hospital grounds. But at home over the coming weeks, when letters from Gus began to arrive, they learned the extent to which their modest investment was reaping dividends for eternity. The day after their visit Gus returned to the eye clinic. He discovered the once-nearly-blind man, in the words of one letter, "up and around. He is a Muslim from an area of the country that is very hard to penetrate. He openly praises the name of Jesus for the miracle of sight." Wide open to the Gospel, he received Christ eagerly when Gus prayed with him.

Overall Gus described an amazing receptivity:

> Revival broke out in the eye hospital since the people could see the resurrection power of Jesus. . . . God has begun to pour out His Spirit and people are getting saved. Almost everyone at the eye hospital accepts Jesus as their Savior and Lord. . . . I think most of the nurses and some of the doctors are now saved.

The love of God spread within the medical complex, and Gus saw doors swing wide as never before.

God has opened nearly every hospital and ward, even the intensive care ward. . . . Muslim people want to see a sign before they
can believe. I know they are saved when they start preaching the
Word to me and take me around the wards to pray for other
people.

The New Life prayer journey team has also received reports that
Muslims healed and saved at the hospital, now discharged, have
returned to their towns and villages to testify to the power of Jesus
Christ. The web of God's sovereign work continues to branch out
into untouched regions, for His glory.

Catching Up with What God Is Doing

Why a separate chapter focusing on power evangelism in the
Muslim world? Because Muslims today, after centuries of rock-solid
resistance to the Gospel, are coming to faith in Christ in unprecedented numbers—many if not most of them as a result of demonstrations of God's supernatural power.

Within the scope of power evangelism, God often uses human
agents ministering under the guidance of the Holy Spirit to draw
Muslims to Jesus Christ. The band from the New Life Church
prayer journey team served as a catalyst for an outpouring of God
when they interceded for healing and salvation at the Albanian
hospital. The Lord moved in power there only after they went on
site personally to pray and minister.

Many contemporary reports, on the other hand, describe how
God Himself is initiating encounters with Muslims through
dreams, visions, angelic visitations and more. The Lord, should
He so choose, can break through with revelations of Himself
directly to closed and resistant peoples.

Even sovereign acts of God, however, do not replace the need
(as we have already seen) for proclaiming the Gospel and cross-
cultural church planting. In one way or another, the Word of God
must dovetail with the works of God in order for people to interpret signs and wonders correctly. But the flood of stories now flowing out of Muslim lands suggests that mission agencies may have
their work cut out just to catch up with what God is already doing.

Late in Joshua's life, the Lord listed for him all the lands remaining to be conquered by the Israelites. He gave the aged leader a detailed outline of the unfinished task. Then He made this interesting statement: "As for all the inhabitants of the mountain regions from Lebanon to Misrephoth Maim, that is, all the Sidonians, I myself will drive them out before the Israelites" (Joshua 13:6). The Lord apparently reserved for Himself the lead role in bringing the Kingdom of God to these regions.

Could it be that God today is driving back the stronghold of Islam sovereignly through signs and wonders pointing to Jesus as Messiah? If so, we His people must seize the opportunity to go in with the light of the Gospel, make disciples and baptize and teach Muslims about the One who has already begun revealing Himself to them.

Within the last generation God has raised up numerous new mission initiatives targeting Muslims. Agencies and resource centers—including Frontiers, the Zwemer Institute of Muslim Studies, Ministries to Muslims, Arab World Ministries, 30 Days Muslim Prayer Focus and Missionary Action/FLAME (Fund for Latin Americans in Muslim Evangelism)—illustrate the wide-ranging strategies now concentrated on the Islamic world.

Bob Sjogren, president of Frontiers Associates, said in a 1994 interview for the video *Light the Window*, produced by the Christian Broadcasting Network, "More Muslims have come to know the Lord in the past 25 years than in the entire history of missions to Islam." The following vignette typifies this new wave of the Holy Spirit.

In a city in Egypt, a Christian woman we will call Eman received an invitation around November 1994 that made her tremble with fear.

Is this a trap? she wondered.

She had been asked to pray for a sick woman at the home of a devout and influential Muslim leader. The ill woman knew Eman to be a Christian, and Eman knew that most Muslims recognize Isa (Jesus) as a healer. But Eman had no idea what she was getting into.

Feeling a little like Ananias being sent by God to pray for Saul, the enemy of the early Church, Eman drove to the home of the

Muslim leader, Mohammed Ibrahim (not his real name). After a short time at the house praying for the woman, Eman hurried back to her car, eager to make her escape. To her horror, Ibrahim followed her out. He forced himself into her car and shut the door.

"I have something very important to tell you," he said in a low voice.

Eman's heart pounded as she listened, every nerve on guard. Ibrahim confessed in strictest confidence that he led an underground fundamentalist Islamic group pledged to destroy all the Christian churches in that city.

"But the week before last, I was visited in the night by a very moving vision," he revealed. "Isa appeared to me in my bedroom as a bright white figure. He showed me the wound holes in His hands and feet. He spoke and said, 'I have shed My blood also for you. I want you to build My Church, not to destroy it.'"

Ibrahim paused. "I was so transformed by this vision that I decided to become a follower of Isa al Masih [Jesus the Messiah]."

Eman's shock only grew deeper.

Ibrahim went on to explain that he had recounted his vision to his group, and to his astonishment all 150 people agreed to follow his decision. The members, already underground, now committed themselves covertly to advance the work of the Church. Eman, filled with wonder, hardly had words to express her praise for God's glory.

Today stories like this are streaming forth as never before from around the world. In some accounts astounding numbers of people are turning to Christ simultaneously. While Western Christians may think this unusual, perhaps even suspect, in many Eastern or Middle Eastern cultures, strong family ties and social networks emphasize the process of mutually interdependent group decision-making. The same close-knit group system that seems at first a hindrance to conversions can facilitate mass movements of whole families or even villages to Christ when the Gospel breaks through in power at the leadership level.

The next story illustrates one of the more private, individual conversion experiences.

Drinking the Water of Life

Parviz could not believe what had happened to his country. His home city of Tehran, Iran's capital where he had grown up, now felt like a foreign culture. As an officer in the Iranian Air Force, Parviz had trained for a year in the United States, and while he was gone in 1978–1979 the Iranian revolution had turned his nation upside-down. The deposed Shah had fled into exile and zealous Shia Muslims had established an Islamic republic under the leadership of Ayatollah Ruhollah Khomeini and other Muslim clerics.

Although Parviz had grown up practicing the Shia Muslim faith, what he saw of religion in Iran now curdled his stomach. In the name of Islam, hundreds of people perceived as enemies were tortured or executed. Violence, unrest, assassination of government officials and demonization of anything Western had slammed the engines of the ship of state into full-speed reverse.

I can't understand how people who call themselves religious can do these things, Parviz thought. *What does it mean when religion turns people into such monsters?*

Meanwhile, border skirmishes with Iraq to the west erupted in September 1980 into full-scale war. Parviz' growing disillusionment with Islam and his Islamic homeland drove him to seek an escape from the nightmare. In October 1983 the 32-year-old officer, with his wife and young son, slipped out of the country.

They defected to the United States, and by December settled near a cousin of Parviz in Tampa, Florida. Grateful for their freedom, they nevertheless found life in their new nation difficult. Grand expectations gave way to culture shock, stress and financial hardship. Parviz lowered his sights from success to mere survival.

Then in 1988 Parviz injured his back on a part-time job. In great pain and unable to work, he began to lose hope.

I'm not good enough, he fretted in his idle hours. *I didn't do well enough for my family, especially my son.*

As day followed aching day, Parviz started planning how he might get rid of himself. He wanted to figure out a way to vanish without leaving a trace of his identity, to spare his nine-year-old son the trauma of learning about his dad's suicide. Yet the idea of leaving his family alone plagued him with guilt.

Back surgery on May 5, 1989, a harrowing and painful ordeal, eventually relieved some of the physical agony. But Parviz' spirit found no respite from suffering. When Parviz had turned from Islam, he had abandoned hope in any religion. God meant nothing to him. Since he was as yet unable to work or even walk well, ending it all still loomed as a seductive option.

Then on the night of May 21, a dream took hold of Parviz as he slept. He saw himself in an old castle standing at the top of a long, stone staircase, so tall it reached to the clouds. Feeling lost and a little frightened, he wanted to go downstairs but did not know if he could make it. Just then a covey of small living creatures—some kind of spirit beings, Parviz sensed—hovered around him in shining white garments, laughing and playing. They took his hands and began to guide him down the staircase, bearing him up so he felt almost weightless.

Parviz noticed someone else, too—an older man dressed in a white robe whose face he could not see well. The older man accompanied them down the stairs to a beautiful courtyard paved with brown brick or stone. The huge area, surrounded by doors and windows of the castle, centered around a small stone fountain with water bubbling out the top. The spirit creatures guided Parviz to the fountain, where a younger man reclined.

Parviz felt a nudge and heard a sound like a voice from the old man next to him. "This is your Jesus. Go close."

Anxiety welled up, but Parviz approached the figure reclining at the fountain. Pale and slender, also dressed in a white robe, the man had brilliant blue-green eyes that shone with intensity in the midst of a well-worn face. When he caught Jesus' gaze, Parviz burst into tears.

The reclining man took Parviz by his left wrist and seemed to indicate with his eyes that Parviz should drink from the fountain. Still weeping, Parviz leaned over to gulp from the water bubbling up.

Just then Parviz became aware of his wife shaking him. "Parviz, what's wrong? Why are you crying?"

He woke up with his eyes moist and a sob in his voice, still feeling the clasp on his wrist where Jesus had held his hand. A few moments passed before he could speak.

"I just had the most unusual dream," Parviz began, and shared everything he remembered.

Both of them recalled how Parviz had received messages before from the spirit world through dreams. In fact, he had dreamed about some of the most important events in his life—including the death of his father in Iran and the circumstances of his family's escape to the United States—right before they happened.

So Parviz needed no convincing that this dream reflected spiritual reality. Yet what a surprise! He might have expected a religious dream to feature Muhammad. But Jesus? He knew almost nothing about Jesus and had never read the Bible.

Still, Parviz' dream made a deep impression. His whole outlook on life changed, and inside he sensed that his search for peace and meaning had somehow found its end. Financial problems still nagged, but with new hope he felt strengthened to face those and other challenges. Thoughts of suicide evaporated like morning mist. And his back improved dramatically, allowing him to look once more for employment.

Over and over Parviz pondered his dream. He did not understand everything it meant, but he knew that this Jesus at the fountain had invited him to join Him and that he had drunk of the water offered. Now Parviz began a quest to find his way to Him.

In September 1990 Parviz and his family relocated to Southern California in search of better work opportunities. His enjoyment of life blossomed. He purchased a cab and started work as a taxi-driver. Then he learned that his long-time aspiration to start a small business, perhaps a convenience store, might find a better chance of fulfillment near Denver. In September 1993 the family moved again.

But his ambition ran into roadblocks, and Parviz returned to cab-driving. Then on Thursday, June 30, 1994, he picked up a passenger at the Marriott Hotel in Denver who changed the course of his spiritual quest.

That passenger, a businessman named Bill Greig, Jr., was headed for the airport. He expressed curiosity about the origin of Parviz' name.

"I'm Iranian—that is, Persian," said Parviz. "I used to live in Tehran."

"Are you a Muslim?"

"No," Parviz answered slowly, "not anymore. But I'm not sure what I am."

He began telling his story as Bill seemed to listen with interest. He also recounted his dream.

"So you drank the water Jesus offered!" Bill exclaimed when he had finished. "Do you know that in the Bible Jesus said He came to offer us living water?"

"No," Parviz replied, turning to look at Bill in surprise. "I've never really read the Bible. I always felt that dream was a message to me, but maybe I haven't responded to that message very well. I didn't really take advantage of it right away, to find my way to Jesus."

Bill leaned forward from the back seat. "I know the Qur'an says more about Jesus—Isa—than any other prophet. But it is in error when it says He did not die on the cross. In fact, He did die for your sins and mine, and all He asks is for us to believe in Him."

When Bill asked if he could pray for Parviz, he agreed eagerly. Parviz felt Bill put a hand on his right shoulder, so he put his own left hand onto Bill's while he continued driving. Bill prayed for him, for his back, for his wife and son, asking the Lord to show them how much Jesus loved them and the meaning of His death and resurrection.

By this time they were approaching the airport terminal. Parviz wrote down his address and phone number for Bill.

"You know," he said, "I tried to visit some churches, but never found one where I felt comfortable."

"I have a friend in the Denver area who can recommend a fellowship here for Iranian believers," Bill replied. "I'll send that information to you."

As Parviz said good-bye and drove away, his heart felt light and happy.

About two weeks later the mail carrier delivered a package from Bill Greig, Jr., president of Gospel Light Publications in Ventura, California. It contained several books, including a Living Bible in which Bill had marked certain passages. What Parviz read amazed him.

Jesus replied that people soon became thirsty again after drinking this water. "But the water I give them," he said, "becomes a perpetual spring within them, watering them forever with eternal life."

John 4:13–14, TLB

Wow, that's just like my dream! Parviz marveled. He turned to the next one.

. . . Jesus shouted to the crowds, "If anyone is thirsty, let him come to me and drink. For the Scriptures declare that rivers of living water shall flow from the inmost being of anyone who believes in me."

John 7:37–38, TLB

Parviz could hardly believe that Jesus had offered him personally this living water to drink. He felt so undeserving. And he continued to read.

Later, when Parviz phoned Bill to thank him for the books, he could sense faith welling up inside.

Parviz and Bill kept in touch. In January 1995 Parviz and his family visited Southern California where his wife's brother lived. He contacted Bill in Ventura, and their families spent the day together on Thursday, January 5. Bill had time to explain the Gospel in a clear, understandable way, and after lunch Parviz prayed the sinner's prayer with sincerity, asking for and receiving God's forgiveness of sins through Jesus Christ.

As a result of a divine appointment with another Christian in Loveland, Colorado, Parviz attended church there and felt immediately at home.

Parviz continues to grow in his faith day by day, having entered a relationship with the One in his dream who offered him the water of life.

Potential and Limitations

Parviz' spiritual journey illustrates both the potential and the limitations of dreams and visions for Muslim evangelism. Many Muslims like Parviz live or used to live in cultures where spiritual communication through dreams and visions is not unusual. Particularly among the Shia and Sufi sects of Islam, many people expect God to speak to them in such a way. Islam began, in fact, when Muhammad received revelation of the Qur'an through dreams, visions and trances.

The first revelation came on the 27th day of the month of Ramadan in A.D. 610, and Muslims everywhere still commemorate this event annually. During Ramadan, particularly "the night of power" on the 27th, many Muslims actively pursue guidance through supernatural means. According to the 1995 "30 Days Muslim Prayer Focus" booklet (published by the group of the same name),

> Muslims often think that this night is a special night when God gives heed to their requests and they are often open to dreams and visions at this time seeking guidance and revelation. Many Muslims will **pray all night** seeking a response to specific requests. One common belief is that angels will shower down the peace and blessings of God on all who remain awake during this "night of power."
>
> emphasis in original

With a spiritual worldview that not only allows for but affirms supernatural revelation, Muslims have more potential to hear from the spirit realm than people steeped in cultures that exalt scientific rationalism. Here is a great opportunity for Christians to pray for God to reveal Himself in the Person of Jesus Christ to Muslims praying for spiritual messages.

Without the protection or intervention of God, on the other hand, Muslims seeking guidance through dreams and visions can easily be deceived by messages of demonic origin. The apostle Paul writes in 2 Corinthians 11:14 that "Satan himself masquerades as an angel of light." The prayers of God's people for Muslims can help raise a spiritual shield against their receiving false and deceptive revelations.

Even when a dream or vision comes from the one true God, the recipient often needs more explanation or counsel in order to respond adequately. Although Parviz recognized the divine origin of his dream and saw his life change as a result, he did not understand the Gospel or how to enter into a relationship with Jesus Christ until Bill Greig, Jr., and other believers followed up on the initial work of the Holy Spirit.

Christians who pray for supernatural breakthroughs among unreached or resistant people groups also need to commit themselves to supporting the ministries of faithful men and women who give their lives to teach the Word of God, disciple new converts and plant reproducible churches.

Forging Trails in Pioneer Territory

As David Henry's plane landed in Banjul, capital of The Gambia, on February 14, 1994, the church-planting coach and trainer wondered what fruit might come of the unexpected opportunity to minister in this West African nation.

The Lord had arranged for David to meet four Australian believers down the coast in Sierra Leone, with whom he had spent four incredible hours at the Lungi Airport in Freetown that very day, helping Muslims come to know Jesus (the story in chapter 1). The Australians were traveling to The Gambia to assist in the distribution of food and medical equipment through a mercy ship ministry. They also planned to participate in nightly outreach meetings.

The team gathered at the Banjul Bible Training Center, established about five months before under the leadership of director Bert Farias. They also met staff member Michael Afolabi, a Nigerian Christian discipled at a Bible institute in Monrovia, Liberia, who now worked with Bert.

Before getting ready for their first outdoor evangelistic meeting that night, the group huddled to pray, asking God to touch those who would hear the message. During prayer a young Australian musician, Ian Farrington, collapsed to the floor, unable to stand. When he recovered enough to find a chair, he told the others what had happened.

"It was like I was lifted up in the clouds above all of Africa," he explained. "I saw an army of huge angels ready for battle, with a bank of ugly demon faces opposite them over North Africa. As I watched, the angels drove the demons back. They retreated north until they disappeared into the Mediterranean. Then I saw a spark of fire flame up and begin to burn all over the continent."

Ian paused, his face still pale. "I sensed in my spirit God saying, 'This is now.'"

David and the others fell silent as they contemplated the awesome vision. What an encouragement that God's Spirit was on the move!

The campaign on the outskirts of Banjul extended for four nights. Risk ran high because the 96% Muslim country was in the midst of the Islamic holy month of Ramadan, when pious Muslims fast from sunup to sundown. Each night police came by asking the outreach team to move indoors, or at least turn down the volume of their music and preaching. But the campaign, held on private property, was allowed to continue in the open air.

The Lord spoke to the hearts of many listeners. At least sixteen or eighteen people each night responded to the Gospel message. Students from the Bible Training Center helped teach the new believers.

David and the Australians wanted to press inland to visit areas more neglected by missions outreach. The five of them, with Bert Farias, Michael Afolabi, a Fula interpreter and a Muslim driver, piled into a little Toyota Hi-Ace van, stashing a guitar, an electronic keyboard, a pair of speakers and the rest of their gear.

For about five hours they followed the road beside the Gambia River, around which the sliver of country fingers inland. At Farafenni, an almost entirely Muslim town of about 7,500 (many of these from the Fula people group), David learned that probably no more than a dozen Christians, including nominal believers, lived in the area. Bert found two young men working under Campus Crusade for Christ who had a small generator and a videotape copy of the *Jesus* film. They allowed Bert, David and their crew to borrow the generator for a couple of nights of outdoor meetings.

The team made the most of rustic conditions. Beside a dusty road they set up a table and strung a few lightbulbs on a rusty old fence made of 55-gallon drums beaten flat. Ian Farrington and his musician friend, Neal Harris, belted out praise song after praise song until they drew a crowd of three or four hundred people, many returning from Friday evening meetings at the local mosques.

Bert Farias preached boldly about Jesus as the Son of God, and at the end invited listeners who wanted a relationship with the Messiah to pray with him. About twenty people indicated their response. But amid the commotion of the crowd, including some heckling and harassment, the outreach team had little chance to follow up.

The next day they got better organized and made arrangements for a room in the town where they could direct people responding to the invitation. That evening seventeen people came forward, then met with the team privately. Bert and David recapped the Gospel message and led each of them in confessing Jesus as Savior. They also encouraged as many as possible to return the following morning for more in-depth instruction in the Word of God.

All seventeen showed up again that Sunday morning, February 20, hungry for teaching. It was hard to miss the eagerness on the faces of these new believers. But David and Bert and the team planned to head in the van back to Banjul about noon to meet obligations there.

During a break in the training, Michael Afolabi, the Nigerian Christian who worked with Bert, drew some of the team members aside.

"Look at the openness we've found here!" he exclaimed. "What receptivity! How can we just leave these people?"

Bert studied his staff member. "Michael, if your heart is burning to minister here, you have my permission to stay."

David pulled a bill from his wallet. "Here, Michael. Use this for food and your eventual return transportation. Stay as long as it takes to get these people on their feet spiritually."

One of the Australians reached into his own pocket. "Yeah, I'll match that."

Michael's eyes welled up. "Oh, man, I *couldn't* leave them! Even if you didn't give me money, I couldn't leave. I've got to stay and help."

At the end of the morning training session, one of the new Fula believers approached Bert and David, frowning gravely.

"I have something to ask you," he said. "I've got a brother back in my village tormented by demons. Twice a day he falls down flailing and foaming at the mouth. When he gets up after one of these fits, he often wanders in a daze into the bush or jumps into the river. It's horrible—and this has been going on daily for twelve years. Can you help my brother?"

Bert and David looked at each other.

"We have to go back to Banjul today," David apologized. He turned to Michael. "Michael, can you minister deliverance?"

"Yeah, no problem."

"O.K., then, go for it. It's your ballgame."

A month later Michael penned a letter, which David eventually received at his home in South Pasadena, California. In it Michael described his experience that same day after the van left for Banjul.

He accompanied the new believer to Yala-Bah, a Fula village within walking distance of Farafenni, to minister to the convert's brother, Lipna Manneh, about seventeen years old. Speaking directly to the evil spirit, Michael rebuked it in Jesus' name and commanded it to leave the boy. Lipna shook like a rag in a dog's mouth and fell to the ground, then lay still. When he got up he was completely delivered.

After they had opportunity to talk, the youth told Michael he believed a demon from the river in their village had been responsible for his oppression. Lipna said he had not attended school since he was small, when the epileptic-type attacks began. Michael directed him to return home to his parents with a message: "Here's your boy, free and well through the power of Jesus Christ. You can send him back to school now."

Soon afterward, however, Lipna's parents sent him back to Michael in Farafenni with their own message: "With our deepest thanks, please enroll Lipna in your school and continue whatever you are doing with him."

Michael moved his home to Farafenni and started a new Bible Training Center with fifteen students, nine of them converts from Islam. Another ten joined evening Bible classes three times a week. Michael explained in his letter to David that many of these "cannot read and write, yet they can hear and memorize." He said he was stunned at the sincerity and hunger of the new believers.

> Even when I ask them not to come, they come, just to know more about this new way and faith. I am not keeping quiet at all. I mobilize them to bring their friends and relations. This is also paying off, as converts are being added to the ones made before.

After praising God for the transformation of Lipna Manneh, Michael concluded his letter, "We shall soon go to the boy's village for outreach. His case is a good testimony around this place."

Almost everyone in the surrounding Fula villages knew of Lipna's former condition. So when they saw the Lord's power in delivering him after twelve years of bondage, they wanted to know about the God who had done this.

In his next letter to David about three months later, Michael described the evangelistic outreaches the new Bible students helped him carry out. The chief of Yala-Bah, Lipna Manneh's once solidly Muslim village, had expressed great openness to the Gospel. On April 28, 1994, Michael and a small team had begun preaching there, and within three days fourteen people had given their lives to Christ. Seven eventually joined the Farafenni Bible Training Center. By May 15 they had established a house church with weekly Sunday morning worship.

This pattern was repeated in other villages in the area. The solid wall of Islamic resistance to the Gospel began to crumble, as anywhere from nine to 24 people in each village responded to the initial outreach presentations. The depth of their new commitment stunned even Michael. "Surprising to us," he wrote David, "they demanded that we create time to teach them the Word of God. Glory to God. We began weekly Bible study with the villagers. The numbers continue to rise weekly."

David Henry could hardly have dreamed that his side trip to The Gambia would result in such a bonanza. He kept in touch with Michael and made plans to return to the country to train another generation of church-planting leaders to mine the rich lode of priceless souls.

Cooperating with God

The severe demonization of Lipna Manneh brings to mind Jesus' encounter with the demoniac in the region of the Gerasenes, east of the Sea of Galilee in the Gentile area known as the Decapolis. The man with the evil spirit

> had often been chained hand and foot, but he tore the chains apart and broke the irons on his feet. No one was strong enough to subdue him. Night and day among the tombs and in the hills he would cry out and cut himself with stones.
>
> Mark 5:4–5

After Jesus cast out the legion of demons, people in the nearby towns heard about it and came out to see the man now at peace, dressed and in his right mind. Awestruck with fear at such authority, they asked Jesus to leave their region. As He was departing, the newly delivered man begged to go with Him. But Jesus knew, like Michael Afolabi, that "his case is a good testimony around this place." He instructed the man,

> "Go home to your family and tell them how much the Lord has done for you, and how he has had mercy on you." So the man went away and began to tell in the Decapolis how much Jesus had done for him. And all the people were amazed.
>
> verses 19–20

Did the deliverance of the former demoniac, and his testimony to Jesus' power and mercy, make a strong impression in his neighborhood? Witness the response, according to the Gospel of Mark, the next time Jesus visited the Decapolis. Now, instead of begging Him to leave, the people brought Jesus another man in need of

His healing touch, whose hearing and speech Jesus restored. As a result, "People were overwhelmed with amazement. 'He has done everything well,' they said. 'He even makes the deaf hear and the mute speak'" (Mark 7:37). Soon Jesus attracted a crowd that included four thousand men.

Healing and deliverance, particularly in well-known and seemingly hopeless cases, can serve as powerful signposts of the one true God, especially among resistant people groups like Muslims. One miracle can open up an area to the Gospel and begin a people movement toward Christ.

Yet God rarely works in a vacuum. David Henry points out that the new receptivity to the Gospel in the Farafenni area "didn't take place without Michael's obedience, without Bert's preaching, without our traveling in there. And so it's sovereign—and yet there's also human cooperation. Even divine dreams and visions usually point people toward someone who can then communicate the Gospel." God has designed the spiritual realm to function in such a way that our obedience and participation carry out the fullness of His will on earth.

For some, obedience may mean crossing cultural barriers, sharing the Gospel, teaching the Bible or being prepared to minister in signs and wonders when the Lord directs. For others, faithfulness in prayer and intercession may be all God is waiting for in order to bring a breakthrough in the lives of others. The Lord gives us the privilege of praying into being things He might not otherwise do out of respect for the free will He has given humankind. Eighteenth-century English evangelist John Wesley is often quoted as saying, "God does nothing but in answer to prayer." If this is true, even in part, God's people have an awesome responsibility to cooperate with Him in bringing to reality everything He desires to accomplish in today's world.

Mohammed and the Bus Driver

Mecca! The man we will call Mohammed shivered with excitement. To think he was really here, at the heart of Islam in Saudi

Arabia, the birthplace of the great Prophet whose name he bore—the dream of a lifetime!

Although Mohammed served as an *imam* (pastor) at his local mosque on the island of Sumatra, Indonesia, he had never before made a pilgrimage to Mecca, as all devout Muslims must do at least once. This first *hajj* in May 1992 fulfilled Mohammed's commitment to the fifth and last pillar of Islam. He went full of expectation that this trip would represent the spiritual climax of his life.

On his first day in Mecca, Mohammed signed up for a bus tour of some outlying holy sites. The next morning he arrived early for one of the many regularly scheduled departures, and he sat right behind the bus driver to get a good view out the front window. He was glad the coach did not fill up and seats nearby remained empty.

The bus shifted into gear and headed down the road toward the city of Medina and the shrines they would visit. In Medina the Prophet Muhammad had established his theocratic state after fleeing a murder plot in Mecca in A.D. 622. With Medina more than two hundred miles north of Mecca, Mohammed had plenty of time to strike up a conversation with the bus driver.

Above the drone of the engine they exchanged chit-chat, using English as a common language.

"Yes, this is my first hajj," Mohammed told the dark-haired driver whose face framed deep, penetrating eyes. "I'm from Sumatra, a Malay—one of the largest Muslim people groups in Southeast Asia."

The driver swiveled his head sideways enough to see Mohammed. "You know, you really shouldn't have spent all your money coming here."

Mohammed figured he had misunderstood. He leaned forward to catch the driver's words. "Excuse me?"

"Coming here on pilgrimage is really a waste of money," the driver repeated unmistakably. "All the rituals seeking to get into Allah's good graces—when you stop to think about it, Islam is full of hypocrisies."

Stunned, Mohammed could only listen as the man went on to point out issues he had never considered. For over an hour they conversed as the bus rumbled on through the desert.

"The truth is," said the driver, turning to look straight at his passenger, "Allah wants to know you personally, as a friend, not just at a distance through rituals. Islam can't give you that kind of relationship."

With their destination approaching, the driver slowed and downshifted to park at the site. Everyone disembarked, but Mohammed's head spun with new, unthinkable thoughts. In a daze he followed the tour group, yet now everything seemed confused. *What did the driver mean? Where did he get such a perspective? How could I possibly run into a person like that in the Holy Land!*

After the tour Mohammed hurried back to meet the returning bus, eager to get a seat by the driver and resume their conversation. But when he boarded, he looked up to see the face of someone new. His spirits sank.

"What happened to the earlier driver?" he asked the man behind the wheel.

He got little more than a shrug in response.

Mohammed found a seat and stared out the window. During the trip back to Mecca, his heart burned with the words of the man on the morning bus. He felt he could recall the whole conversation from beginning to end.

Mohammed's hajj lasted more than a week, but the excitement and anticipation he had brought with him fizzled like air from a leaky tire. Everything he saw and did etched fresh questions and doubts into his mind. As he continued his pilgrimage, he scanned all the buses lined up at each tour site, but never saw his driver again.

Back at home Mohammed's family wondered why he had not returned bubbling with joy from his spiritual zenith. In the solitude of his thoughts he pored over the events of his hajj. He could not forget the driver's words or his face. Yet Mohammed's spirit grappled with perplexities. *If Islam is not the true faith, what is?*

A few days later Mohammed dropped by the home of a neighbor we will call A-Ching, a Chinese Christian, to borrow something. A-Ching welcomed him inside with customary Indonesian hospitality. As they chatted, Mohammed's eyes lit on something hanging from A-Ching's wall. There within a picture frame he saw the face of his bus driver from Mecca!

Mohammed gasped, pointing to the picture. "A-Ching! Do you know this man?"

"Yes, I do," came the reply. "That's Jesus. You know Him as Isa."

Mohammed sat still as a stone. *Isa! The second-highest prophet in Islam—the Christians' Messiah! Could it be—?*

When he found his voice, he spoke up quietly. "I have a story to tell you, A-Ching."

His neighbor, just as shocked at the tale, listened in silence. When Mohammed finished, he began to choke up, suddenly overcome with conviction of his sin. A-Ching explained the truths Jesus had declared about His own identity and purpose.

"Mohammed, you can receive salvation as the free gift of God through Jesus Christ," A-Ching told him. "You can have a personal relationship with God."

Mohammed prayed and committed his life to Christ. When he returned home, he gathered his family and spilled out the whole account. Awed at his story and his transformation, they, too, confessed Jesus as Lord and Messiah.

A-Ching introduced Mohammed privately to the pastor of his local fellowship. Then, for their own protection, a network of believers spirited the new convert and his family to a safe house in another city where they could receive biblical teaching without risking retribution from angry Islamists.

Mohammed's trip to Mecca indeed proved to be the turning point of his spiritual life. But he never expected supernatural revelation to come through his bus driver.

Sovereign and Creative Breakthroughs

Even in the heart of Mecca, at a time when millions of devout Muslims are reaffirming pacts with the demonic strongholds of Islam, God in His sovereignty demonstrates creative ways of breaking through to those He has called to be His own. Stories like this one blast holes in our usual conceptions of what God can or will do.

Theologians may debate whether the bus driver in Mohammed's story could actually have been Jesus in human guise or some kind of angelic being. But their scholarly arguments would make no difference to Mohammed. One way or another, God communicated to him an immediate, penetrating, unforgettable message through His emissary at the wheel of the bus.

Here again the supernatural visitation alone did not bring the recipient directly into the Kingdom of God. The heaven-sent message tore the veil of darkness off Mohammed's mind enough for him to see, for the first time, the futility of Islam. Then when Mohammed learned the identity of the driver during his visit to A-Ching's house, his friend shared the way of salvation and prayed with him to be born again in Christ. Without A-Ching's role, the miracle might have produced nothing more than a stillbirth.

Although divine intervention in the Muslim world has apparently revved into high gear recently, signs and wonders during the hajj have historical precedent. Notice in the following account the key role of the believer:

> In 1855, Yahya Baqui, a zealous Afghan Muslim, made the long pilgrimage to Mecca, and in a dream was told that he should follow Christ. On his way home he met a Christian doctor and was soon baptized as the first Afghan convert to Christ. He returned to Afghanistan boldly proclaiming the Gospel!
> Day 9, 1995 "30 Days Muslim Prayer Focus"

What an encouragement to know that God's hands are not tied, no matter how hopeless a situation may seem for the advance of the Gospel! No power, earthly or demonic, can begin to match His as the Creator of the universe or thwart the ultimate will He has purposed to accomplish, to save some from every people group on earth. Let His declaration of omnipotence boost your faith: "I am the LORD, the God of all mankind. Is anything too hard for me?" (Jeremiah 32:27).

10

What Then Shall We Do?

The wild man living out in the desert attracted a lot of attention. His rustic clothing and strange diet set him apart as a prophet like the ones of old. Just about everyone in the territory nearby trekked out to hear his provocative proclamations and get baptized by him in the River Jordan. Addressing the religious leaders with blunt, shocking language, John the Baptist pulled no punches, offending some and chastening others. "And the multitudes asked him, 'What then shall we do?'" (Luke 3:10, RSV).

Distinct groups of listeners came in turn and asked John the same question as it applied to their particular situations. Tax-collectors and soldiers wanted their own specific instructions. All felt the same burning conviction: "If what you say is true, what does this mean for me personally?"

John's audience recognized that his message demanded a response. They found it impossible to hear him, receive baptism and then go back to their workaday lives unchanged. They needed to incarnate their new understanding into their choices, actions and perspectives.

In today's on-line, drive-through, hurry-up world, we frequently fail to take time to reflect on what we see, hear, read or experience. Yet even in small events God may have a message for us, making it appropriate for us to ask, "Lord, is there something here You want me to learn or remember or do?"

In this book we have seen the power of God at work in an amazing variety of ways to bring people to salvation through His Son, Jesus Christ. In light of all God has done, perhaps the Holy Spirit wants to prompt us, like John's disciples, to consider a fitting response. I hope this chapter will help you turn this book from a collection of stories into a catalyst for action.

A Smorgasbord of Styles

Power evangelism can have as many variations as the limitless power of God may initiate. We have looked at several of them:

- *Divine Healing.* One of the main themes in supernatural healing is how God's compassion for the sick and suffering, in conjunction with His ability to bring physical relief, draws people to Him as they see He is both loving and powerful.
- *Prophetic Messages and Words of Knowledge.* Through supernatural messages, God shows His personal concern for individuals, whether warning them from sin or assuring them they are known and loved. Prophetic messages can also give believers inside information on how God wants to minister to specific people at specific places and times.
- *Dreams and Visions.* God sometimes uses dreams, visions or trances to bypass emotional or analytical barriers to the Gospel. A dream or vision may represent the most effective way for some people to receive and understand the truth about Jesus Christ.
- *Angelic Visitations.* Angels, whether appearing in supernatural form or disguised in human form, can serve as God's spe-

cial messengers to convey truth, protect from danger or lead people to an encounter with the good news of Christ.

- *Miracles.* Miracles—including improbable "coincidences" of timing and circumstance, divine appointments, unexplained nature phenomena, and language or healing wonders—often break through intellectual resistance to the Gospel, rearranging worldview grids.
- *"Extraordinary Miracles."* On occasion God demonstrates His sovereignty over the universe by temporarily suspending the laws of nature He has established. In so doing He intervenes to meet people's most desperate needs, showing extraordinary love and compassion and eliciting heartfelt response.
- *Spiritual Warfare.* Spiritual warfare serves to bind evil forces that fight against the Gospel. The Lord works through a variety of methodologies, including deliverance, power encounter and intercessory warfare, to show the power of His Kingdom triumphant over the strongholds of darkness and to release Satan's captives to respond to Christ.

This book represents by no means a comprehensive survey of power evangelism. The smorgasbord of stories here can give just a taste of what God is doing around the world in using signs and wonders to facilitate salvation.

The Limits of Documentation

One purpose for this book is to provide a careful record of a few dozen conversions occurring in conjunction with supernatural signs, boosting their credibility and the consequent praise to God.

St. Augustine, writing in the fifth century, had a similar aim. Yet he recognized the limitations of this approach. While affirming God's ongoing ministry of miracles, Augustine lamented the lack of publicity and authoritative documentation that thwarted contemporary signs and wonders from generating all the glory to God He deserved.

The truth is that even today miracles are being wrought in the name of Christ. . . . The fact that the canon of our Scriptures is definitively closed brings it about that the original miracles are everywhere repeated and are fixed in people's memory, whereas contemporary miracles which happen here or there seldom become known even to the whole of the local population in and around the place where they occur. Especially is this the case in the more populous cities, where relatively few learn the facts while most of the people remain uninformed. And when the news does spread from mouth to mouth, even in the case of Christians reporting to Christians, it is too unauthoritative to be received without some difficulty or doubt.

The City of God
Book 22, chapter 8

The need for careful documentation represents only one hurdle on the road to acceptance for power evangelism stories with the potential to glorify God. We discussed in chapter 6, in the context of miracles, the issue of worldview and having "eyes to see." We acknowledged that no amount of historical evidence—or, indeed, eyewitness experience—will convince skeptics whose worldviews disallow the possibility of miracles. In extreme cases skeptical eyewitnesses may decide they were suffering a hallucination. Only the Spirit of God working to bring about a paradigm shift will allow people to see what otherwise they cannot see.

Why doesn't God make Himself and His works so unmistakably clear that no one can deny Him? Blaise Pascal, the seventeenth-century French mathematician and Christian thinker, wrestled with this question in his *Pensées*. Pascal noted that the Lord will, in fact, reveal Himself plainly when He comes again at the end of the age, on the clouds with trumpet blast and great glory. But for now He elects not to compel belief out of those with no desire to relate to Him, preferring not automatons but children who choose freely to love and obey.

Pascal concluded,

It was therefore not right that he should appear before them in a manner that was obviously divine and absolutely bound to convince all mankind. Neither was it right that his coming should be in such hiddenness that he could not be recognized even by those who sincerely looked for him. But he wished to make himself perfectly recognizable to such. Instead, wishing to appear openly to those who seek him with all their heart, and yet hidden from those who shun him with all their heart, God has given signs of himself, which are visible to those who seek him, and not by those who do not seek him.

There is enough light for those who desire only to see, and darkness for those of a contrary disposition.

No. 132 (Multnomah Press edition)

Unbelievers have their own set of worldview issues to deal with. But even Christians who believe in the divinity of Jesus sometimes shake their heads at reports of contemporary signs and wonders. One key guide in discernment is to examine the fruit of these incidents. The greatest significance of a story lies not in the supernatural event itself but in whether someone moves toward a relationship with Christ as a result. If so, then God is behind it, for Jesus Himself said, "No one can come to me unless the Father who sent me draws him" (John 6:44).

While our focus must remain on Christ and not the miracles in themselves, believers desiring to see Him exalted throughout the world will investigate the potential of power ministries for evangelism. If souls saved for the Kingdom of God represent the Lord's bottom line, the ministry of the supernatural can multiply the harvest of new believers when we partner with God according to His will. In many areas around the globe today, this is happening at an unprecedented rate.

Why Signs and Wonders?

Why does God intervene sovereignly, powerfully in the lives of unbelievers? We will highlight two reasons.

Compassion for the Lost

First, God's intervention in the lives of unbelievers relates to His compassion and sensitivity to people's pressing desires and difficulties. Many would never understand their deepest need for a Savior until their immediate felt needs are met. When God steps into people's lives—through healing, a prophetic word at a moment of desperation, a dream, vision or miracle that brings assurance that He cares about the situations and problems most important to them—people recognize more readily the reality of God and their need for a personal relationship with Him.

Edgardo Silvoso, in his book *That None Should Perish*, illuminates this concept masterfully. He reminds us that the Good Shepherd leaves the 99 sheep safe with the flock to search out the hundredth sheep lost in the briar patch of bondage to sin (see Luke 15:1–7). God's passion for the lost drives Him to any lengths to redeem these beloved ones and draw them to Himself. This divine zeal explains why brand-new believers just making the transition from darkness to light sometimes see sign after sign of God's supernatural power. Then, with their eternal destinies secured, the Good Shepherd transfers them from the "Club of the One-Hundredth Sheep" into the fold with the 99. Now the new believers may find dramatic miracles less frequent, because less is at stake in a crisis for a believer whose salvation is assured and who can turn to the Lord for spiritual resources.

As God's children, we can learn from the model of His Son, Jesus, by letting Him develop in us a radar sense for the needs felt most desperately by those around us. When we offer to minister to those needs through intercession in the name of Jesus Christ, as well as through acts of compassion, people's hearts unfold to the Gospel like roses blossoming in the summer sun.

Silvoso writes,

> Meeting the felt needs of the lost opens their eyes to the reality of God and allows them to make a vital connection between His power and His love for them (see Mark 1:40, 41; Acts 4:9–12). Most unsaved people believe in the power of God. The universe itself is clear testimony of God's power. What most of them do not believe is that God loves them. When God's power, shown through an answer to prayer, is released on their behalf, they are finally able to make that connection. As Paul explained to King Agrippa, once

their eyes are open, they have a choice to turn from darkness to life and from the dominion of Satan to God (see Acts 26:18).

page 80

We can help open those eyes as we pray for God to show Himself strong at the point of people's needs.

Advancing the Fulfillment of the Great Commission

The second reason God intervenes sovereignly, powerfully in the lives of unbelievers is specifically to bring them to Himself. The Holy Spirit is casting His net wider and deeper and faster as the return of Jesus Christ approaches. Patrick Johnstone, editor of *Operation World*, writes in the 1993 edition,

We are living in the time of the largest ingathering of people into the Kingdom of God that the world has ever seen. . . . For the first time in history we can meaningfully talk of the real possibility of world evangelization in our generation. What a privilege, what a responsibility to be a Christian alive today!

pages 25–26

"I believe," says C. Peter Wagner in *How to Have a Healing Ministry in Any Church*, "that in the twentieth century we have been witnessing the most powerful outpouring of the Holy Spirit on the world Church that history has ever known. At least in magnitude, if not also in quality, it surpasses even the first century." He explains that the contemporary waves of the Holy Spirit he identifies "have seen, and I believe will continue to see, explosive church growth" (page 16).

All over the world the Lord is working toward the day when "a great multitude that no one could count, from every nation, tribe, people and language, [will stand] before the throne and in front of the Lamb" (Revelation 7:9). In God's desire to save some from every people group, even the most obscure, He demonstrates that His purposes are global in scope. And, as Johnstone notes, those of us believers alive today have both the privilege and the responsibility to co-labor with Him toward fulfillment of the Great Commission.

Power evangelism can play a role in advancing those goals. For instance, in close-knit societies that make important decisions through group consensus, a demonstration of the power of God may result in a quick, widespread turnaround within a family or larger unit. Then, as these new believers touch other lives through a web of social relationships, an entire people may move toward Jesus Christ. This strategy reflects the way many intercessors are praying for certain nations—for instance, the country of Japan.

At the same time, the front-line troops in the army of the Lord must stand ready for dispatch at a moment's notice to wherever the Holy Spirit is breaking through enemy territory. Advance soldiers already on the scene will have the first opportunity to begin liberating captives from the devil's prisoner-of-war camps. In this role God's people must then distribute the Bread of Life to the starving throngs.

World evangelization, while on one hand a sovereign work of God, involves human cooperation. God has chosen to make us responsible participants in His work. For power evangelism, too, both the ministry of divine power and our proclamation of the Word of God should go hand in hand. Jesus' last message to His disciples reflects this: "You will receive power when the Holy Spirit comes on you; and you will be my witnesses in Jerusalem, and in all Judea and Samaria, and to the ends of the earth" (Acts 1:8). The apostle Paul described his ministry in Thessalonica in similar terms: "Our gospel came to you not simply with words, but also with power, with the Holy Spirit and with deep conviction" (1 Thessalonians 1:5).

The words of the Gospel bring necessary knowledge of Christ's atonement for sins on the cross. Demonstrations of spiritual power can help quicken faith. Then the Holy Spirit, working through both the words and the power, plants a deep, inward conviction in the hearts of the new believers. This inner conviction, resulting from the combination of both Word and works, is what sustains new believers through periods of persecution, trials and spiritual dryness.

God's witnesses find greatest effectiveness in missions and evangelism when they use all the spiritual resources available. Those proclaiming the Gospel faithfully may also pray that the Lord intervene in power confirming His divinity. Those involved in ministries of power, and those who observe sovereign supernatural acts of God, should seize the opportunity to proclaim the clear message of the Gospel regarding the power source.

Prayer: Key to Releasing God's Power

In the act of intercessory prayer, we acknowledge that we have no power in ourselves to bring about change, and we recognize God as the only omnipotent authority who can act on our behalf.

Arthur T. Pierson, who helped found the Student Volunteer Movement for Foreign Missions in 1886, believed that this dependence on God through prayer represented the key to world evangelization. As editor of *The Missionary Review of the World*, he wrote in the August 1890 issue,

> Every time the Church has set herself to praying, there have been stupendous movements in the mission world. If we should but transfer the stress of our dependence and emphasis from appeals to men to appeals to God—from trust in organization to trust in supplication—from confidence in methods to importunate prayer for the power of the Holy Ghost, we should see results more astounding than have yet been wrought.
>
> pages 585–586

Author Richard J. Foster observes something similar in *Celebration of Discipline* (revised edition, Harper & Row, 1988) about the discipline of prayer: "We are working with God to determine the future! Certain things will happen in history if we pray rightly. We are to change the world by prayer" (p. 35).

Without compromising His sovereignty, God has structured His relationship with His people so that we may take part in what He is doing. He specifically invites us to ask Him to accomplish His will, and often waits for us to do so. "Ask of me," the Lord beckons in Psalm 2:8, "and I will make the nations your inheritance, the ends of the earth your possession."

Paul suggests in 1 Corinthians 3:9 ("For we are God's fellow workers . . .") that we co-labor with God in His goal of bringing salvation to the peoples of the world. In this process we may part-ner with the Holy Spirit in His desire to touch someone with a miraculous sign of God's love and power. We also partner with the risen Lord Jesus in His ongoing work of intercession (see Romans 8:34; Hebrews 7:25).

The 1995 "30 Days Muslim Prayer Focus" booklet, published to encourage Christians to pray for Muslims during the month of Ramadan, states in the introduction, "You will never learn to know the nations of the world as fast as you will through intercession." The more we intercede for people and nations, the better we come to know them. As we come to know and care for them in prayer, we will love them more. Then our love for them will draw us back into intercession as we long to bless them and see their needs met.

Richard Foster closes the circle: "If we truly love people, we will desire for them far more than it is within our power to give them, and this will lead us to prayer. Intercession is a way of loving oth-ers" (*Prayer: Finding the Heart's True Home,* HarperSanFrancisco, 1992, p. 191).

Prayer can release God's supernatural power for salvation on those who need His grace and mercy. Prayer can also bind the pow-ers of darkness and break demonic bondages that keep people from coming to Christ. After ministering to a violently demonized boy, Jesus explained to His disciples, who had made an unsuccessful previous attempt at deliverance, "This kind can come out only by prayer" (Mark 9:29).

Prayer for God's power in the salvation of the lost may well require persistence, as a number of Jesus' parables taught. The Bible also stresses the importance of agreement and unity in prayer. One hallmark of the first-century Church was its practice of united, cor-porate prayer—not only praying similar petitions for the fulfill-ment of the Lord's will but actually meeting to pray "all together in one place" (see Acts 2:1). Every prayer principle that applies to individual intercession can be put to use with multiplied effectiveness in the context of corporate prayer.

Practical Steps to Take

At this point we recognize that power evangelism (in its many forms) demonstrates the compassion of God and helps to speed fulfillment of the Great Commission. We acknowledge that God's power is released through prayer.

What then shall we do?

Be Open to New Roles

Does God want every believer to emphasize a ministry of power evangelism? Not at all. The diversity of functions in the Body of Christ, like sections of an orchestra, reflects the polyphonic beauty of the Lord, and when each of the parts is represented, they harmonize well. But believers who are ready to minister in new and different ways than in the past can enhance their potential usefulness to the Spirit of the Lord. Our God, while unchanging in essence, is never static in His relationship with His children. At any time He may ask us to move out in new ways, into new roles—sometimes for a brief season and sometimes as a no-turning-back life change.

With so many different gifts and ministries in the Body of Christ, no one of them, including any of various forms of power evangelism, will ever become a primary ministry for the majority of believers. But just as members of a large family, each with assigned chores, may also pitch in and help one another when needed, so members of the family of God should be ready to step in and function in whatever way the Lord needs hands and feet at the moment.

Ignatius of Loyola (1491–1556), founder of the Society of Jesus, wrote a devotional volume called *Spiritual Exercises*, an examination of the life of Jesus for people desiring to order their lives and imitate Christ through prayer. Philosopher and theologian Karl Rahner, in his commentary on Ignatius' work, writes:

The Spirit of God breathes where He will; He does not ask our permission; He meets us on His own terms and distributes His charisms as He pleases. Therefore, we must always be awake and ready; we must be pliable so that He can use us in new enterprises. We cannot lay down the law to the Spirit of God! He is only present with His gifts where He knows that they are joined with the multiplicity of charisms in the one Church. All the gifts of this Church stem from one source—God. What Paul says in the twelfth chapter of his First Epistle to the Corinthians is still true today! This should give us the strength to overcome every form of clerical jealousy, mutual suspicion, power-grabbing, and the refusal to let others— who have their own gifts of the Spirit—go their own way. That is what the Spirit wants from us! He is not as narrow-minded as we sometimes are with our recipes! He can lead to Himself in different ways, and He wants to direct the Church through a multiplicity of functions, offices, and gifts.

Spiritual Exercises (Herder & Herder, 1965)
page 255

As we open ourselves to possible "new enterprises" of the Holy Spirit, the Lord reminds us to show grace toward others with gifts and callings different from our own. Those in front-line activities like power evangelism should not project their ministry focus onto others. But neither should those ministering in other roles accuse believers God has called to the front lines of overstepping proper bounds or acting in presumption. Jesus commissioned disciples just like us with a breathtaking investment of authority:

"I tell you the truth, anyone who has faith in me will do what I have been doing. He will do even greater things than these, because I am going to the Father. And I will do whatever you ask in my name, so that the Son may bring glory to the Father. You may ask me for anything in my name, and I will do it."

John 14:12–14

Even when power evangelism is not a regular emphasis, the Holy Spirit can work through us in expanded ways when we stand prepared to add prayers for the release of supernatural power to our palette of ministry options. Perhaps the best way to learn to pray and minister with the power of God is to come alongside those doing it—whether prayer for divine healing, hearing and speaking prophetic messages, spiritual warfare, or intercession for release of dreams, visions, angelic visitations or miracles. Observe, ask questions and begin to model such people. Methodologies differ, so find a style that could become comfortable. But do not shrink back reflexively from unfamiliar practices or manifestations. Ask the Holy Spirit to reveal what comes from God and what does not.

Empower Your Prayers through Faith

Believers concerned for the advance of the Gospel of God's Kingdom will scarcely find any asset more valuable than an unshakable faith in God's power to answer prayer and work His will in the world in sovereign ways. A. T. Pierson and his co-editor of the *Missionary Review*, J. M. Sherwood, wrote in the August 1890 issue,

> The Editors of this REVIEW are thoroughly convinced that no one obstacle stands in the way of the progress of missions so prominently as *lack of faith in the supernatural power of God*. There is too much dependence on appeal, on organization, on human instrument, on Governmental patronage, on the influence of education and civilization; and too little simple looking unto that real source of success, the POWER OF GOD IN ANSWER TO PRAYER, first to open doors of access, then to raise up and thrust forth laborers, and then to break down all opposition and make the truth mighty in converting, subduing, saving and sanctifying.
>
> page 630, emphasis in original

Faith builds our effectiveness in prayer. James 5:15 cites faith as necessary in prayer for healing: "The prayer offered in faith will make the sick person well; the Lord will raise him up." Jesus Himself said, "If you believe, you will receive whatever you ask for in prayer" (Matthew 21:22) and "Everything is possible for him who believes" (Mark 9:23). If prayer is the primary means by which we participate in advancing God's purposes in the world, then faith in God and His power to answer prayer (sometimes in miraculous ways) will turn our intercession from a dusty ritual into a high-voltage generator empowering His Kingdom to come and His will to be done.

Faith also honors and pleases God. Hebrews 11:6 asserts, "Without faith it is impossible to please God, because anyone who comes to him must believe that he exists and that he rewards those who earnestly seek him." At times we may hesitate to pray for divine healing or miracles because the situation seems impossible and we do not want to disappoint ourselves or the person who needs intercession. But Hebrews 12:2 reminds us to "fix our eyes on Jesus, the author and perfecter of our faith." We need not try to manufacture faith inside our own hearts. Jesus initiates faith within us and develops it into fullness and maturity.

The power to work signs and wonders in the process of people's salvation comes only from the Holy Spirit. Recognizing that the power source lies outside ourselves can help us feel less self-conscious or vulnerable when we ask God to manifest Himself in supernatural ways. Yet our role does not come without risk. We must stay sensitive to the will of God and neither go beyond nor lag behind Him. Jesus gave us a model during His earthly ministry: "'I tell you the truth, the Son can do nothing by himself; he can do only what he sees his Father doing, because whatever the Father does the Son also does'" (John 5:19).

Walking by faith, particularly in power evangelism, requires keen spiritual insight. According to Jesus' philosophy of ministry, the exercise of signs and wonders depends on God's will for a particular time and place and people. On the one hand, we dare not presume to do anything the Father has not purposed to do. In ourselves we can do nothing—and if we try outside God's will, we may bring on worse than nothing. On the other hand, whatever the Father does, He wants and expects His children to enter into. We have the privilege—indeed, the responsibility—of taking part with Him in His work, even ministering in supernatural power to the lost.

Walk in the Power of Godly Living

Power evangelism represents but one tool in a toolbox full of strategies God may use to bring people to salvation through Jesus

Christ. We have focused in this book on the role of supernatural signs and wonders in conversion, partly because many Christians have overlooked the potential of power evangelism, particularly in the West. A comprehensive survey of missions methodologies would go beyond the scope of this book. Yet one important evangelistic strategy demands mention in counterpoint: the power of godly living.

The apostle Paul expressed his heartfelt ambition in Philippians 3:10: "I want to know Christ and the power of his resurrection and the fellowship of sharing in his sufferings, becoming like him in his death. . . ." In Paul's desire for deep, personal intimacy with Christ, he mentioned two aspects of his Savior's life he wished to know in greater fullness: the power of His resurrection and the fellowship of His sufferings. Both are vital. Either alone can spell ruin.

Through sharing in Christ's sufferings, we learn holiness, obedience and godly character. A turn in the furnace of the Refiner's fire costs us pain and sacrifice. But by God's grace He does not leave us in the smelter, and we emerge more like the Lord we love, reflecting greater purity.

The power of Christ's resurrection represents the highest power of the universe. Paul declares that this power is available to us who believe in the Lord (see Ephesians 1:18–21). But power alone, like an unharnessed nuclear explosion, can prove deadly. Only within the disciplined confines of a nuclear generating plant can the power of atomic fission help, rather than harm, humankind.

The Lord wants to exercise His mighty resurrection power through vessels scrubbed clean by the fellowship of Christ's sufferings. The more we reflect His character, dying to sin and allowing His life to flow through us, the more powerfully the transformation of our lives will witness to those around us.

Paul G. Hiebert, now professor and chair of the Department of Mission and Evangelism at Trinity Evangelical Divinity School in Deerfield, Illinois, wrote an article entitled "Spirituality of the Indian Road" for the October 1994 issue of *Theology, News and Notes*, the alumni magazine of Fuller Seminary, where he formerly taught. In this article he told the story of a group of first-generation converts to Christianity in the village of Pedda Danvada in south India. As members of the despised Untouchable community, the believers suffered daily trials and persecutions at the hands of the high-caste village leaders. Yet they maintained their uncomplaining trust in God.

When the Hindu elders prevented the Christians from drawing water at the village well a half-mile outside town, the believers raised money to dig another of their own. Twice they struck rock. After prayer they decided to dig next to their church right in the village. Ten feet down they again hit granite. But they determined to spend the rest of their money blasting through the rock at this same site. After thirty feet they reached abundant water.

Both Christians and Hindus recognized this as God's miraculous provision, since all previous attempts to find groundwater within the village limits had failed. Now the believers faced a decision. Following discussion and prayer, they went to their persecutors in the high-caste community and offered the whole village access to their plentiful supply of water.

Hiebert reflects on the impact of this powerful witness to the transformation of character through Jesus Christ:

> This is why the decision by the Christians at Pedda Danvada to invite the others to draw water from their well spoke louder than words. Hindu and Muslim villagers claim that at times their gods, too, answer their prayers. But it amazes them to see Christians whose lives have been transformed by honesty, faithfulness, diligence, and, above all, love and compassion. They are rarely won to Christ by argument or dialogue, but they are drawn to Christians who are truly godly.
>
> page 23

The Bottom Line

Signs and wonders are never ends in themselves. When the delegation of 72 disciples returned in triumph from their mission, Jesus welcomed them back with thought-provoking words:

"I saw Satan fall like lightning from heaven. I have given you authority to trample on snakes and scorpions and to overcome all the power of the enemy; nothing will harm you. However, do not rejoice that the spirits submit to you, but rejoice that your names are written in heaven."

Luke 10:18–20

Jesus did not want His followers to glory in their participation in miraculous signs. The Bible exhorts us in numerous places, by contrast, to rejoice in the Lord and exalt Him for His own mighty deeds. And the most glorious work of God deserving our praise is the salvation of souls through the death and resurrection of Jesus Christ.

The motive of the apostle John for writing his Gospel, which echoes a prayer of mine, underscores the primary purpose for the manifestation of God's power in the world:

Jesus did many other miraculous signs in the presence of his disciples, which are not recorded in this book. But these are written that you may believe that Jesus is the Christ, the Son of God, and that by believing you may have life in his name.

John 20:30–31

All glory to God!

Index